NORTH SOUTH EAST WEST

BY WATER

RON GREINER

Copyright © 2021 Ron Greiner

All rights reserved. No part of this book may be reproduced, stored, or transmitted by any means—whether auditory, graphic, mechanical, or electronic—without written permission of both publisher and author, except in the case of brief excerpts used in critical articles and reviews. Unauthorized reproduction of any part of this work is illegal and is punishable by law.

ISBN: 978-1-956373-26-4 (sc)
ISBN: 978-1-956373-27-1 (hc)
ISBN: 978-1-956373-28-8 (e)

Because of the dynamic nature of the Internet, any web addresses or links contained in this book may have changed since publication and may no longer be valid. The views expressed in this work are solely those of the author and do not necessarily reflect the views of the publisher, and the publisher hereby disclaims any responsibility for them.

CONTENTS

Preface ix

Chapter 1   1988 Eagan to Cairo, Illinois, & back to
            Eagan, Minnesota 1

Chapter 2   1989 Lake Itasca to Eagan, Minnesota 21

Chapter 3   1990 Minnesota River (Renville-Shakopee) 31

Chapter 4   1991 Saint Croix River (Mile 97 to Mile 39) 34

Chapter 5   1992 Miss, Cairo, Gulf, Mobile, Tenn-Tom,
            Tenn, Cum, Ohio, Cairo 37

Chapter 6   1993 Saint Croix River (Gordon Dam to Hwy 70) 64

Chapter 7   1993 Missouri, Mississippi, Illinois, Lake Michigan 67

Chapter 8   1994 Ohio, Monogahela, Allegheny,
            Muskingum, Tennessee, Kentucky 85

Chapter 9   1994 Big Stone Lake to Renville Co
            Park #2 Minnesota 112

Chapter 10 1995 Arkansas, Tennessee, & Cumberland Rivers 117

Chapter 11 1996 Missouri River from Fort Buford,
            North Dakota to Sioux City, Nebraska 145

Chapter 12 1997 Jefferson River from Twin Bridges to
            Three Forks, Montana 159

Chapter 13 1997 Missouri River from Three Forks,
            Montana to Fort Buford, North Dakota 171

Chapter 14 1997 Bois de Sioux, & Red River to
            Lake Winnipeg, Ontario Canada 183

Chapter 15 1998 Bois De Sioux, Mud Lake, Lake Traverse,
            Minnesota 199

Chapter 16 1998 Big Hole River 205

Chapter 17 1999 Colorado River(Powell, Mead,
            Mohave, Havasu) 211

Chapter 18 2000 Yellowstone River 226

Chapter 19 2001 Chadakakoin, Cassadaga, Conewango,
            Allegheny 229

Chapter 20 2001 Buffalo to Troy to NYC to Albany New York ...237

Chapter 21 2001 Pend Oreille River 265

Chapter 22 2001 Columbia River 277

Chapter 23 2002 Clark Fork, Pend Oreille, Flathead, &
            Yellowstone Rivers 300

Epilogue 317

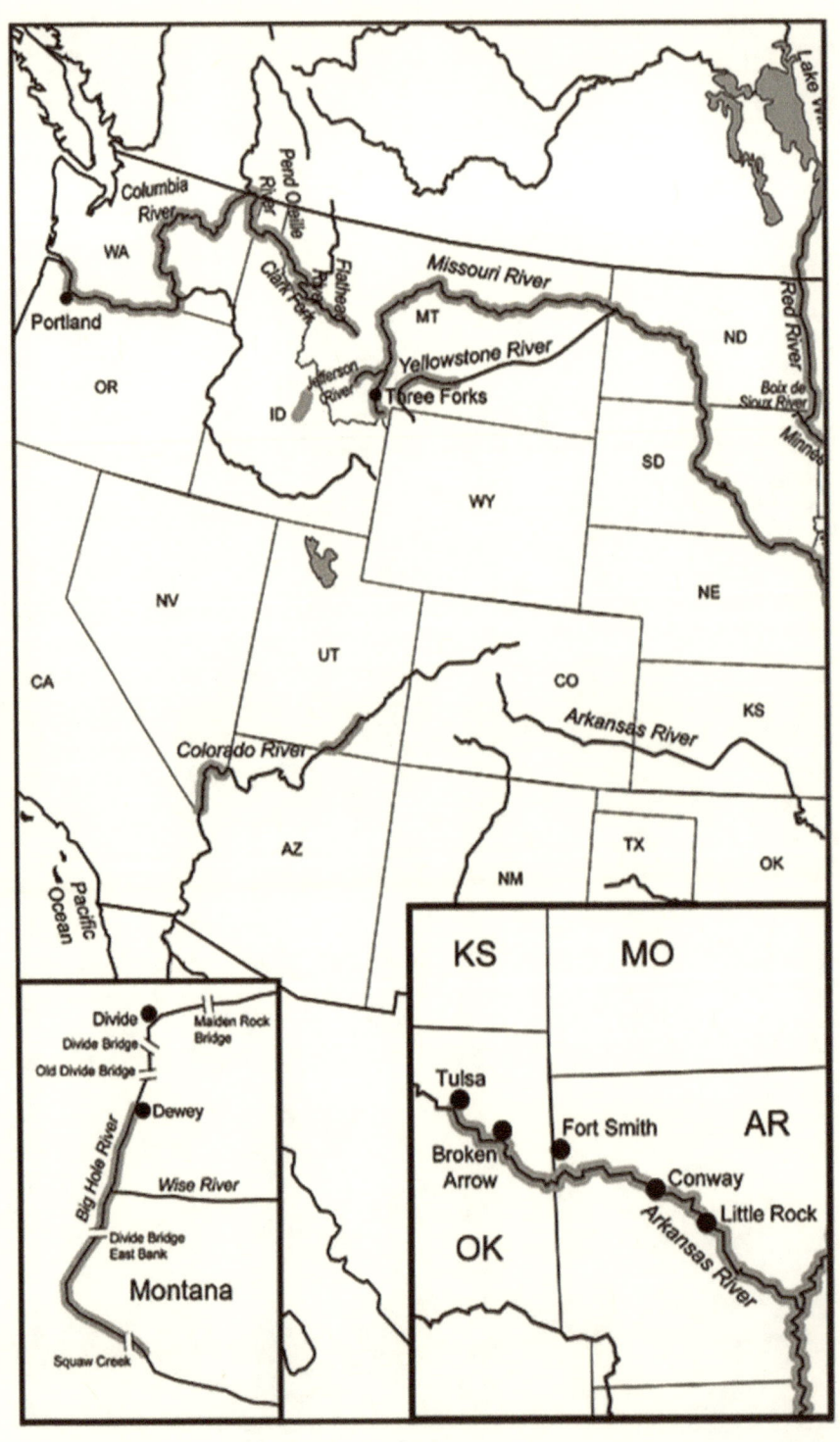

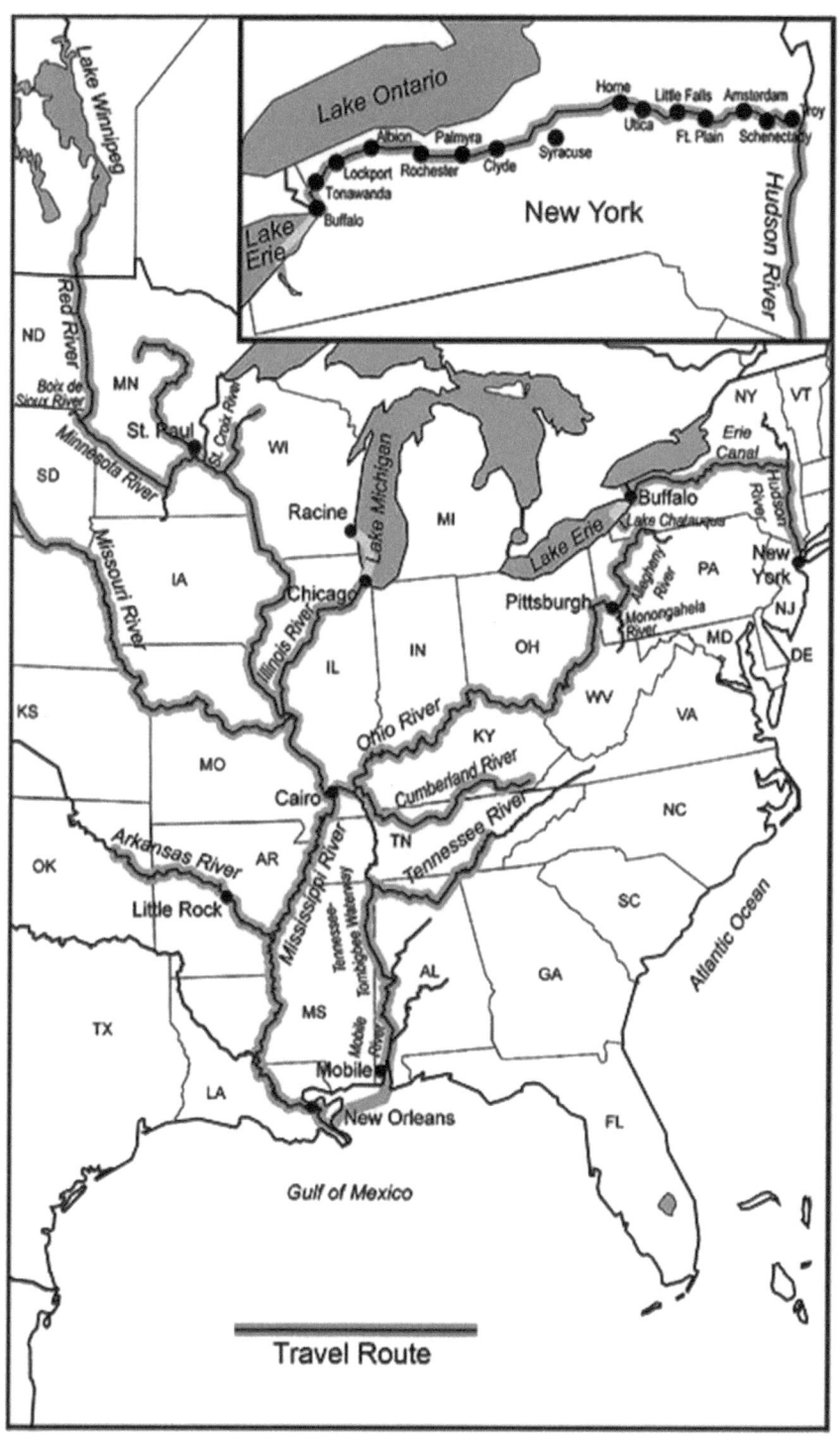

Travel Route

I want to thank Merry Gudmundson, Martha Erickson, Jan Brandes, and Virginia Greiner who were 'test' readers. They each provided insights on how the book looks in its final form

PREFACE

Initially writing a book was not in my mind, with few notes taken on early trips. Then while boating the lower Mississippi River, and in being asked if I was writing a book, thought about it, and started to take more extensive notes. After boating the length of the Mississippi, be it by motorized means, and having touched on major portions of other river systems, I set upon the thought of doing North, South, East, West, by water. There are more people than you might imagine who have canoed the length of the Mississippi. I understand that there have been a couple transits of East to West, but I have heard of nobody who has boated from Lake Winnipeg to the Gulf. Having said that I realize that their trips were probably done from start to finish with only a couple breaks. Mine was done over a period of fourteen years. One of the reasons for wanting to get my story out is to show that you don't necessarily have to quit your job to accomplish personal goals. Most of the rivers I boated were done in less than a two week period. It did take persistence and dedication.

Persistence and dedication not only applies to the actual doing of NSEW but to the writing about it. With help from test readers giving me direction, I did the actual writing. It took me over twenty years from the time I first started taking real trip notes to reach the point where I considered it ready for publication. Kevin, the oldest son, said that I write like I talk. So while other books are probably better written, this story truly reflects me, giving my best effort towards both boating and writing.

1988 EAGAN TO CAIRO, ILLINOIS, & BACK TO EAGAN, MINNESOTA

Where should my story about travelling rivers begin?

With where I viewed the Mississippi River for the first time? A sand bank levee that separates the Mississippi River from Lake Odessa in southeast Iowa where my folks had built a cabin.

With when I had rheumatic fever at age seven? That is when I started reading adventure books, such as Tom Sawyer, while bed ridden for almost a year.

With seeing the big United States Map that hung in every schoolroom of our *small rural Iowa community*? I visualized it while doing the chores on our 160-acre farm.

With the year 1961 when my parents bought a small resort on Indian owned land on Leech Lake in northern Minnesota? That is when I really started to develop my love of being around water.

With when I first viewed the source of the Mississippi at Lake Itasca sixty miles from our resort? Or when I saw the Mississippi at New Orleans during Mardi gras in 1973? Having seen the source and being within one hundred miles of its end, I wondered what the river was like in-between.

With small trips, using canoes and home made kayaks on Iowa rivers after graduating from a one-year technical college in Des Moines, Iowa? The urge to travel an entire river system haunted me.

With when I bought my first powerboat? An 18-foot wooden Thompson lap-strake with a 95 horsepower Mercury outboard in 1976. In spite of spending more time maintaining the boat and fighting more mechanical problems than I cared to, the rare trouble free day spent on the water usually made up for it.

Or with the birth of our second son on June 27, 1986, at 2:59 PM? We named him Nathan. Kevin is his five-year-old brother, born May 12th, 1981 at 5:19 AM.

What does all of this have to do with boating and river trips? Well, I'd sold the Thompson the year before, coming off the water more disgusted than relaxed. Debbie, my wife of six years, and I missed being on the water and had agreed to buy a new boat next year.

Six weeks after Nate's birth, Kevin and I went out to 'just look' for a boat. Our first stop was at King's Cove Marina, twenty miles away and located on the Mississippi. I walked into the showroom and laid eyes on a boat that I instantly liked. Compared to the other boats King's Cove sold, this 1986 model, made by Sea Sprite, was by far the smallest at seventeen foot five inches in length, and seven foot two inches across. Having been around boats since birth and now thirty-seven I pretty much knew what I liked and disliked. I **liked** this boat! While it was affordable, we left to look at what other boat dealers had to offer since we were 'just looking.'

2

We'd gone about ten miles when I turned to Kevin and said, "This is ridiculous, *I like that boat!*" I turned around and went back. After further negation with the salesman, I called Debbie. "Debbie, you gotta come and look at this boat." She was on her way out the door and could not come and look. Asking, "What color is it?" I said, "Blue/Grey over White." "Just buy it!" So I did.

My only reservation was if our 1985 Nissan pickup would be able to tow it. Under the Terms and Conditions section of the Purchase Agreement for the Sea Sprite, I had written 'Subject to test ride & Trailering, $500.00 Deposit Returnable'.

The on water test drive confirmed I *liked* this boat, with the towing test showing the pickup adequate on the road. We completed the purchase and the family was excited about using it. I did experience trouble with the pickup being too light to pull the boat up slippery wet ramps, so I added weight to the bed to help compensate.

When my boss at Early American Life Insurance Company heard I was having trouble ramping, he volunteered me the use of his new Chevrolet Suburban four-wheel drive company vehicle while he was away on a two-week European vacation.

While many people name their boat, Debbie and I have always referred to the Sea Sprite as 'the boat'. When referring to it, I'll call it, The Boat, an unpretentious name that fits its small size.

On a Friday afternoon, while Debbie was doing teacher preparation as part of her job as a general music teacher at Valley Middle School, Kevin and I went exploring lakes in the southern metro area. I backed our two-week-old boat up using the new Suburban into Lake Marion, which is about fifteen miles south of where we lived in Eagan.

As I pushed The Boat off the trailer on the gravel ramp, two fishermen were waiting in their boat to load. One said, "Nice boat!" while the other said, "Nice vehicle!" I replied, "One is mine, while the other is not!"

We did a quick loop around the lower portion of the lake. The only reason I bring this specific launching up is because in the fall of 1989 we bought a house on Lake Marion, and this was the only time I was ever on it until we moved there.

The Boat saw a lot of use on Minnesota lakes and rivers over the next two years.

It was during the winter of 87-88 that I got a 'wild hair', as my father would say, about running the Mississippi River between the Twin Cities and Cairo, Illinois, where the Ohio River flows in.

A set of 'Upper Mississippi River Navigation Charts', available from the US Army Corps of Engineers, provided most of what I needed to know. The chart purchase also included a separate guide that detailed marina and fuel facilities along the way. I studied them; finding it was a one-way distance of 852 miles, requiring passage through 26 locks. The trip would start from the Cedar Avenue boat ramp on the Minnesota River, five miles from our house in Eagan.

I installed a marine VHF radio so we could communicate with the locks to arrange passage. It also would be useful in the event of an emergency.

Debbie's father, Frank May, a math teacher in Evanston, Illinois and Eldonna, Debbie's mother, agreed to take care of Kevin and Nate while we made the journey.

THURSDAY, AUGUST 4TH, 1988

At 12:45 Frank, Donna, and the boys saw us off from the boat ramp underneath the Cedar Avenue Bridge on the Minnesota River, about seven miles upstream from its junction with the Mississippi River.

Little did I realize that in starting my boy hood dream of boating the length of the Mississippi that I was actually embarking on the first leg of 'North, South, East, West, by Water'.

While passing Turtle Island, a strip of sand off the marked channel about twelve miles above Lock 2 that we had nicknamed due to its numerous turtle tracks, I was reminded of the times spent there picnicking and swimming. Kevin in his life jacket, and Nate, just turning two, held up in the water.

Arriving at Lock 2, we found that it would be a two-hour wait. We wondered if this was going to set the tone for the rest of the trip.

There are three locks above Lock 2 at Hastings, Lock 1, and Upper and Lower Saint Anthony Falls, with the Minnesota River entering downstream from them.

As we locked through Debbie read aloud from the brochure about Lock 2 put out by the Army Corps of Engineers. She would do this for the next ten locks, since these were the only locks we had brochures for. Excerpts are included to give perspective of what we would be encountering.

LOCK & DAM NO.2 HASTINGS MINNESOTA

"A major rehabilitation program is underway at Lock and Dam No. 2 to assure the stability and functioning of the installation for another 50 years. In addition, the Corps is allowing the city of Hastings to construct a hydropower plant at the dam."

We were the last boat in at Lock 3, catching it just as they were ready to lock down.

LOCK & DAM NO. 3 RED WING MINNESOTA

"The St Croix River enters the Mississippi River at Prescott, Wisconsin, 14.4 miles above Lock and Dam 3. The upper reaches of this scenic waterway are part of the national wild river program and provide excellent canoeing and camping opportunities. The lower reaches of the St. Croix afford a paradise for the power boater and fisherman alike."

About ten miles below Lock 3 is Lake Pepin, which stretches over twenty miles in length. It is a very popular boating spot, especially for sailboats, as it is over two miles in width for two thirds of its length. This is the widest spot on the river for hundreds of miles. It was calm and sunny as we passed through, which is not always the case. In passing Hok-si-la, a former Boy Scout Camp on Lake Pepin where earlier that summer we had trailered The Boat. I remembered that Nate had to be carefully watched as he kept crawling towards the firepit, wanting to play with the ashes. While taking a break from cruising we listened to a Twin Cities radio station that announced a major windstorm due to hit Lake Pepin. Even though the sky was clear, we immediately headed back to camp. Almost as soon as we got to shore, a major storm came through. From our safe vantage point, we saw a sailboat under full sail go over.

While in Lock 4, I hit my knee against the key in the ignition, breaking it off. For the rest of the trip I would have to mate the broken halves together to start or stop the motor.

LOCK & DAM NO. 4 ALMA WISCONSIN

> "The dam, completed in 1935, is 6,867 feet long, including 1,367 feet of movable gate sections and 5,500 feet of non-overflow earth fill dike. The movable gate section consists of six roller gates and 22 tainter gates extending from the auxiliary lock to the right bank of the main channel."

Roller and Tainter gates? Do you need to be an engineer to understand this? **Yes!** Therefore, I will paraphrase from the 50th Anniversary publication, Old Man River 1938 - 1988, published by the U.S Engineer District, St. Paul, Minnesota.

A dam can contain a number of elements; dikes, spillways, and both Tainter and roller gates. By incorporating the use of both types into their dams on the Mississippi River, the Corps established a precedent in dam engineering.

Invented by Wisconsin lumberman Theodore Parker and patented by Jeremiah B. Tainter in 1886, Tainter gates became the principal component of the dam. The Corps chose these gates mainly because they were cheaper than roller gates and still offered dependable operation. A Tainter gate resembles the blade of a large bulldozer and is hinged on the downstream side for raising or lowering. Tainter gates are ineffective for spans greater than thirty-five feet with some channel openings needing to be wider to accommodate the passage of ice and debris. Tainter gates are difficult to maneuver during cold weather because ice often forms on them. Roller gates solved both the problems of length and icing. Swedish engineer M. Karstanjen invented the roller gate about 1900, and the Krupp and M.A.N. companies, in Germany, patented it. The gates are large cylinders with toothed ends that mesh with an inclined track set into the piers at the ends of the gate. Large electrically operated gears on top of the piers raise and lower the gate.

LOCK & DAM NO. 5 MINNESOTA CITY MINNESOTA

> "Pool #5 is a typical Mississippi River Pool. The high bluffs show signs of glacial action. Terraces below were formed by glacial stream outwash. For about 2 ½ miles above the lock and dam, the pool and the main channel are confined within a narrow area between high ground and an earth dike. The pool is nearly 15 miles long and has a shoreline of 50 miles. During high river flows, much of the valley floor is covered with flood waters."

As we left Lock 5 at 7:24, Debbie urged me to find a spot to set up camp for the night. I said if there were a wait at Lock 5A, we'd find a spot above there.

LOCK & DAM NO. 5A FOUNTAIN CITY WISCONSIN

> "Some 10,000 lockage's are made annually for both commercial and recreational craft. Commodities shipped include grain, coal, petroleum and chemical products. Millions of tons of cargo pass through here each shipping season. Pleasure craft use the lock extensively, and range in size from canoes to large houseboats and cruisers."

There is a Lock 5 and a Lock 5A, but not a Lock 23. The Army Corps of Engineers did the study for the Lock and Dam system in the late part of the 1920's. They pre-numbered the locks according to where they thought they needed to be. It turned out they needed an additional one between 5 and 6 and didn't need 23.

LOCK & DAM NO. 6 TREMPEALEAU WISCONSIN

> "Surrounding forests and plenty of fresh water combine to produce a natural wildlife habitat for fish, waterfowl and wild game. Recreational sites provided by the Corps of Engineers, the U.S. Fish & Wildlife Service, the state of Wisconsin and the City of Winona ensure easy access to the area. In addition, small federally-owned islands provide day-use for boaters and fisherman."

We breezed through Lock 5A and with Lock 6 ready upon arrival, locked through. It was 8:50 and in semi-darkness when we found a nice camping spot on the sandy beach of the right descending bank (RDB). Debbie wasn't happy with such a late night campsite decision, saying so as we pitched the tent.

In retrospect, a better discussion of trip expectations should have occurred. It turns out that Debbie's was that of stopping by seven o'clock and having a leisurely meal around a campfire, while mine was that of covering as many water miles possible each day. My thinking was that since I didn't know how long it would take to cover the approximate 1700 mile, 52 lockage round trip, I made the decision to put in long days on the river, which would allow time for unforeseen time delays.

While on a weekend river trip on the Iowa River in SE Iowa using homemade kayaks in September of 1974 with Denny Wolfe, a high school buddy, a fast approaching rainstorm and accompanying darkness forced us to find a campsite quickly. The tent, being pitched in soft mud, collapsed within 15 minutes. After several futile attempts to keep it upright, we gave up. This was one of the most miserable nights of my life. I slept fitfully, if at all, awaking in a pool of water at least three inches deep. The tent had collapsed with the window flap facing uphill causing the rainwater to collect in my corner. This was before the day of internal self-supporting frames. Expecting the same tent staking conditions, I had made a portable wooden interlocking frame for our non self-supporting two-man tent to fasten to so it would not collapse.

A side note about how to make the kayak. It is fairly simple. First you construct a lightweight wooden frame in the shape that you want the kayak to be. Then cover the frame with a continuous canvas material for the lower half above the midline, fastening with staples. Then cover the upper half the same way. Use a water base paint to soak the canvas, followed by two coats of oil base. In 1973 we built them for $25, selling mine three years later for the same amount. This type of kayak is fairly durable if properly handled and not punctured.

Getting back to the present trip, it was cloudy during the day with rain holding off until nightfall.

As I slept, a dream that I was in Vietnam crept into my subconscious; this in spite of the fact I was never called to the armed forces due to a heart murmur resulting from rheumatic fever.

FRIDAY, AUGUST 5TH, 1988

While Debbie made breakfast, I learned the source of my dream. A noisy group of Vietnamese fisherman had encamped from the roadside after we fell asleep.

LOCK & DAM NO. 7 LA CRESCENT MINNESOTA

> "The lock chamber is 110 feet wide and 600 feet long. Tainter valves at the upstream end of the lock allow water to flow into the lock chamber by gravity for filling. Likewise, valves at the downstream end of the lock allow water to flow out of the lock for emptying."

LOCK & DAM NO. 8 GENOA WISCONSIN

> "Pool 8 has an excellent reputation for sport fishing of walleye, sauger, pike, and pan fish."

Shortly after clearing Lock 8, I heard a subtle change in the sound of the motor. Looking at the dash gauges, I noticed that the battery charging needle indicator was not in its normal position. Finding a safe place to stop outside the main channel, I lifted the motor hood and found that the alternator belt had broken. While having a spare, I'd never replaced one. Acknowledging my limited ability to fix anything mechanical, I referred to the manual. A motor support bracket needed removed to install a new belt, which was easy. Putting the bracket back in place required raising the motor slightly. Fortunately, I had a long heavy-duty screwdriver that took the place of a pry bar.

LOCK & DAM NO. 9 LYNXVILLE WISCONSIN

> "Pool 9 is the only pool in the St. Paul District with boundaries formed by three states -Minnesota, Iowa, and Wisconsin."

At 12:15 we arrived at Lock 10 and ate lunch while waiting for a 'double lockage.'

A 'double lockage' occurs when the length of a tow exceeds the length of the lock chamber, requiring two locking operations. The tow first pushes the barges into the lock. Depending on the length of the tow, a number of barges are uncoupled from the tow. The towboat then backs away from the lock chamber with the remaining barges. The first part of the tow, known as the 'first cut,' is pulled out of the lock chamber by an electrically driven winch, after being raised or lowered. The locking cycle is then repeated for the push boat and remaining barges. When the water level is again the same, the lock gates open, and the push boat and barges couple with the 'first cut' using steel cables called 'wires.' The tow then continues on its journey.

LOCK & DAM NO. 10 GUTTENBERG IOWA

> "Southernmost of the 13 locks in the St. Paul District, Lock & Dam No. 10 is located in an area rich in historic

interest. Several of the largest pioneer outposts and settlements flourished here as river cities servicing the upper Midwest, such as Prairie du Chien, Wisconsin, and Guttenberg, Iowa."

LOCK & DAM NO. 11 DUBUQUE IOWA

"The Mississippi River is divided for navigational purposes into two parts, the Lower Mississippi River and the Upper Mississippi River (UMR). The UMR extends from Mile 0 at the confluence of the Ohio and Mississippi Rivers at Cairo, Illinois, to River Mile 857.6 at Minneapolis, Minnesota."

The fourth fuel stop since starting was at Point Pleasant Boat Landing in Bellevue, Iowa at 7:03 PM, just ½ mile below Lock & Dam #12. Debbie again prodded to find a place to camp while I said, "Just one more lock".

And one more lock it was. Immediately after locking through #13, we found a sandy moorage area on the Iowa side and were in our sleeping bags by 9:40.

SATURDAY, AUGUST 6TH, 1988

It is 29.4 miles between 13 & 14, with the original lock (14A) maintained at a five foot depth for recreational boats with limited weekend hours. Today being Saturday, the auxiliary (14A) opened just ½ hour before our arrival. So even though a barge was locking through the main chamber, our only slow down was passing through a long no-wake Army Corps of Engineers staging area on the approach to 14A.

There was a major delay at Lock 16 while waiting for a double tow to lock down, and a single tow to lock up.

At 2:30 we arrived at River Mile 441. This flat area used to have a wide flood plain, creating several channels over a period of time. With the decision made to have a nine-foot navigation channel, levees were built to contain the river in low-lying areas. Behind this levee system is Lake Odessa, where my parents built a cabin. From before my birth until when they bought the resort in Minnesota, this is where the family spent its recreational time.

Walking up the levee from the Mississippi side and seeing Lake Odessa fulfilled a goal I had as a youth, 'To be on the other side by boat.' It also brought back other remembrances from my child hood.

Fall was hunting season, with Dad being an avid duck hunter. There were preferred places to have a duck blind; who got them being determined by a boat race. The boat arriving first to their favorite spot laid claim to it for the season. In 1958 my father, Carl, bought a boat with 50 HP Mercury. On its first trip out, he hit a submerged log, causing the motor to come off. Recovery was possible by pulling on the still attached control cables. Taking it in for service due to being submerged, he traded it for a 70 HP Mercury. He never lost a race after that, with the boat and motor taken to the resort on Leech Lake. The motor didn't have a neutral, having two starters, one for forward, and one for reverse.

Winter was when ice blocks were harvested and preserved by covering with sawdust in a storage area to be used the following summer. Remember, this was the 1950's with electricity expensive and refrigeration at a cabin considered extravagant. It amazed me that even through the heat of August, the ice blocks stayed almost the same size as when they were cut.

Spring was unpredictable. Twice, that I remember, the levee broke and flooded most of the cabins next to us. Dad had the foresight to build a two level, the lower level being a four bay storage area designed to handle flooding, with the upper level having a kitchen, single bedroom, a large communal area, and a bay containing a jukebox.

Summers on Lake Odessa were spent fishing, boating, and swimming. That is with the time left over from operating the farm, a forty-mile drive from the cabin. Many a party was to the sound of Patsy Cline, Hank Williams, and Earnest Tubb on the jukebox. There was also the impromptu singing and playing of guitars from Uncle Howard, and his buddies, Lampy, and Durian. Those are times and places that are too much reminiscent of the past and not the present.

Just below Lock 19, we stopped to buy gas and beer at the Purple Cow in Alexandria, Missouri. I was intrigued by the name because forty miles from our farm there had been a fast food drive-in place by the same name. It lived up to my expectations of being somewhat offbeat and yet a place I'd feel comfortable spending the evening. Except it was only 7:15, and with at least one hour of daylight left, I said we'd stop by on our return for gas and a beer. The bartender said to go to the red house to the North and ask for Joe if they were closed.

It was 7:40 by the time we found a campsite off the river in an area known as Smoots Chute, about 2 ½ miles below Lock 20. Because of being off the main channel and close to the upper end of the pool formed by Lock & Dam #21, I was concerned about water depth. A pool is formed by the amount of water backed up by a dam.

Back in 1976, while camping with my parents in their converted school bus just off a side channel of the Mississippi, I had an experience from which I learned a lesson. Unloading my recently purchased Thompson boat at a downstream ramp, I piloted it up a side channel and anchored about one hundred feet from shore in about two foot of water. After the evening meal and mandatory late night pitch card game with some of their acquaintances camping nearby, we settled in for the night.

Looking out the next morning, we found the boat resting on the muddy river bottom with **NO** water in sight. The pool had been lowered at least two feet by the lock below. With the aid of a pickup pulling on two ski ropes tied together and three people on either side doing their best to help while sinking in the soft mud, we were able to get it to the bank. Then with the boat trailer backed up to the banks edge, we cranked the boat on using the winch.

So as we entered Smoots Chute, I had Debbie in the bow checking the depth with a paddle so I would not make that mistake again. Instead of pitching the tent, we slept in the boat, laying out the back-to-back seats making passable individual beds.

SUNDAY, AUGUST 7TH, 1988

Upon arriving at Lock 24 at 10:00 and finding out via VHF radio that it would be at least an hour wait, we took a quick three-mile trip back upstream to Silo Park to refuel and take a quick shower for a nominal charge. Lock 24 still had a minor wait upon our return.

Because of not getting a response on Channel 14 from Lock 25, the channel used since starting, I was ***not happy*** thinking there was a radio failure. We locked through quickly with other pleasure boats.

Being Sunday, many pleasure craft were out creating quite a chop that normally I relish bouncing over and Debbie usually hates. Except I was pissed thinking about the radio, and Debbie was thoroughly enjoying herself as we passed through an especially scenic part of the river.

Just as my attitude started to improve, a Missouri water patrol boat hailed us to stop. Without out any prerequisite questions, the officer said that we needed to change our Minnesota boat registration. "What do you mean?" "When you move down here, you need to reregister your boat." I let him know that we had not moved, were passing through on our way to Cairo, and held up a recent edition of a Twin Cities newspaper. Saying that normally a boat of 'our size' doesn't make such a trip, off he went.

Lock 26, Mile 202.9, responded on channel 14, setting my mind at ease. Being novice VHF radio operators, having just installed it before leaving, we didn't realize that some locks use a different 'working' channel than others. Locks also monitor 16, the emergency channel, so it can be used. The lockmaster will tell you to switch to a certain channel to actually converse.

A new lock & dam, Melvin Price, was under construction two miles to the south.

The Illinois River joins the Mississippi seventeen miles above Melvin Price, with the Missouri River joining the Mississippi five miles below.

Lock 27 at Saint Louis, Missouri is the last lock on the Mississippi, accessed via a nine-mile long canal called The Chain of Rocks Canal, bypassing a four-foot high rock dam in the main channel.

1988 was a low water year, evidenced by how dramatically different the river looked upon leaving the lock. No longer a 'pool of water' held back by a dam; it was now a narrow channel dictated by the flow released from above. While not actively monitoring VHF radio traffic, I would guess that only one barge at a time through the area- was possible.

We spent a HOT night in the tent tucked behind a wing dam, which normally are not visible.

Since this is the first time the term wing dam is mentioned, I will explain what they are. Back in 1878 with the authorization of a 4-½ foot deep navigation channel, (now 9 foot), the river was forced into a narrower passage. Building obstructions horizontally from the bank out of wood, and later rock, did this. This forces the river to flow in a tighter channel at a higher current speed, not as easily allowing sediment to drop. Closing side channels also helped attain the required channel depth.

With the water level low, wing dam structures were clearly visible. This further reiterated the importance of staying within the red and green navigation channel markers during normal water level. Straying outside the channel not only exposes the danger of shallow water, but also puts you at risk of hitting a submerged wing dam.

MONDAY, AUGUST 8TH, 1988 THE SLIGHTLY HAZY DAY STARTS WITH DEBBIE SINGING, "GOING TO CAIRO".

> Going down to Cairo, Goodbye and a bye, bye
> Going down to Cairo, Goodbye Liza Jane
> Black my boots and make them shine, Goodbye and a bye, bye
> Black my boots and make them shine, Goodbye Liza Jane.

At mile 103, while refueling the main gas tank and Debbie on watch for approaching barges, I glanced up and saw several barges shoot by on their way upriver. I yelled at Debbie for not keeping a proper watch. She pointed out that there was not a towboat behind them. We pondered how there could be barges under weigh without a towboat, coming up with the answer being they were 'loose.' Seeing a towboat behind a string of barges twenty miles downstream, we alerted him to the danger via channel 16. Expressing skepticism, he thanked us for the alert.

After further thought and discussion, we realized our ***stupid, stupid, mistake.*** Since leaving Lock 27 at St Louis, this was the first time we'd refueled while drifting in the low water fast current. What appeared to be 'loose barges', actually was us drifting by them at such a speed as to seem that they were moving and we were not! On returning upriver, we looked at the barges again. The current could be seen running into and under.

At 10:45, we arrived at Huckstep Oil Company, Cape Girardeau, Missouri, 52.3 miles above the Ohio. The normally floating platform that dispenses fuel was high and dry. I had to clamor the rocky bank about ten vertical feet to reach the stranded fuel platform, then pick my way up the rip-rocked bank another forty vertical feet before reaching them, although we could not tell how they were moored so far away from the bank, the fifteen foot high concrete floodwall built to protect the city from floods, climbing steel steps up and over the wall to reach the office on the other side. The fuel attendant drug the hose to the water edge and put in nineteen gallons priced at $1.309. He said they'd be open until 5:00 so we planned to buy fuel on our way back.

On Greenleaf Bend, an S curve fourteen miles above Cairo, we met an oncoming barge named the Keith Davis navigating a tight turn in the narrow channel. Due to the low water and length of the barge string pushed, the pilot needed the entire bank-to-bank width to accomplish the turn. I nosed our bow into the east bank and kept under power while the Keith Davis eased by, its powerful backwash throwing water over our stern.

At 1:00, with Mile Marker Zero indicating the junction of the Mississippi and the Ohio in the background, we took pictures of each other in the bow of the boat. We were elated, having boated 850 miles in four days.

As we rounded the tip of Illinois, it was obvious that there was one at a time barge traffic on the lower Ohio since a dredge obstructed most of the channel.

After traveling twenty miles upstream on the Ohio to view the sights, I was concerned about having enough fuel to return to Cape Girardeau. A major seawall separates downtown Cairo from the Ohio River, with a blockable opening to allow access to a boat ramp. Deciding to search for a gas station, I had walked most of the way up the very long concrete ramp carrying a gas can when it occurred to me that I wasn't wearing a shirt. Thinking of the "No Shirt, No Service" rule, I shouted at Debbie to meet me half way with a shirt. Not understanding, she still met half way, took off, and gave me the T-shirt she was wearing over her swimsuit.

While walking back to the boat she heard a loud whistle coming from a towboat named the "Trojan Warrior". A crewmember waved her over, yelling to bring a gas can. Debbie shouted for me to come back. Having been offered a ride by a guy sitting in his vehicle just outside the floodwall I was reluctant, however, return I did. The Trojan Warrior was holding itself against the bank under power, not having barges under tow. The crewmember said that he figured we needed gas and would fill the container I was carrying. While towboats use diesel engines, they also have gas engines aboard to run other equipment. Returning with the full container, I asked what we owed. At first, "Nothing", then he quickly reconsidered and asked if we had beer? Saying yes, "Just bring two beers", which I did.

Although we arrived back at Huckstep's at 4:30, beating the closing deadline by ½ hour, the office was closed! I found a gas station two blocks south where I filled and carried two six-gallon containers back up over the seawall and down the rocks to the boat. Twice! According to the VHF weather channel, the heat index was over 105 degrees! The only consolation was that gas was $93.9 instead of the $1.309 Huckstep's charged. I rewarded myself for making the multiple sixty-five foot vertical climbs over the rocks and sea wall by making another trip, this time buying *cold* beer and ice.

We spent the night behind a wing dam at mile 101 on the Illinois side. **It had been a good day!**

TUESDAY, AUGUST 9TH, 1988

We met a towboat named the 'Kevin Michael', the same as our seven-year-old son. We wanted to stop at "The Arch" in Saint Louis, but in seeing signs that indicated the limited dock space was only for tour boats, we continued on.

Due to again pushing the maximum travel distance possible, we spent the night sleeping in the boat tied to a log on the Illinois side, with rain pattering the mooring cover most of the night.

WEDNESDAY, AUGUST 10TH, 1988

After waiting an hour for a Hannibal, Missouri marina to open, we set off in search of our first meal away from the boat. While waiting for breakfast at Becky Thatcher's Restaurant, neither Debbie nor I felt comfortable. It was as if the whole town was 'rocking,' having spent so much time in the boat.

The morning was cloudy and rainy, with the afternoon being somewhat cool.

Although I'd promised myself to spend some time at the Purple Cow on the return trip, being it was only 1:45, we refueled, had a quick beer, and continued upstream.

Due to an especially long wait at Lock 18, I asked the lock attendant about the delay. His rely was, "Those boys are from the South. They move slow."

At 7:15, I talked Debbie into using the Coleman stove while we waited for Lock 17 to clear. This was the first time she'd done so prior to stopping for the night. I was hungry! She said I had finally reached my limit of starvation.

Lock 17 is also the down side terminus of the levy system that forms Lake Odessa, so it is time for the 'Iowa Jokes' to start. While awaiting lockage, we conversed with 'Iowans' in two other boats. One passenger was the 'typical dumb blonde.' When the topic of 'cow tipping' came up, she fully bought into the story as it was being told. For the uninformed, cow tipping can occur when a cow falls asleep and is so out of it that you can walk up and literally push it over. Not true, but there is a myth out there that says so. She also agreed with the storyteller who said the reason mosquitoes disappear after midnight is because the dew is too heavy for their wings. The members of the two boat group egged her on, giving us an especially memorable experience.

THURSDAY, AUGUST 11TH, 1988

We slept in the boat below Lock 16, and left at 6:45 in the early morning haze.

FRIDAY, AUGUST 12TH, 1988

While passing through the No Wake Zone where the Saint Croix River enters the Mississippi, Debbie radioed Lock 2, three miles upstream, to request passage. As this was the last lock separating us from the boys after eight days on the river, we were understandingly in a hurry to get home. Upon hearing our exact location the lockmaster said; "Well, you have five minutes to get here before we close the gates. Otherwise, it will be three hours. And remember, you are in a No Wake Zone!"

Within sight of the open lock gates and out of the No Wake Zone, running at wide-open throttle, I felt a small thud. Knowing I'd stayed within the marked channel and not feeling any adverse effects, kept going at the same speed. I looked back at a boat closely following our wake and right at the spot where I'd felt the thud they slowed abruptly and headed to shore.

I believe we tapped a 'deadhead' with the skeg, the bottom most point of the lower unit. A 'deadhead' is a log submerged just below the surface, having just enough buoyancy to keep from sinking. With a planing hull such as ours, the faster you go the less water it draws. The faster than normal speed we were traveling at might have saved the lower unit from damage. Seeing the boat following us able to head to shore, and with the lock gates still open, we made the lockage deadline.

Just across from downtown St. Paul is the 'No Wake Café,' a food and gas stop, where we called Frank who met us with the trailer at the same boat ramp from where we had started.

We loaded and were home by 4:00, having covered approximately 1725 miles in eight days and completing 52 lockage's. Needing to be back at work Monday, and wanting to attend the closing weekend of the Dakota County Fair and spend some time with Debbie's parents, I'd pushed to make it.

1989 LAKE ITASCA TO EAGAN, MINNESOTA

After completing the Cairo trip, my next goal was to travel the Mississippi from its source at Lake Itasca to the Twin Cities. The type of watercraft, how many water miles, and how long it might take, were all questions that needed answered.

The answer to how many water miles was easy to find out since the Minnesota Department of Natural Resources publishes Canoe Route maps, with the Mississippi being one. The Mississippi route is a series of fourteen maps from Lake Itasca to the Iowa border. Using those maps I found it to be 503 miles from Lake Itasca to the Minnesota River, and then up the Minnesota to the Cedar Avenue Bridge.

The type of watercraft would have to be portable, as there are numerous dams to portage around. It would also have to be of shallow draft as the depth to be navigated would be in inches, not feet. While reading the classified ads, I spotted a canoe that fit our needs to a T. On October 3, 1988, we bought a 1982 sixteen-foot Oswegan square back canoe for $300, which included two paddles, car top blocks, two life jackets, and an anchor. A square back canoe is designed for use with an outboard motor. In November, we bought a new 1988 four HP Johnson short shaft outboard motor for $635. It is worth noting that the 4, 6, & 8 HP models use the same lower unit and basic power head, resulting in the 4 HP being over built for its corresponding horsepower. Since the only time Debbie and I were ever in a canoe together had been eight years ago and resulted in us tipping over; I was a little apprehensive about a long trip.

Shortly after closing on our new house in Eagan, with Debbie and me spending innumerable hours painting the interior and exterior as part of a down-payment agreement, we went with two other couples for a short canoe trip on the Cannon River. The current was fast due to recent rains. As we pushed away from shore, I told Debbie that I was taking this trip to relax and not race downstream. Totally ignoring me, and seemingly intent to set some downstream speed record, she paddled furiously, but only on one side, resulting in us quickly being at the opposite bank and fast approaching a low overhanging limb. I told her to duck, *but no*, she opted to stab at the limb with the paddle, overturning us within five minutes of starting. Our friends helped by retrieving her wooden shoes and other miscellaneous things that escaped.

FRIDAY, JUNE 9TH, 1989

During a visit to my parents, I found out that Cousin Dick was looking for a father/son to accompany him and Mike, his oldest son, on a fly in Canadian fishing trip. Kevin and I went, leaving June 9th, and returning June 16th. It was a life changing experience for seven-year old Kevin since the bush pilot allowed the boys to pilot the dual control pontoon plane. He loved being in the air and started to explore careers associated with flying.

SATURDAY, JUNE 17TH, 1989

After a brief night of sleep upon returning from the fishing trip and leaving the boys with friends, Debbie and I took off for Lake Itasca in two vehicles. Me pulling the canoe on a single place snowmobile trailer with the Nissan pickup, and Debbie driving our 85' Chevrolet Cavalier. Debbie didn't think we could travel the entire 503 miles in nine days, so we would be leaving the car at Crow Wing State Park, 353 water miles downstream from Lake Itasca. It is only about seventy-five miles as the crow flies between Lake Itasca and Crow Wing State Park so that gives you an idea how the Mississippi meanders initially.

It was 5:00 PM when we left a boat ramp on Lake Itasca, which is a good size lake at over four miles long. One mile from the ramp is the 'official' start of the Mississippi, 1347 river miles above its junction with the Ohio River, and 2552 miles to the Gulf of Mexico, according to the sign at the headwaters. There is a short set of rocks over which the river flows, where annually thousands of tourists gingerly cross. A picture of pulling the canoe over them officially signified the start of our trip.

Just three hundred feet downstream is a log crossover for those who don't want to get their feet wet, necessitating our first portage.

For the record, the rock over which the river now flows is not the original source of the Mississippi. It used to leave the lake a little ways west through a marshy area not conducive to easy walking. The rocks were set in place, the small channel dug, and the marshy area damned so the Mississippi would leave over the rocks, making for a much better tourist attraction. If you go about ¼ mile downstream and look left the original riverbed is visible.

The next two obstacles encountered were low clearance bridges, which we got under by pushing the bow down. This was easier than carrying the eighty-two pound canoe, fifty-pound motor, and about one hundred pounds of gear and gas around.

Then we let the canoe float through a concrete viaduct, maintaining control with ropes.

At Wanagan, a designated canoe campsite six miles from the boat ramp, we set up camp in the unkempt grassy area. Hearing a sound similar to an airplane in trouble coming down the river, we left the enjoyable solitude of our campfire to investigate. It turned out to be a gentleman testing an airboat propulsion system mounted on top of two canoes with his wife and another couple. They ran a canoe rental operation and gave us invaluable information about how to get around a couple dams.

SUNDAY, JUNE 18TH, 1989

At 9:00, with a leisurely breakfast behind us, the days boating started by trying to use the motor in shallow water drive. Proving to be more trouble than it was worth, we switched to walking the canoe through the intermittently deep and shallow water for the next two miles. Debbie was in front helping pull the canoe through very shallow areas. Occasionally she would suddenly hit deep water, and struggle to climb back in. Knowing where the drop off was, and because I was pushing from behind, I'd casually hop in the back just as the depth dropped off.

Encountering a low wooden dam with a very narrow spillway, we opted to portage around it since there were railroad type spikes protruding from its interior. It appeared that at one time having been used to sluice logs.

Oh Yes, TICKS, I need to mention ticks. While packing up we found several wood ticks amongst the gear, and for the next seven days continued to find them. I felt almost paranoid not knowing if the crawling feeling I felt was or was not a tick. As often as not it was!

At a very well constructed beaver dam holding back at least three feet of water, we pulled the canoe over while watching for any pissed off beavers.

Having gone thirty-one miles, with another twenty-six to go before reaching Bemidji, we stopped for the night at Bear Den canoe campsite. Anyone thinking about doing the sixty-mile stretch above Lake Bemidji should be aware that it is next to impossible to get to dry land as the river goes through a series of swampy lakes. While dry land is in sight it is next to impossible to get there since the channel tends to flow through the middle of the swampy areas.

MONDAY, JUNE 19TH, 1989

The only reliable way to find your way through the wide, windy, weedy, swampy areas is to follow the slight bend in the tips of the vegetation caused by the very slow current. I believe it was just above Bemidji where we passed through a short section of river that didn't 'fit' with that above or below it, literally passing through a cow pasture with the rivers width being as little as three foot. On one tight turn, Debbie pushed off the bank with a paddle to keep the bow on track while I ran the motor in shallow water drive.

About 3:00, we stopped underneath the Highway 2 Bridge at Bemidji and bought two ½ gallons of gas and some fast food a short walking distance away. While making our first major portage of 200 yards around a dam, we caught up with a man motoring to the gulf from Bemidji. He had rigged up a system so that he could sit in the middle of the canoe and steer a motor via cables. We wished him luck!

It was 8:30 by the time we got the tent pitched at Joe's Lodge on Lake Andrusia, where we ate pizza and played cards in their lodge. We'd covered thirty-six miles, with less than three being across open water. Tomorrow would be different, with eight miles of Cass Lake open water to be crossed.

TUESDAY, JUNE 20TH, 1989

We awoke to the sound and feel of wind battering the tent, and were not in a hurry to leave after hearing from the lodge owner there was a constant wind speed of 20 - 35 mph. Since there is a 3/4 mile section of river separating Lake Andrusia from Cass Lake the actual effect of the wind on Cass was not visible. Hoping the wind would die down, we waited until 10:30 before leaving.

Entering Cass, a 15,596-acre lake, and somewhat in the protection of Star Island, it was obvious that a beeline crossing was out of the question. So I headed southeast, the direction providing the most protection for the longest period of time. When the full force of the wind blowing towards us was no longer avoidable, I turned into the minimum three-foot waves to attempt a crossing. We had left Joe's somewhat prepared, wearing full rain gear with life jackets on. I had also made a bailing bucket out of a ½-gallon plastic milk jug. Realize we were in a fully loaded canoe with a freeboard clearance of 8" at best.

I bailed as fast as I could, but each oncoming wave would add more as they crested on the way by. Debbie, sitting in the forward seat, got a face full of spray with almost every wave. I tried to take the waves at an angle, which minimizes dropping the bow into the next wave, but this was not always possible. Only making it about ½ mile from shore, one wave half filled the canoe. At that point I knew we'd be lucky to not capsize and decided to turn back. I initiated a turn midway between wave crests. Debbie started to turn around to ask what I was doing, unaware of how much water had poured into the canoe. I yelled, "Don't move!" as *any* unnecessary movement would capsize us. I continued to furiously bail while heading to shore, now concerned about the waves that were washing over the stern.

Fortunately, right at the spot where we made it to shore was Marclay Point Campground. It was only 1:00, we paid $11 to pitch the tent, played cards, and took a nap, all the while hoping the wind, and waves would subside enough to attempt the crossing again before dark.

About 5:00 the wind dropped off to no more than 20 mph, so off we went, skirting the main part of Cass by following the south shoreline around. It was still rough, but at least we'd be within swimming distance of shore. Waves were at somewhat regular intervals along the south shoreline. After Debbie got used to the way I quartered them to avoid taking on water, she commented that she was enjoying the ride. We arrived at 8:30 to Knutson Dam, which controls the Mississippi outlet on the northeast side of Cass, with the campground host and a friend of his helping us carry the canoe to our campsite. It took us all day to travel the nine river miles.

I figured we were forty-three miles short of where we needed to be in order to complete the 353-mile trip by Sunday.

WEDNESDAY, JUNE 21ST, 1989

It was into a very dense morning haze that we headed at 7:30, having ten miles of river before hitting Lake Winnibigoshish. 'Winnie', at 18,904-acres, is notorious for having rough water, and we would have thirteen miles of open water. Fortunately, the wind stayed under 10 mph, generating only light waves. Halfway through the crossing we caught up with three older men, each in their own rubber raft, one with a motor pushing the rest. They spent one week a year together towards the goal of travelling the length of the Mississippi, admitting they were not in a hurry since this was their third year.

Shortly after portaging around the dam at Lake Winnibigoshish and barely entering Little Lake Winnibigoshish before the channel leaves, we came to several areas where fallen trees covered the entire width of the river. After getting out and pushing the canoe over the first couple of trees, I decided to try to power the canoe over, coming off the throttle just in time to tilt the motor up to clear the log. I did this without telling Debbie of my idea. She freaked out when I did not slow down, and in fact sped up. It worked slick, and this became a normal procedure. Most canoes would not take this kind of abuse, but the Oswegan is especially well built.

It was surprisingly difficult to find enough space just below the first dam at Grand Rapids to pitch a tent amongst the many others. It figures since we had to do it in pouring rain.

The days seventy miles of water covered encompassed a wide variety of scenery; from a big wide-open lake, to a very narrow twisty Maple canopied channel.

THURSDAY, JUNE 22ND, 1989

At 7:30, under the threat of rain, we arrived at Blandin Dam, named after the paper mill that built it so they'd have a reliable source of water. We'd learned on Saturday that since Blandin is a private dam they are required to shuttle people around. With the takeout spot on the opposite bank from the mill, it was not easy to attract their attention. Once we did, two trucks and four men swiftly loaded the canoe, drove us to the put in spot, and carried everything to the waters edge. This would be a tough portage to do unassisted, and not just because of the distance. Due to fenced yards preventing access back to the river, you need to use city streets.

Before leaving Grand Rapids, we tied up underneath a bridge and walked to a nearby service station to buy food and gas.

The Mississippi is very twisty and turny from Grand Rapids to just above Brainerd. Around Mile 1120, we met three kayakers, their professed goal being to make it to the Gulf.

At 7:30, having traveled ninety-seven miles, we set up camp just outside the small town of Palisade. The round trip walk to town to buy fuel and groceries was less than a mile.

FRIDAY, JUNE 23RD, 1989

We caught up with two canoeists who were on their way to - - - - ? If you guessed the Gulf, you would be half-right. Just one was attempting it, with the other accompanying him partway. I have no idea how many people actually complete their attempt to paddle the Mississippi's entire length. If you are trying to do it in one summer, an early start is necessary.

The Potlatch Dam, another private dam, was our final portage for this portion of the trip. It is reasonably short so we didn't ask at the paper mill for help, opting to do it ourselves. Immediately below the dam, we ran a short set of boulder-strewn rapids. Exhilarating!

While passing through Brainerd, with the gas tank on empty and ten miles to go before reaching our car at Crow Wing State Park, I asked Debbie if she was ready to paddle. She was, so I didn't climb the very steep, high bank looking for a gas station. It was 7:00 when we arrived at Crow Wing, paddling the last five miles.

After eating a big meal at Mr. Steak, we settled in for a good nights rest at the Dell Motel completing the trip one-half day ahead of my self-imposed schedule.

SATURDAY, JUNE 24TH, 1989

We drove back to Lake Itasca to get the pickup and were home late Saturday night with the boys. During the night, Debbie woke up to find me sitting up with my feet over the side of the bed, right hand thumping the mattress, and left hand grabbing the nightstand. "What are you doing?" "I'm fishing, but I can't find my pole!" Evidently having spent so much time on the water the last two weeks; fishing in Saskatchewan, and boating the Mississippi were taking their toll.

FRIDAY AUGUST 11TH, 1989

Wanting to finish the upper Mississippi yet that summer, we headed back to Crow Wing State Park with the Nissan pulling the trailer hauling the canoe.

As we crossed a bridge spanning the Mississippi, I got my first inkling of what we were in for. The water level was very low! The thought of low water had never entered my mind. We arranged to leave the pickup and trailer in a secure area at Crow Wing and camped for the night.

SATURDAY, AUGUST 12TH, 1989

Back in June we'd taken a picture looking downstream from Crow Wing, and compared to one taken now showed an amazing difference. What had been a bank-to-bank river was now a boulder-strewn stream!

I berated myself for not following the original plan of travelling the entire upper length in June. We would be attempting to finish the final distance to the Cedar Avenue Bridge on the Minnesota in the same period we had left before, except now in low, low, water.

Starting with the motor in shallow water drive, it became a challenge to guess where the deepest part of the river might be. While the 'official' depth finder is a paddle, the actual depth was obvious as the prop kept hitting bottom.

We completed the portage around the dam at St. Cloud *late* Saturday night. Debbie used a flashlight to pick our way amongst boulders while trying to find a spot to camp.

Finding a flat area on the left bank, we hurriedly pitched the tent while a light evening rain fell. The tent collapsed sometime during the night, with Debbie getting up to fix it. Over night the water table came up and filled the depression where Debbie had removed a rock, resulting in her awaking in a pool of water, with me high and dry.

SUNDAY, AUGUST 13TH, 1989

As we got closer to the Twin Cities, the flood plain of the river got wider. There were islands that separated the slight current into two channels, with the deeper side not obvious. I would ask Debbie which side of an island to go. She would judge from her forward position in the bow, and say either left or right. I would then study the river myself, and ended up taking the opposite direction. Not once or twice, but all nine or ten times that I asked her. And every time I was right! After passing the island and looking back upriver, the side Debbie had chosen was blocked with either brush or the water rejoining the river was almost nonexistent. The last time I asked her I did not even look at the flow and did just the opposite of what she said, and I was right.

The approach to Upper Saint Anthony Lock & Dam is intimidating, especially in a canoe. You must stay to the right bank as you approach the lock chamber. The sight and sound of water going over Saint Anthony Falls is amazing. The combined drop of Upper and Lower Saint Anthony Locks, only 6/10 of a mile apart, is about 75 feet. Then 5.6 miles further is Lock and Dam No 1. As we left it, Debbie and I celebrated locking through all twenty-nine locks on the Mississippi in a one-year period. We were now on familiar water and within ten miles of the Cedar Avenue boat ramp where we ended this trip, traveling 159 miles.

From the ramp, I walked about a mile to where we'd left the Cavalier parked at a neighbor's parent's house. After dropping the canoe off at home, we had a six hour round trip to Crow Wing to retrieve the pickup, getting back after dark.

Just as a note, I did not mention all of the portages from Lake Itasca to the Twin Cities.

1990 MINNESOTA RIVER (RENVILLE-SHAKOPEE)

Just three weeks after finishing the Upper Mississippi, I saw an ad in our weekly local paper that piqued my interest. It described a 'fixer upper' on Lake Marion in Lakeville and listed at twice the value of our Eagan home. I called the listing agent to get further details. Chuck Zweber said that while the house needed work, most of the value was in the one-acre heavily treed 125-foot lakeshore frontage lot. I jotted down the address and said we might drive down and look.

If first impressions count, ours turned negative upon driving up the very rutted gravel driveway. However, the mostly brick rambler seemed solid, and it *was* an excellent lot. We drove around the rest of Lake Marion, seeing another for sale in much better shape. It only had a 50-foot wide lot and listed $100,000 higher than the first.

Debbie and I discussed the pluses and minuses of buying a 'fixer upper'; coming to the conclusion that we would have to look at the interior before making a final decision. I called Chuck to set up an appointment, finding out that an offer was pending that the seller would probably accept, but he took my name and number. Within a half-hour, Chuck called back and asked if we were serious in our inquiry. "Yes", but we had to see the inside before we knew for sure. Since there was an outstanding offer, we went to look at it that evening. To make a long story short, we bought it, moving in the following March.

The only reason I mention buying the lake home is that it directly affected our budget, leaving very little extra money to spend.

In late July, I felt the need to get away, having spent every spare moment away from work on the house and separate garage; scraping, caulking, and painting the exterior, while Debbie cleaned the interior, with both of us raking and hauling away years of accumulated leaves.

With both time and money an issue, I decided to travel the last 197 miles of the Minnesota River I hadn't yet boated using the canoe and four-horse. This time Kevin, now nine, would be my companion.

Due to a very rainy summer, river and lake levels were up. Being 'new' on the lake and in putting out our dock for the first time, I followed the same procedure as we had at the resort and set it high enough to allow three-foot waves to pass underneath. Neighbors later said that they thought I was nuts for putting the dock so high! It had rained so much that my dock now had less than a foot clearance. In their defense, Lake Marion is 1/20th the size of Leech Lake. The Minnesota River was at flood stage, even though it was late July.

The four of us drove to Renville County Park No. 2, which is one hundred miles as the crow flies from Lakeville. The reason for picking Renville as the starting point is that just upstream is the last marked rapids. The DNR map states, "Patterson's Rapids (river mile 225.9) is a short stretch of white water tumbling over a bed of glacial drift boulders. The rapids fall about five feet in one-third of a mile and are of intermediate difficulty at normal water levels." Debbie was concerned, and rightfully so, that Kevin would not know how to react, having no experience in a canoe.

While carrying the canoe to the rivers edge on a Saturday morning, Nate, four years old, learned that he was not going and was not happy about it! As Kevin and I pulled away from the bank, he was in tears.

Within two hours of starting, Kevin and I encountered a ***major*** logjam. Since the opposing banks were steep and slippery, it made sense to pull the canoe up and over the twenty-foot deep and five-foot high jam. Because the logjam had shifting logs and an underpinning current that could suck you under, I put Kevin on shore. While pulling the canoe up and over, I kept an eye on Kevin since he had a habit of wanting to help.

We had a couple minor logjams after that, not a big deal.

I did my best to be a good camper example to Kevin while pitching the tent and settling in to spend the night on the muddy bank, but truth be told, I do not like tent camping.

While I try to keep track of where I am at any certain time, part of the beauty of river travel is to be 'lost' in the abstract world where civilization is a thought as opposed to a fact.

Sometime on the second day we passed through a cornfield, it being a better passage than the blocked logjam alternative.

At Chaska, five miles upstream from our end destination of Shakopee, we had to work our way around a final small logjam.

While waiting at Shakopee for Debbie to pick us up, we watched a tiny boat with a rather large man cutting 'doughnuts' through his own wake. His boat resembled a bathtub, and he was only able to fit into it by positioning his feet over the steering wheel. Considering the size of his boat, I anticipated a smaller tow vehicle, but not a lawn tractor towing a very small trailer. Normally you back a vehicle with a trailer down the entire length of a ramp; with his unit so small, he did a 180-degree turn at the bottom and had only five feet to backup. Then, after loading his boat, he took off on city streets to go where I assume he lives not too far away.

We traveled 159 miles in 1-½ days.

1991 SAINT CROIX RIVER (MILE 97 TO MILE 39)

As we looked towards a summer vacation, money was a major issue. While the house now looked nice from the outside, only two burners on the kitchen stove worked and the oven door had to be propped shut. You also had to be careful to not trip on the hole in the threadbare living room carpet, and the list goes on. Then came the letter from city hall requiring us to hook up to city water and sewer within thirty days due to our failing septic tank system. That was a large bill because the contractor had to dig and tunnel over 200 feet through a hill to reach the basement of our walkout rambler. Oh well, we loved lake life and had excellent neighbors. Since I'd already traveled the upper 1347 miles of the Mississippi and the lower 224 miles of the Minnesota, the next logical trip was the Saint Croix River. Using The Boat, we had already gone upstream forty-one miles to where it becomes shallow. Now we would use the canoe and four-horse motor to start from some point upstream and end up at the closest access after Mile 41.

This was meant to be a family trip, space and weight for the four of us in the canoe would be an issue considering we'd end up at different campsites by water.

When Nate was twenty-two months old I'd tried to organize a Memorial Day weekend camping trip using The Boat, but the logistics were a nightmare. What we did instead has become a cherished family memory. We camped in the backyard of our Eagan home, which adjoined a sixty acre heavily wooded undeveloped park. With the city of Eagan's blessing, I had cleared out a good section of brush that created an area better conducive to camping than many a paid site. Rules were established; the house was now the 'lodge,' and you where only allowed to go there to use the bathroom or take a shower. The only exceptions were that Debbie could use the house microwave to heat up baby formula and the refrigerator to keep the food cold. We slept in a tent, played games in the extended yard/park, and swam in the 'pool'. The pool being an 8-foot inflatable boat that instead of floating on water was filled with water.

I digress. The plan for this trip was to start from the boat ramp at Highway 70, ninety-seven miles upstream from where the Saint Croix joins the Mississippi and use the Nissan and Cavalier to shuttle a vehicle to our stopping point. The reason for picking Highway 70 as our starting point is that the canoe map showed Class II rapids eight miles upstream from there, and this was the easiest access below them. Class II rapids, as defined in the Canoe Route pamphlet, are 'Rapids with waves up to three feet high. Some maneuvering is required.' We did not want to put the fear of water into the boys due to tipping over.

One of the benefits of my job was a 37 ½ hour, four and a half day workweek, with the office closing at 12:30 on Fridays. With Debbie being a teacher and having summers off, we were able to drive to St. Croix Wild River State Park and set up camp with plenty of daylight left.

Day One's plan called for the tent to be left up, and use the Nissan to haul the canoe to the Highway 70 water access. It was an enjoyable thirty-mile run back to our campsite at Wild River State Park. Then we had to drive back to Hwy 70 to pickup the Nissan, returning to Wild River in darkness.

Day Two's agenda was less aggressive, with only twelve miles of river between St. Croix Falls and us. There is a dam requiring a ¼-mile portage around the falls. To avoid the portage, we drove to just above the falls and left the Cavalier and all of the camping gear inside, and went back to Wild River in the Nissan.

Our time spent in the canoe was leisurely, paced to enjoy the scenic surroundings. Upon arriving above the falls, we tied the canoe on top of the Cavalier and drove less than two miles to Interstate State Park. We found a campsite, dropped the canoe off, went back to Wild River to get the Nissan, and arrived back at Interstate State Park in time for Debbie to cook in daylight.

Day Three, our final day on the river, would end at William O'Brien State Park sixteen miles downstream from St. Croix Falls. After shuttling the car, we headed upstream against the swift current, following a paddle wheel excursion boat. We got as close to the falls as was reasonable, and then enjoyed the scenery while passing through the braided downstream channel. After finding the side channel to William O'Brien boat ramp and retrieving the Nissan, we settled into camping mode again.

While driving home the next morning, I wondered if the result was worth the effort spent. We'd spent far more time in vehicles than on the water. The conclusion I reached was, 'Yes,' although only going fifty-eight river miles in three days, a good time was had by all.

1992 MISS, CAIRO, GULF, MOBILE, TENN-TOM, TENN, CUM, OHIO, CAIRO

Over the winter, we managed to scrape up enough extra money to replace the kitchen stove and living room carpet, but not enough to think about taking a major vacation. That is until July 28th. I had been frequenting the Indian owned and operated casino called Mystic Lake, fifteen miles to the west of us. On Saturday, July 25th, I won $600, and the following Monday night I picked up an additional $900 playing blackjack. The unexpected windfall quickly put me in the mindset to boat the rest of the Mississippi, which had become my goal.

Debbie had not been with me at the casino on Monday night, and when I arrived home was sound asleep. I tossed and turned until 3:00 AM when I awoke her and told of my winnings. I then laid a real bombshell by saying that I wanted to finish the rest of the Mississippi now that we had the money. She asked when we would leave. I said, "Tomorrow!" Debbie brought up the fact that we had committed our place for a snowmobile club party the following Sunday. Canceling the party was not an option so I slowed my time line down a bit.

My spontaneity was not due to lack of thought or planning that needs to be done prior to undertaking such a trip. Over the course of the winter, I'd laid the trip out using the 1988 Flood Control and Navigation Maps of the Lower Mississippi put out by the Corps of Engineers. These cover the area from Cairo Illinois to the Gulf of

Mexico. I also found a publication called Quimby's, proving to be invaluable over the years. It is like AAA for boaters.

Now I had to get permission to take two weeks off from work on such short notice. With no major projects going on, and having a boss that believed me when I said a relative new hire could cover my job, resulted in another hurdle cleared. My parents and two of my three married sisters live in Washington, Iowa. They agreed between them to take care of the boys.

We left Minnesota Sunday night after the snowmobile club party. After dropping the boys off in Washington, Iowa, we continued onto Cairo, Illinois arriving at 9:00 PM, on Monday, August 3rd. We were already 730 miles from Lakeville.

Downtown Cairo had many abandoned buildings, and the active businesses had barred windows and doors. Stopping outside Smith and Groves Bar, which is two blocks from the Ohio River, I told Debbie I was going inside to inquire about river conditions. Initially saying she would wait in the pickup quickly changed her mind when I opened the pickup door, saying she would go inside, but not for very long.

I asked the bartender about river conditions, who said, "Ask those two guys. They are US Coast Guard." So we did. Over the two pitchers of beer I bought, I told them of our plan to boat the Mississippi to mile zero and then return using the same route. They tried to discourage us by saying there were very few pleasure boat facilities on the lower Mississippi.

Hearing that I was well aware of the lack of facilities on the lower Mississippi, they then asked if we knew of the Tenn-Tom waterway, which I didn't.

It is a canal system that connects the Tennessee River to the Tombigbee River, which then joins the Mobile River, which then flows into the Gulf of Mexico. Built by the Army Corps of Engineers and finished in 1985, the two Coast Guard guys referred to it as the 'ditch.' They encouraged us to consider coming back that way since the Tennessee connects to the Ohio and that would get us back to Cairo.

However using that as a return route also required crossing approximately 125 miles of the Gulf of Mexico between New Orleans and Mobile, Alabama. Another seed planted that germinated and flourished in my mind over the next few days! With Debbie already apprehensive about boating the lower Mississippi, crossing the Gulf was the last thing she wanted to hear.

As I tried to fall asleep in a motel on the northern outskirts of Cairo, I mulled over the idea of doing the loop. Periodically during our trip down the lower Mississippi, I would shout over the sound of the motor, "Do the Ditch! Do the Ditch!"

TUESDAY, AUGUST 4TH, 1992

From what we had seen of Cairo last night, where we could leave the Nissan and boat trailer became an issue. An officer at a police station suggested a nearby junkyard that had a security fence. They wanted $5 a day and we would be limited to their business hours to pick them up. Money and hours of operation aside, it just did not feel right. We found a parking spot on a city street next to a fire station where I felt more comfortable to leave them.

Having made that decision, we went to the Municipal Landing on the Ohio side to launch. There were two ramps leading off from the cement road that passed through the high floodwall surrounding lower Cairo. Both ramps had piles of driftwood blocking access. While cleaning up the steeper of the two, since it had less debris, we recognized that we might have to use the other to load. The shallow-angle ramp had a *major* log lying across it.

After unloading the boat, I drove back six or seven blocks and parked on the street next to the fire station. As I locked the Nissan, I thought maybe I should tell the firefighters that I was leaving it there. They gave permission for me to pull up on the grass and park the Nissan and boat trailer right underneath their 24-hour security light. What a deal! I walked with a much lighter step back to the boat since any concern about leaving the pickup and trailer were now gone. Debbie said she had gotten a whistle from a passing tug while organizing the boat.

We were underway shortly before 10:00 AM. As we entered the confluence of the Ohio and Mississippi, Mile 953 descending, the civil defense test sirens went off, almost as if announcing our departure. As a point of reference, the Mississippi River mileage used in this book is the same as that used in the Upper and Lower set of the Army Corps of Engineers Charts. Mile 0 on the Upper Mississippi set of charts is where the Mississippi joins the Ohio and increases from there, and Mile 953 is the start of the Lower Set and decreases from there.

The width of the river was so much wider than when we had been here in the drought year of 1988. Now it was flowing fast and high requiring me to alter course often to avoid floating debris that varied in size from small sticks to entire trees. We also *enjoyed* the distinct odor of diesel fuel and a smell similar to that of rotten eggs.

Barges become much larger on the lower Mississippi because there are no locks below Saint Louis and the channel widens.

In addition to the fifteen-gallon onboard tank, I had brought 6 six-gallon gas containers. This gave us a **maximum** range of just over 229 miles based on the 4.5 mpg averaged in 1988.

At 2:30, we saw people fishing off the bank at Caruthersville, Missouri, Mile 845.5, and stopped to buy fuel. With the next known marina still over 100 miles away, I pulled up to the bank and grabbed two empty containers intending to walk to the closest gas station I could find. A large black man volunteered to drive me there. With no knowledge of where or how far away the nearest gas was, I gladly accepted. Between him and a young boy who got in the other side of the pickup, they totally filled the cab leaving only the pickup bed for me. They waited while I filled the two containers and took me back. It was probably a one mile round trip, and he would not accept any money.

We arrived at Mud Island Marina, Mile 735 in Memphis at 7:00 PM. Just in time to witness a photo shoot with female models posing on a boat. I could not decide whether they were promoting the boat or the models, but it was a pleasant view in any case. Our overnight moorage was right next to the gas pumps. After showering and getting dressed up to go out for dinner, we found out that the monorail connection servicing Mud Island Mississippi River Museum to downtown closed. We could have called a cab, but elected to use the Coleman stove to heat up the evening meal.

The museum is well worth visiting, touring it on a land trip three years later.

It was a comfortable night in the boat, not needing the warmth of sleeping bags until early morning.

WEDNESDAY, AUGUST 5TH, 1992

While putting in 27.2 gallons of gas at Mud Island, a man told us that we would be able to tie up to a dock in Vicksburg, Mississippi next to an excursion boat, the John Hoseman. We were on the river at 8:30.

It was 3:00 when we arrived at Greenville, Mississippi, 198.6 miles downstream. All the auxiliary cans were empty and the gas gauge was on E, but from experience I knew the main tank still held five gallons upon hitting E. I knew I had cut it close because it took twelve gallons to fill the fifteen-gallon tank.

Shortly after leaving Greenville, lightning lit up the sky. A major rainstorm quickly followed. Lightning is my second worst fear, behind rough water, in a small boat since it is indefensible and indiscriminate. We went to shore and debated whether to stay put, go back to Greenville, or continue onto Vicksburg.

I remember being on Lake Odessa when a major storm came up. Doing the wise thing, Dad pulled up on shore to wait it out. A large lightning strike hit a tree, crashing within sight of us. I have had respect of lightning ever since.

With the storm seeming to abate, we continued. Then a major squall hit while passing a large string of barges. Not having windshield wipers, visibility was almost zero. With lightning strikes closely followed by extremely loud thunder, my heart rate must have closely matched that of the tachometer.

The storm had passed over by the time of our arrival to Vicksburg where we then headed up the Yazoo River, expecting to find the John Hoseman.

Not finding the tour boat John Hoseman, we idled past numerous identical small boats moored next to the towboat 'Christy.' Upon seeing 'John', a crewmember of the 'Christy', we asked permission to moor overnight saying we were traveling the lower Mississippi and headed for the Gulf. He gave the OK.

John walked over while we were in the midst of organizing for the night, asking where we had started. While talking, he noticed Debbie setting up the Coleman stove. He said to put it away and invited us aboard to use their shower and stove, which I accepted. After John left, Debbie said she did not feel comfortable about being on the boat with the all male crew.

With the boat covered, we boarded the Christy. I went to take a shower, while Debbie checked out the cooking facilities. After showering, I came back to the cooking/dining room area. Robert, the engineer/cook, was frying huge steaks, saying no one but he cooked aboard.

As we prepared to eat, I asked if they cared for a beer. They accepted so I brought the cooler in from the boat. While Debbie and I had our beer in plain sight, they put theirs in a brown paper sack, which I thought was rather odd. I found out that they were going out the next morning and were not supposed to drink alcohol in the 24-hour period preceding.

They told us about the owner of the Christy, and referred to him as J.O. He owned a few car dealerships in the area and was chair of a bank. The small boats we had tied next to were river survey boats that J.O. leased to the government. He also owned two other push boats that were currently on the Tenn-Tom, the Betty Pierce, and the Melvin L. King. The crew had a lot of respect for him saying that he would still work on even the dirtiest job if needed. They also said he is always on the phone and always had a smile on his face.

While eating, drinking beer, and swapping stories, one of J.O.'s sons stopped in to ask why a private boat was tied to their dock. It was an uncomfortable moment as it was obvious they were drinking beer and had invited us aboard. J.O.' son did not say much, but when he left John called J. O. to explain the situation. J. O. said that John should not have given permission for us to dock without calling him as it was **his** dock. John said he just did what he thought J.O. would do. J.O. said he would not make John look like a fool and we could go ahead and stay.

However, J.O. said to be sure that John guided us back to our boat over the uneven dock so that we would not fall in the darkness. He'd been sued once before by a pleasure boater who had gotten hurt on his dock.

Robert gave me a tour of the Christy, while Debbie took a shower. It held 25,000 gallons of diesel fuel, and had two engines of 6,000-horse power each. The propeller, called a wheel, was four feet in diameter.

John had not told J.O. that he would take me into town with the company pickup to buy gas, which he still did. John and I took all six of our gas containers, stopping at the station he knew to be the cheapest. He also helped carry them to the boat.

In asking what we would encounter down river, there was a dispute between Robert and Charles over which side of the river Natchez was on. They placed a fifty-dollar bet between them. Charles was trying to tell us about a bar in a restored 1860 building with Civil War memorabilia in it. After politely sidestepping why he was so sure, Charles finally blurted out, "I know it's on the right as you go down river. I was just there. I have to say it straight out! There is a cathouse there too, with a red light on one of the four tall buildings. It has a bar just like on Gunsmoke where they slide beer down." This was an especially memorable conversion while aboard the Christy. For the record, Charles was wrong. Natchez is on the east side of the river.

THURSDAY, AUGUST 6TH, 1993

It rained heavily at 3:00 & 7:00 AM, accompanied by lightning and very loud thunder. The mooring cover sagged and dripped water everywhere, making it a miserable night. We were up at 9:00, and learned from the VHF radio weather station that some areas of the Mississippi had received 12 inches of rain. Noticing water above the sub floor, I turned on the bilge pump. The pump didn't work so I used a coffee can and sponge. When the rain changed to a drizzle we packed up and left by 10:00.

Packing up is a major operation itself. Given a choice, and if there is sufficient dock space, we always take the gas containers out. Even with them gone the stench of gas is always present, since the mooring cover completely encloses the boat to keep out rain and bugs. The two fire extinguishers aboard probably would not quell a fire quickly enough to avoid jumping overboard. The gas containers are carried two aside and three deep in front of the motor cover and between our two seats.

We convert our individual beds back to seating position, and stow the sleeping bags, pillows, sheets, etc in a big vinyl bag kept in the bow alongside the folded mooring cover. Our two coolers then fill the only remaining aisle space.

The remaining limited storage was utilized as follows; Debbie kept food and cooking utensils under the open bow cushions. Under the back-to-back seats, we kept fleece jackets and rain gear. Under the two rear seats, I kept a basic set of tools, extra prop, and extra motor oil. In the glove compartment were cameras, charts, sun tan lotion, etc. Alongside one seat, we squeezed the propane two burner Coleman stove. Then there are always the things that need to be handy; such as life jackets, a flare gun, and numerous cassette tapes.

There is *just* enough space for our needs, and to reach any one thing required moving two or three to get to it.

With wet sleeping bags draped over the seats and rain threatening, we headed to Natchez, Mile 364.

Our view of Natchez from water level was typical to that of other cities that have turned their backs to the waterfront after having their heyday because of the river. We drifted by eating a typical lunch consisting of sausage/cheese with crackers, carrots & celery, and a Little Debbie snack product for dessert.

In approaching Baton Rouge, Louisiana, we found the side channel where we had planned to spend the night rocked shut! The threatening rain started falling right after we finished putting up the canopy. This only offers protection from the elements in the middle third of the boat.

Four miles later we arrived at Red's Boat Shop, tucking in behind their dock just as a very heavy rain started to fall. We stashed our just dried sleeping bags under the folded mooring cover. It was a good thing we had also put on rain gear as the driving rain still found its way in.

While waiting for the storm to abate, we decided to find more secure moorage. The current was running very fast through the narrow channel by Red's and barge traffic was causing a lot of river chop. Using Quimby's, we found a place allowing overnight dockage three miles downstream called Cargo Carriers and radioed them. An anonymous female voice answered, telling us to go to an old paddle wheel steamboat that was their office. As we approached, 'the voice' said to go around the front of the steamboat, cross under the cable holding it to shore, (we only had about one foot clearance), and tie up to the walkway connecting it to shore. Before 'the voice' signed off, it said gas was available in the morning.

Because the old steamboat was just downstream from another barge, it provided a safe secure calm spot from river traffic. While happy to be there, it was also a very strange situation. We felt like vandals, having crept in without actually seeing anybody, and at the same time like potential victims in the heavily industrialized area.

While Debbie warmed up chili, we listened to barge traffic on the VHF radio. There were two guys talking about moving barges around to create an upstream tow. One rattled off directions to move specific barges with almost the same numbers, (4260, 4262, 5672, 5962, etc) while the other tried to clarify what he was saying. Also the Tater Bug gave wrong boat numbers to the lockmaster at Port Allen, an access point to the Mississippi less than a mile upstream, which really teed off him off.

We had went 209 miles without being able to purchase fuel, and the gas gauge had hit **E** once again.

FRIDAY, AUGUST 7TH, 1992

Partially due to using the day canopy to support the mooring cover, the boat was so tight it was dripping condensation due to high humidity.

Wanting to get out as early as possible to avoid local barge traffic, I grabbed gas cans upon seeing activity. We bought 30 gallons, enough to get us safely to New Orleans, and gave $40 cash for the $38.52 metered charge since they only accept cash. Their till was not officially open and since the amount was minimal, I said to forget the change. That is until the two men helping us found out we were from the Twin Cities. Both used to live in Minneapolis, working for Cargill, before transferring to

Cargo Carriers. Having established Minnesota connections they felt bad about being unable to make change, and dug into their pockets finding $1.20 between them to give back. They also offered free coffee, and ice from a machine like you'd find in a hotel, both of which we gladly accepted.

I asked if they ever saw canoeists go by, as we had seen several on the Upper Mississippi who said they were going all the way to the Gulf. They told of one who last year had tipped in the fast choppy water right next to them. He yelled for help, but was swept under a parked barge before he could be reached. The canoe came up downstream and the body sometime later.

They are not in the business of selling gas or providing transient dockage. They ship grain products all over the world, and sometimes allow transients to dock as a good will gesture.

At 8:00 we were on our way, coolers full of ice, and coffee in hand. It was calm, with few barges on the move as we passed through heavily industrialized Baton Rouge. We saw the Delta Queen heading up river, and the African Carmilla, an ocean going boat at anchor. We passed the Steal Leader pushing a load of rock the fourth time in four days, and the Butch Borras the third time. The large pieces of floating wood encountered at Cairo were smaller, put still plentiful.

At 9:45 we met our first ocean-going freighter actually underway, the Fantasy L. I told Debbie to take a picture, as it may be her last! Its wake was very different than I had expected it to be. Instead of the sharp, short, closely spaced, punishing wake of the barges, the freighter left very large swells, with no real high or low point. It was nice not having to slow way up, and bob up and down waiting for wakes to subside. The marked channel was now much wider which made it much easier to stay out of the worst part of any chop.

A strange phenomenon of the Deep South is the regular appearance of local heavy rainfalls around two or three in the afternoon, irrespective of any regional storm systems. The rainstorms previously experienced were the result of a major weather system passing through. Now there were times when we would see rainfall dumping ahead of us. We'd put rain gear on, and then as often as not the river's course would change and we'd miss it. It could be pouring rain on one side of us with the sun shining brightly on the other.

It was a beautiful day with very little water traffic or wind making a mostly calm river. During a stop to add gas just below the Vieux Carre, French for Old Quarter, I reminisced on being here during Mardi Gras in 1971.

I had gotten separated from the two guys I was with, but we'd agreed to meet back at the car in the parking ramp if that happened. I got back to the parking ramp around 4:00 AM, only to find the car gone. I slept in a wheelbarrow at the ramp entrance with my shirt pulled up over my head while waiting for my friends to return. Around 6:30, a maintenance worker woke me and said, "I let you sleep as I long as I could, but now I need my wheel barrow." They came back around 8:00, having been kicked out of the ramp for sleeping in the car.

Immediately across from the U.S. Naval Docks is a lock that opens to a canal leading to Lake Pontchartrain, where we planned to stay the night. Debbie, being the navigator/radioman, tried to call Algiers Lock on Channel 14 to arrange passage. She never actually talked to the lockmaster, and we followed a tug into the lock. Fortunately it was headed to Lake Pontchartrain, contacting the lift bridge operators along the way. We could hear their two-way conversations, with the bridge operators choosing to ignore us. Three very low lift bridges needed to be raised. The last one got stuck, and we listened on the VHF radio as the bridge boss talked to the tug on Channel 13 about the delay.

Upon entering Lake Pontchartrain, we turned left, with New Orleans Lakefront Airport being to our right. We encountered numerous small white spherical floating objects, and saw several tall brightly colored markers shaped like a crayon off in the distance. I was freaking out! They were like nothing I had ever seen, with their meaning not identifiable using our charts.

We found transient dockage at Municipal Yacht Harbor, a Five Star Hotel compared to spending the last two nights moored next to the Christy and the old steamboat. When I asked what the unidentified markers meant the answers showed how naïve we were. The small white spherical buoys were crab pot markers, and the tall crayon type markers were used by sailboats for races, as checkpoints or turn-around identifiers.

While preparing to go out on the town, we talked to a man with a large boat about what it was like to be on the Gulf. He showed us his twin-engine boat capable of running 65 mph and tried to talk me into buying it to finish our trip. With the mileage gauged closer to gallons per mile instead of miles per gallon, a deal was so far out of the realm of possibility that price never came up. Having talked to him about what it was like to be on the Gulf, we both felt more comfortable about the possibility of crossing it to Mobile Bay, following the Intracoastal Waterway. Most of the area we would be covering is referred to as the Mississippi Sound, and is somewhat protected from the wide-open Gulf by barrier islands.

Pat, a marina security guard, gave us a ride to the bus stop, and from there we made it to the French Quarter, getting off at Bourbon Street. I was not 'up' to being a tourist, but enjoyed an excellent steak at Morton's Steakhouse.

During the cab ride back to the marina, I told the driver about our trip. He said that his father had done some river canoeing and had traveled across Lake Pontchartrain by canoe with some of his adventures appearing in the local papers.

SATURDAY, AUGUST 8TH, 1992

We finally had a night without rain, but there was still water in the bilge. Since the pump didn't work, I'd been bailing by hand daily. As I sponged the last of it out, I noticed a trickle coming in through the lower unit housing. It could only come in when the boat is not on plane, so I decided not to spend time figuring out why. It did make sleeping for the rest of the trip more difficult because now I had to worry about sinking at the dock.

Over dinner last night, we discussed crossing the Gulf and decided that if the waves were below three feet and the weather prediction was favorable, it was a go. Since the Municipal Marina did not sell fuel or charts for the Gulf, we went to nearby Schubert Marina to do both.

The charts produced under the direction of NOAA, (National Oceanic and Atmospheric Administration), were unlike anything we had seen before. They had so much more cryptic information than the river charts we were accustomed to using. The marina attendant gave us a 'short' course on how to interpret them. We bought the three that would get us from New Orleans to the entrance of Mobile Bay, costing $13.25 each.

We still had ninety-two one-way miles of the Mississippi to finish before our goal of traveling its length was complete. It is a common misconception that the Mississippi ends at New Orleans. It probably did at one time, but due to erosion, the delta continues to expand every year.

In transiting back to the Mississippi, we again had trouble communicating with the lift bridges, slipping through with tugs. While again trying to contact Algiers Lock, Debbie found out that our intended locks name is locally known as the Industrial Lock. Upon closer examination of the 1988 US Army Corps of Engineers Mississippi River chart page that shows the area, we found that Algiers is 4.6 miles further downstream and part of the Intracoastal Waterway. Also in looking at the 1988 US Army Corps Mississippi River chart, we did not see the name Industrial Lock, it being identified as the Inner Harbor Navigation Canal Lock. Quimby's had it listed as the Industrial Canal Lock, but we had not been using it for navigation purposes.

By 11:00, we were back on the Mississippi and headed for Mile Zero, more of an artificial ending than its name indicates. At Mile Zero, referred to on the chart as the Head of Passes, you have a choice of three channels to reach the Gulf. After passing three or four freighters and two barges in the New Orleans area, the water became smoother.

We darted in and around thunderstorms and the further south we went the increasing wind caused us to have a rough ride, especially when the channel was at maximum exposure to it.

At Mile 10, known as 'The Jump,' we stopped to fuel up at a place that was busy servicing charter, shrimp, and pleasure fishing boats. The pleasure fishing boats were the first small boats seen on the river since leaving Cairo, other than a couple small Jon boats that were obviously day fishing.

The fuel attendant there told me that the Loutre/North Pass was the closest route to the Gulf from Mile Zero, with boats of all sizes coming in there.

It was 3:00 when we got to Mile Zero; from there we followed the Loutre channel. The area looked much like the beginning of the Mississippi, with reeds growing along either side, only much wider.

About three miles from the Gulf, the channel split and I took the right branch. As we quickly approached an oil rig, I noticed water breaking on rocks just before it. I immediately throttled back and settled into less than two feet of water. It was 3:30 and we had literally hit the Gulf! We got out in the soft sticky mud and pushed the boat back to deeper water.

We popped the cork off a bottle of champagne to celebrate the occasion and reveled in the moment.

We had traveled the entire length of the Mississippi, Lake Itasca to the Gulf!

Looking back, I realized the gas attendant said Loutre/**North** Pass. *If* I had taken the left branch, it would have been the North Pass, but I took the **South** Pass. Oh, well, it was more symbolic that we started out touching bottom, and finished the same way. As we ran the unmarked Loutre channel back, I followed another boat's wake. In varying only five feet off its course to the north, we came to another quick stop by hitting hard sand. It was ironic hitting bottom twice **after** Mile Zero and not at all between the Twin Cities and Mile Zero. The boat we had been following stopped, but upon seeing us back off with out damage continued.

We raced against the sun, attempting to get back to New Orleans by dark. Due to thunderstorms, it got dark much earlier than normal. Freighter and barge traffic was lighter, and with the wind mostly coming from behind, it made for a quicker and smoother return trip.

7:40 found us making our third transit through what we now knew was the Industrial Lock. They still would not talk to us on the VHF radio, so we slipped through with two short barge/tug combos.

It was dark as we exited the lock. Our plan was to overnight at the Gulf Outlet Marina, location known because of Quimby's. This required following the Intracoastal Waterway east fifteen miles, leaving it to follow the Mississippi River Gulf Outlet for a mile, find the entrance to Bayou Bienvenue, and go another twisty two miles.

With Debbie using a flashlight to coordinate our progress against NOAA Chart #11367 to the various flashing and blinking lights and bridges we were passing by and under, I stayed in the center of the channel running at 30 mph. It was scary as we zipped by moored barges in the relatively narrow channel, although everything was matching up perfectly.

I started to relax upon finding the entrance to Bayou Bienvenue, only to see yellow flashing lights warning of a swift current between the walls of a dike under the bridge entrance. We made it through only to encounter mosquito's intent on sampling Minnesota blood and getting lost in a maze of milk jug buoys. I could not determine if their intent was to mark the channel or warn of obstructions. After pushing off mud more than once, we encountered a family fishing for crab who gave us good directions to the marina. It being well after closing time for the marina, we tied up to the seawall next to a busy seafood restaurant.

SUNDAY, AUGUST 9TH, 1992

After listening to the VHF weather report of clear in the morning with PM thunderstorms and just one to two foot swells predicted, the decision was **GO. Do the Gulf, and the Ditch!**

Departing from Gulf Outlet Marina at 8:00 with a full load of fuel, we rejoined the Intracoastal Waterway at mile 15(Rigolets-New Orleans Cut). Debbie's job was to keep track of the directional and mile marker buoys and inform me of course changes, while mine was to run a straight course without the use of a compass.

Since our original plan had not included crossing the Gulf, we were unprepared in several ways. Surprisingly the Gulf is shallow in many places and a depth finder would have helped us stay in the shipping channel. We did not have a compass, since prior to the Gulf crossing all we really needed to know was if we were heading upstream or down, easily determined by current or mile markers. Finally, we had not brought binoculars, which simply was an oversight. They would have been helpful to pick up the widely spaced navigation markers, some as much as eight miles apart.

At one point we lost tract of where we were on the Intracoastal Waterway. Coming upon a buoy that did not match expectations, Debbie tried to persuade me that it was mis-marked and we were still on course. I said, "No, If that buoy # is?, then that is where we are at." "We need to locate that # on the chart and that is where we are." Moreover, I was correct. We were off course about five miles, and headed north into Biloxi, Mississippi instead of being on course to Mobile Bay.

Overall, I did a good job of navigating between waypoints. While each freestanding navigation tower confirms a location, very often course adjustments are required. I'm ashamed to admit that with each change of course, I would simply study the approximate degree of change and head off on the new course. I would glance back at the boats wake to see if I was running a straight course. The normal procedure is to align and follow the new compass heading.

The seas never got higher than one to two foot, making it an excellent day to cross. While adding gas just outside Mobile Bay, two porpoises surfaced and playfully followed us into Mobile Bay.

Needing gas, we blindly explored every marked channel heading west on Mobile Bay. I had scrimped and not purchased the NOAA chart that covers Mobile Bay. I kicked myself for being cheap since the bay is huge! It was Hot! A patrol boat encountered in a 'No Wake Zone' gave us directions to the side channel that lead to Dog River where Quimby's had noted several facilities. It was the next west channel and three miles away.

At 3:30 we arrived at Grand Mariner Marina, where we had a friendly conversation telling of our unusual loop trip. We bought enough gas to reach Lady's Landing, the planned overnight destination that was still another 100-mile distance away.

We bought the Army Corp river charts covering the Mobile, Tombigbee, and Tenn-Tom Waterway systems. They copied the small portion of Mobile Bay still left to travel and gave us old charts of the Tennessee and Ohio left behind by previous boaters.

My dock departure was uncharacteristically amateurish, banging into it several times. Either the tide was going out, or the Dog River's current swept towards the dock, or a combination of both.

Upon getting back to the shipping lane, it was a race to reach the protected area of an inland river before the thunderstorms visible against the black sky let loose.

While passing through Mobile, we saw numerous ship and barge facilities, idle due to being Sunday. Debbie noticed the chart marked channel depth changed from 55,' to 40,' to 9' within a three-mile period of the Mobile River.

Mile 45 is the head of the Mobile River, formed by where the Alabama and Tombigbee Rivers meet. Since the Tombigbee connects via the Tenn-Tom Waterway to the Tennessee, we followed it upstream.

From a brochure put out by the US Army Corps of Engineers called Black Warrior & Tombigbee Lakes, we learned Tombigbee derived its name from a creek, the Etomba-lgaby (box makers creek). The French had a fort on this creek in the 18th century, and they corrupted its name to Tombecke. English-speaking settlers simplified it further, calling it the Tombigby. Then it ended up being Tombigbee. Mile numbers do not start over at the junction.

At Mile 55.5, we had our closest encounter yet with a towboat pushing a small string of barges. While rounding a tight, narrow, 90-degree right turn in the midst of some of the heaviest rainfall we had ever experienced, we met an oncoming barge!

I headed as far to the right side of the bank as I could. Then to make matters worse, two huge lightning strikes, simultaneously followed by two correspondingly loud thunder cracks hit, seemingly occurring as one. The stern of the push boat passed within ten feet of us as it maneuvered into the turn. I honestly doubt the pilot even knew we were there. After it went by, I nosed the bow into the side of the river with the highest bank. Debbie yelled at me about going into shallow water. I explained that the side of the river with the highest bank is typically the deepest. We stayed there until the rain let up, keeping the motor in slow forward to hold us against the bank.

It was to a clearing sky that we arrived at Lady's Landing, not much more than a long dock on a sweeping bend of the river. While concerned about exposure to 24-hour barge traffic, we decided that it was better to tie up to a dock than some tree along the bank. We climbed many steps and passed three goats grazing the steep bank to reach the mobile home office. The owner said his land was in a hunting area that included deer, bear, and even a panther or two. He also mentioned that an alligator had sunned itself on the dock just two weeks ago.

I tied up with our 'best' lines', nothing more than pieces of old polyurethane water-ski towrope. Debbie gave permission to buy new ones since I expressed doubt about their holding ability. Just after falling asleep, the passing of the first barge caused me to wake up and start grabbing for stuff. After that, even with the passing barge's annoying spotlights and large wakes, we slept well.

MONDAY, AUGUST 10TH, 1992

Even though we were up at 6:30, untypical of me, I didn't push to get started. While Debbie fixed breakfast, I threw sticks for Hershey, their chocolate Labrador retriever. One of the goats liked being petted, and I nick named him Billy Bob. It took another 2 ½ hours before we left Lady's Landing with a full load of fuel and a supply of spring water that the owner insisted we take.

The Tenn-Tom Waterway opened in 1985, part of its purpose being a shorter water connection to the eastern part of the Gulf. Due to the nature of any changed river system, the Tombigbee has areas of high eroding banks, and evolving sandy beaches. We met barges carrying coal, and others with logs, with many logs piled along the bank awaiting transport.

While adding gas to the main fuel tank at Mile 184.6, we heard over the VHF weather station that it was 90 degrees, with a heat index of 100, and 100 % humidity. When I went to start the motor, all that happened was a whir. We paddled off to the side in case a barge happened by to let the motor cool off, hoping that would make a difference. While periodically trying the starter, we ate a sausage/cheese/cracker lunch.

In checking electrical connections and finding no apparent problems, I resorted to creative problem solving. I got out a hammer, tapped the starter, and then turned the key to see if anything had freed up. Debbie thought I was nuts! Not getting the desired result, I got out and started to pull the boat African Queen style to a boat ramp two miles upstream.

Upon seeing a barge coming upstream, we contacted them on VHF Channel 16. The Alabama Star answered back. I asked if they would send help from Demopolis Yacht Basin, thirty-two miles upstream, since we were out of VHF range. Just a note: The weather channel can be received over a much greater distance than I can transmit on. After I explained the problem, they told us to stay put. The captain nudged the front of their tow into the opposite bank, and then idled the stern close to us, whereupon I pushed the boat to close the remaining distance between us.

The three-man crew checked the same things I had. One had me turn the key, while he tapped the starter with a hammer. It started! Almost the same thing I had tried, except **I** turned the key while **they** tapped the starter.

The captain said that if it was up to him we could have tied onto the towboat for the upstream trip, except insurance reasons prohibited it. We asked if they knew anybody from the 'Christy' at Vicksburg, with the captain knowing Robert, the engineer.

With heartfelt thanks given, we continued onto Demopolis Lock, Mile 213.4, careful not to shut the motor off. While waiting to lock through, I contacted Demopolois Yacht Basin just upstream of the lock. It was 4:00 and I wanted to arrange repair. Their plan was to pull the starter first thing in the morning, have it rebuilt, and back in by closing, which seemed almost too good to be true.

We also talked to the Betty Pierce, one of J.O.'s tugs, waiting to lock downstream.

Demopolois Yacht Basin put us in the only available covered slip next to some very nice boats and only charged $8.50. Dinner was at the Riverview; Debbie had crab claws while I had my third steak of the trip. It looked skinny compared to the ones eaten on the Christy, and at Morton's, while still being very good.

TUESDAY, AUGUST 11TH, 1992

Gus came by and removed the starter, taking it to town to be worked on.

During the downtime, we called Iowa and talked to the boy's. They were having a good time and not in a hurry for us to return. We greatly appreciated the covered slip since the temperature under it was at least 10-15 degrees cooler than the hot day.

A young man studying for a Captains license gave us a tour of a new for sale large houseboat, having just piloted it here. At sixteen feet wide, seventy foot long, three bedrooms, two baths, more cupboards than at our home, dishwasher, trash compactor, full size refrigerator, washer/dryer, wet bar, generator, hull storage, A/C, etc, very nice and once again out of our price range.

Gus reinstalled the starter at 1:30. The repair shop had not gotten the starter to fail, but replaced the brushes and bushings worn from use. The cause of the starter problem was quite possibly due to the continually wet conditions experienced over the last seven days. I was still bailing every morning because of the leak around the I/O boot, and then there were the daily rains.

With full gas tanks, and hearing the call of the river, we were back on the water at 2:00. We locked through Gainesville at 4:30, Mile 266 and arrived at Tom Bevill Lock at 6:00, Mile 307. While locking through Tom Bevill, we talked via VHF radio to the 'Snow Goose' a recreational boat staying the summer at a local marina. Originally from Minnesota, they alternated between Florida in the winter, and points north during the summer. They wanted us to stop by, but I continued onto the 'Tote-N-Float' having heard from the two Coast Guard guys at Cairo that it is a real party place.

At 8:00, we arrived at the 'Tote-N-Float,' Mile 338.8, after locking through Columbus, Mile 335, to a dark and quiet spot with just one boat tied to the dock. It had closed early and was obviously not going to be a wild spot tonight.

While Debbie readied the boat for sleeping, I talked to the two men aboard the Shamrock.

Jerimy invited me aboard his at forty-foot boat, with Debbie joining soon after. Jerimy had been a fire chief in Florida, until he was blown out of a burning auto parts store in a fiery explosion. He had had eight back operations since and was unable to work. With the help of his friend Dale, they were transiting the Shamrock to SE Ohio where Jerimy's wife had a job. The plan was for Jerimy and his wife to live aboard the Shamrock since she is from there.

While passing by Pensacola, Florida, they rescued two swimmers unable to swim back to shore against the outgoing tide.

Dale had brought a female acquaintance, but since she did not like to do any work and was bitching and drinking was debarked at Demopolois and given $100 to get home. Telling Jerimy she was not getting off, he said that that is the quickest way to be evicted.

Dale, a sailboat owner, kept saying that the Gulf was easy; but then would tell another story about storms, rough seas, and running aground.

Just before going to sleep, we put up the canopy and placed a polyethylene tarp under the mooring cover since it no longer shed water as it should and storms were approaching.

I fell asleep quickly, awaking with a start when rain started pounding down. I sat straight up, pulled the tarp and canvas off my side, and in seeing land started yelling about being aground. Debbie tried to tell me I was dreaming and we were safe at a dock. I said, "This is a two person operation. You should be looking out for land too!" She said, "You're not driving". "Yes I am. I'm driving right now!" She proved her point by shining the flashlight on our gas cans tied to the dock, bringing me out of my nightmare.

WEDNESDAY, AUGUST 12TH, 1992

When I turned the key to leave at 7:00, the starter would not *disengage* for a while, just the opposite of the original starter problem.

Aberdeen Lock 7:30, Lock A 8:30, Now the Tenn-Tom **really is a ditch**, straight and narrow, with Lock B visible even though five miles from Lock A.

Lock B 10:00 – Played Gin Rummy while waiting for a tow to lock through.

At 10:30, we arrived at Smithville Marina, finding nobody 'minding the store.' We talked to two men, one a teacher, who told us about good eating spots on the Tennessee River. While waiting to buy gas, we played cribbage in the shade of the porch. Forty-five minutes later the friendly little old man who ran the marina returned in his pickup. While fueling, we told him of our trip.

Apologizing for not having a good stock of groceries, he offered the use of his pickup. "Want to take my truck and go the Piggly Wiggly store?" Still not used to southern drawl we naturally got a kick out of it. Not really needing anything, we kindly thanked him for the offer. There is nothing quite like southern hospitality, and we truly appreciated it.

11:30 – Headed for Lock C. The five locks lettered A through E are referred to as the Alphabet Locks, separated by thirty-five total miles. The lockmaster at each asked if we were going through to the next, and upon hearing confirmation called ahead to alert the next one.

Lock C 12:00, Lock D 12:30, Lock E 1:00. Lock E referred to us as, "An RV in the chamber."

1:40 Bay Springs Lock, Mile 412, Lift of 84 feet. We were the only ones in the 600' X 110' very clean water of the lock chamber, the same dimension but not lift as all the locks since leaving the Gulf. While sitting in the high lift lock, I told Debbie "I feel like the Tidy Bowl Man."

The following information is word for word from a brochure published February 1989 and produced by the 'The Tennessee Tombigbee Waterway Development Authority'.

425.9-418.9 – The Divide Cut is the topographic divide (line of hills) between the Tennessee and Tombigbee River basins separating Bay Springs Lake on the Tenn-Tom and Pickwick Lake on the Tennessee River. Over 150 million cubic yards of earth were removed to form the 39 mile long Divide cut – more than that excavated for the Suez Canal. A total of 350 million cubic yards were removed from the entire waterway, or nearly twice that removed for the construction of the Panama Canal, making Tenn-Tom the largest earth excavation project in history. At the deepest point (near River Mile 425) excavation depths reached 175 feet'

All remaining lockages to Cairo would be down, while all since the Gulf had been up. At Mile 419, we entered a twenty-four mile narrow channel referred to as the 'Divide Cut' with a normal elevation of 414 ft. The view is of red colored side hills, and rock cut banks

3:00 – Swimming in the clean cool water of the ditch took the place of our missed morning shower.

3:30 – We arrived at the end/beginning of the Tennessee-Tombigbee Waterway, mile 450.7 and its junction to the Tennessee River, Mile 215.2.

4:30 – Left Pickwick Lock. Around Mile 170, Debbie said the limestone cliffs looked at lot like those of the Wisconsin Dells. There were numerous old cabins, and fancy new homes built along the river bluff.

7:30 – With the gas dock closed upon our arrival at Cuba Landing Marina, mile 115.5, I went looking for someone to point us to an unassigned slip. The manager, who lived in a nearby mobile home, told me to tie up to the gas dock. We had just gotten the boat secured and extra gas cans set out on the dock when the manager walked down. Not realizing we were in a canvassed boat, he then gave us a covered slip since it looked like rain. When had it not rained since starting?

Dinner was at Dot & Doug Donaldson's houseboat, a couple we met at the gas dock. Dot, a retired high school English teacher, and Doug, a retired oil rigger, were transiting a houseboat for their son. He had been looking for one similar to what Dot and Doug had, finding it through a broker at Miss Croix Marina, just upstream from Kings Cove where we bought The Boat.

The route chosen to transit the houseboat from Hastings, Minnesota, required taking the Mississippi to Cairo, up the Ohio to the Tennessee, to the Tenn-Tom, to the Mobile, crossing the Gulf and to Lake Charles, Louisiana.

Over a meal of New England Boil (Pot Roast), we exchanged notes about our trips. They broke two props while passing the mouth of the Missouri River because of floating debris.

THURSDAY, AUGUST 13TH, 1992

It did not rain overnight! We almost had ourselves a cat. While having a final conversation with Dot and Doug, I pushed off the dock without starting the engine. About eight feet from the dock I turned the ignition key which caused mad scramble by a previously unseen cat to leap onto Debbie, jump on me, and then to the safety of the dock.

At 8:00, we were on the choppy river with the wind in our faces.

It was 11:00 when we arrived at Kentucky Lock and Dam, with only twenty-two miles separating us from the Ohio River. Debbie radioed for passage, finding out it was at least a 2 ½ hour wait. The Kentucky Lock suggested we go upstream to the Barkley Canal, cross to the Cumberland River, and use the Barkley Lock. It is a good twenty miles further, but would be faster if we could lock through Barkley quicker.

We stopped at Light House Landing to buy 12 gallons of gas, enough to get us to Cairo and the end of the trip. I bought two 3/8 inch nylon-mooring lines, filling the promise made to myself at Lady's Landing.

While waiting to lock through Barkley at 11:30, we talked to a couple from Indiana who had been up the Cumberland visiting parents. They broke a prop turning off the Ohio and up the Cumberland when they missed the channel in a rainstorm.

As we cruised on the Cumberland, Debbie said it felt like we were boating downhill.

We entered the Ohio at Mile 924, and in passing by Joppa, Illinois, thirty miles upstream of Cairo, Debbie noted a usable boat ramp in case Cairo was full of driftwood.

Having traveled over 2000 miles in ten days and completing fifteen lockages, we arrived back to Cairo at 3:30.

The trip had taken an entirely different tone due to our chance encounter with the Coast Guard at Smith & Groves.

The boat ramps were not bad so we cleared the wood debris off the shallower angle of the two. We chatted with a man watching his grandson throw rocks in the river. He said that he had a cabin and a pontoon boat on Kentucky Lake. Debbie was going to walk to the pickup, while I cleaned the scum off the boat, but the grandfather offered her a ride. His grandson was disappointed, as he still wanted to throw more rocks.

Debbie found the pickup in the same shape as we had left it, and thanked the fire department for allowing us to park there. It took forty-five minutes to finish cleaning, load the boat, and pack for the road after Debbie returned.

The only thing different on the boat was a couple small dings to the aluminum prop. One of the pluses about a small boat besides price and fuel economy is maneuverability. When I saw debris, a quick flip of the steering wheel is all that it usually took to avoid it. Besides hitting bottom at the end of the Mississippi, I tapped something only once when I took too wide of a turn on a curve and ended up outside the channel.

We made a quick stop at Smith & Groves and told the same bartender and two other men who worked for the utility company how our trip turned out. One said, "I've always wanted to go on the river and do that." It was said in such a way that he already knew he would never do it.

It was too late and I was too tired to drive nonstop back to Washington, Iowa, so we found a room at the Budget Inn at Cape Girardeau. We cleaned up and walked to Mr. B's for their Mexican Buffet, having a nice conversation with a retired female teacher from the area.

After eating a fine meal and settling into a comfortable bed after ten days on the water, you would think I would sleep soundly. But no! I woke up and did not know where I was. My first thought was I was in the hull of a freighter! There was a dull drone as one might come from the sound of muffled diesel engines. And there was an oblong shaped light coming from what appeared to be a hatch cover.

I thought, "How the hell did I get in here, and how am I going to get out!" Debbie woke up to see me sitting up.

I told her we had driven into the hull of a freighter!

She tried to convince me that we were in a motel room. "Put your foot on the floor and feel the carpet!" I very tentatively slid my foot to the floor, expecting to find bilge water or a cold metal hull. After a couple taps with my foot, I was reassured.

She pointed out what I thought was a hatch cover, was actually the sliding glass door with the curtain shut and light coming in around from outside.

The diesel hum was actually the sound of the air conditioner running. I guess the stress about crossing the Gulf was worse than I had thought.

FRIDAY, AUGUST 14TH, 1992

Left for Iowa at 9:00 and spent the night in Washington with relatives and the 'boys'

SATURDAY, AUGUST 15TH, 1992

Returned to Lakeville and unpacked

SUNDAY, AUGUST 16TH, 1992

Relaxed for one day, returning to work Monday

TRIP NOTES
1. The starter did not cause any more problems. Had conditions been just too wet?
2. The only thing wrong with the bilge pump was a piece of the broken alternator belt from the 1988 trip inside blocking it from turning.
3. The reason for the trickle of water coming in around the lower unit was due to a small hole in the rubber boot that covers the drive shaft. I do not know if it was there before we started the trip because the boat normally sits out of the water on a boatlift. I had the boot replaced and a tune-up done at the same time.
4. We used 412 gallons of gas, traveling at a usual speed of 32 mph at 4400 rpm, averaging over 4 ½ mpg.

5. The delicate chain holding the gas cap to the fill spout had broken during the trip. So every time I added gas I had to be careful and not lose it. A simple chain splice fixed it.
6. Standard procedure is to change the motor oil and lower unit grease before and after a trip.
7. Not itemizing all trip expenses, I remember thinking that the total cost; boat & pickup gas, 2 nights of motel, dockage fees, food, maps, ice, booze, all repairs, etc was almost exactly the $1500 I had won at the casino.

1993 SAINT CROIX RIVER (GORDON DAM TO HWY 70)

It had been a winter of somewhat normal snowfall followed by abnormal spring and summer rainfall. I had to raise our dock several times. Lake Marion was declared a no wake zone for a period of time. Due to our sandy lakeshore frontage eroding in several places, I worked on a long term solution.

Dad had built a harbor at the resort, protecting it from wave erosion using field rock. I liked the look and tried to find a cheap way to get them. I called Linda Moe, who coordinated getting permission from local farmers to allow trails across their fields for our snowmobile club. She suggested calling Octor Leiny. Octor said he had just sold all his field rock to a landscape firm and said I should call Lyle Ruh.

Lyle, a third generation farmer of the same land, said that over the years they had picked rocks from the tillable soil and piled them next to where the milk cows grazed. Lyle gave permission to take what I wanted and directed me to the tree/hedge line where they were piled.

While returning for a fourth load, I blew a tire on the Nissan while crossing railroad tracks. No problem, I had a spare. After taking off the flat and in lowering the spare from under the pickup, the crank broke. A couple minutes later, a big car coming down the dusty gravel road stopped and offered ne a ride. As I got in the driver extended his hand and started to say his name was Octor - - - - -, I interrupted by saying

"Leiny". And I was right! But then again how many Octors can there be within any given radius? Octor took me to my next-door neighbor's son business, who then drove me home to get a bolt cuter to cut the chain to drop the spare tire.

With the family pitching in to help load/unload, we hauled enough rock in the early summer to stabilize the shore, going back for more in September to fill low spots. The last Saturday in September, Kevin asked if we could go back and get more rock. The question really surprised me until I realized his underlying motive. I'd always let him drive and spin the pickup in Lyle's muddy field road and he wanted to do it some more. We went. We made at least eighty trips over a ten-year period, with both boys learning how to drive and shift a manual transmission in his field.

Even though we were thoroughly enjoying our third summer on the lake, a small family vacation was in order. In late June, we decided to finish boating the rest of the Saint Croix River starting from its upper navigable point in Wisconsin to the Highway 70 Bridge, a distance of about eighty miles.

Leaving Lakeville on Friday, June 26th, at 3 PM, we checked out potential river access meeting points along the way. Not wanting to take two vehicles, Debbie would meet us along the way. It was 8:00 PM by the time we reached Gordon Dam Park, setting the tent up while being swarmed by mosquitoes. While Debbie fixed a late meal, we boys took a dam walk. Wait, Wait, what I mean to say is we took a walk to the dam. Kevin and I told Nate that tomorrow we would be shooting the canoe over the ten-foot drop of the spillway. Nate took us seriously.

Putting the canoe in above the dam the next morning, we motored up to the point where it becomes very shallow, and then headed back to the dam. I made a fake run to shoot over the spillway, with Nate hanging on for the drop. He was just seven years old at the time.

We did inadvertently go over an old rock dam known as Coppermine about six miles later, having missed the portage to our right. From upstream, the old dam appeared to be just a bunch of boulders. It was only after the canoe was half-way over the drop that I realized it was a dam. Kevin yelled from the front, "Dad there is no bottom!" I kept the throttle wide open as we went over. We took on minimal water during the four-foot drop as the canoe took a slight dip at the stern. The boys egged me on to portage back upstream and do it again. Due to the serious possibility of drowning by being sucked under by the undertow, I didn't.

The boys got goofy after that. Kevin grabbed some weeds from the shallow bottom and draped them over his head. He did a takeoff of Adam Sandler's Sea Weed character as portrayed on Saturday Night Live. It was hilarious! Nate was funny in his own way. We truly had a great time on the water.

We camped at Riverside Landing, about twenty miles downstream from Gordon Dam. Five miles upstream, the Namekagon joins the Saint Croix, another popular canoe river. Our next day of travel would include sections of Class II rapids. High water can cause river travel to either be easier by exposing fewer obstacles and a wider channel or more difficult, especially if there is a significant drop of altitude.

Reaching Nelsons Landing at 3:00, our planned overnight destination, we decided it was too early to stop. The boys tried paddling for a while, but due to quickly being tired of it, I used the motor to finish the trip to the Highway 70 Bridge. After loading up, we went home and spent the night pitched in the tent of our backyard.

It had been a pleasant three-day family vacation. Combined with the two year ago motorized canoe trip, and a day jaunt using The Boat four years ago I had now covered what is considered the navigable length of the Saint Croix.

1993 MISSOURI, MISSISSIPPI, ILLINOIS, LAKE MICHIGAN

Having completed my original goal of traveling the entire length of the Mississippi and still enjoying the challenge of boating new waters, I thought about where to go next.

It had been a very rainy spring and summer in the Midwest causing the Mississippi, Missouri, Illinois, and the tributaries that feed them to be in flood condition.

In order for a reader to understand what conditions were like, I searched the internet and found a six-page article titled 'The Great USA Flood of 1993' presented at a conference in 1996. I will paraphrase the information gathered from the NOAA website and written by Lee W. Larson, Chief, Hydraulic Research Laboratory, Office of Hydrology, NOAA/National Weather Service, 1325 East-West Highway, Silver Spring, Maryland 20910.

Rainfall amounts were 200-350 percent above normal from the northern plains southeastward into the central United States. A critical factor was the near continuous rainfall, with many locations in a nine state area experiencing rain twenty days or more in July. With the soil saturated, water had no place to go but into streams and rivers. Over 1,000 levees either failed or were topped, with the Mississippi River at Grafton Illinois being at flood stage for 195 days.

The bottom line of his report understated how long lasting and widespread the flood was. Fifty people died, 10,000 homes were destroyed, and at least 15 million acres of farmland was inundated.

As more and more the news media covered the floods, the more and more I wanted to go in behind the receding water to see the flood damage first hand. A newspaper clipping from the 1st or 2nd week of August is shown below exactly as it appeared.

U.S officials plans to reopen riverways Associated Press St Louis, Mo. Federal officials outlined plans Wednesday to reopen the Midwest's flooded riverways but offered no firm timetable because they don't know what they will find when the rivers go down – besides broken levees.

"The normal channels may not even be there anymore," Army Corps of Engineers spokesman Wally Feld said", And sandbars may have moved from one side to the other."

The flood closed all or parts of six rivers in the western system above Cairo, Ill. As of yesterday, the Mississippi remained closed from Keokuk, Iowa to Cairo, Ill.; the Missouri was closed from Courtney, in western Missouri, to St. Louis; and the Illinois was closed from Havana, Ill., to Grafton.

Shippers estimate that 5,000 barges, some loaded with such commodities as grain, fertilizer, and coal, have been stopped by the flood, and the barge industry says it is losing $3 million every day the rivers are closed.

"As far as any of us remember, this has to be the longest interruption of business ever," said Norb Whitlock, senior vice president of American Commercial Lines in Jeffersonville, Ind. "In essence, the upper Mississippi has been closed since the last week of June and is probably not going to reopen until the end of August."

In the meantime, President Clinton was to visit St. Louis today to sign a federal flood relief bill and pay tribute to the heroes of the 1993 flood.

At yesterday's news conference, Coast Guard Cmdr. Scott Cooper said locks and dams on the Mississippi River above St. Louis are operational and the river will be opened to traffic there as soon as levees are checked for damage. That section of the river could be open next week, he said.

"The Missouri River awaits the same assessment," Cooper said. "We may have word on the conditions there by the end of this week."

But the Illinois River, which handles cargo to and from the Chicago area, probably will be closed longer.

Cooper said, because it is the system's slowest-draining river.

Below St. Louis, officials can't begin to assess damage on the Mississippi until the water recedes some more.

In Washington, D.C. yesterday, the conservation group American Rivers held a news conference to say that the levees along the Mississippi should not be rebuilt because they only create a false sense of security.

Kevin Coyle, president of the group, said that the Clinton administration should instead develop long-term flood management policies for the country's major rivers and designate natural flood plains into which excess water could spill from the river during heavy rains.

As noted in the article, the rivers were close to being officially opened to traffic. I decided to start from the upper end of navigation on the Missouri and go as far as I could, with no definite end destination in mind. I bought the Army Corps of Engineers two chart set that covers the last 753 miles of the Missouri and made a subset of the information that I consider the most valuable. After being stranded on the Tenn-Tom last year, I had a motor bracket installed to carry a 7 ½ Mercury outboard as a backup.

After numerous calls to various agencies about when the Missouri, Mississippi, and Illinois rivers would be open, and receiving conflicting and vague answers, I just decided to go.

Debbie agreed to drive me to Sioux City, Nebraska, where I would start the Missouri River from, and pick me up wherever I ended up. Due to returning to school for teacher workshops, after dropping me off she could not pick me up until the following Friday.

FRIDAY, AUGUST 20TH, 1993

I left from Scenic Park River Access in South Sioux City, Nebraska, Mile 723.2, about 5:15 PM. At about Mile 681 I stopped to assist a boat with a lower unit problem. With the stainless steel prop off and motor in gear, you could hold the drive shaft from turning.

The main problem with using a stainless steel prop instead of aluminum is that when you hit a solid object it does not break, taking out the lower unit drive gears instead. An aluminum prop is less efficient but I would rather sacrifice a prop than tear up the outdrive, especially while on a major trip.

I agreed to tow the husband/wife couple about thirty miles to the Cotton Wood Marina. With twenty miles to go and darkness approaching, I had him steer The Boat while I sat in the stern running the 7 ½ Mercury outboard to speed things up. Due to safety and practical reasons, I could only run the I/O about 1500 RPM. Their boat was probably twice the weight of mine while only about three feet longer. After securing the boats at the Cotton Wood, The husband bought a round of drinks called a watermelon, a local specialty, and bribed the cook to make 'burgers' since the kitchen had closed. I found out his wife worked in the underwriting department at Woodman Life Insurance Company in Omaha, Nebraska.

SATURDAY, AUGUST 21ST, 1993

Dave and Heidi, who have a 24ft Bayliner-Microwave, TV/VCR, A/C etc, served coffee. The five of us talked for a good hour and a half, mostly about all the damage caused by the flood. I had agreed to take the towed boat couple to Dodge Memorial Park where their vehicle and trailer were. The gas attendant, who talked through a mike in his throat, had to be roused from bed.

We left Cotton Wood at 9:30 and boated to Dodge Memorial Park, Mile 627.9. In the interest of space, I carried only one life jacket. The couple forgot their life jackets when I dropped them off, and not remembering their names, I sent them via UPS to the underwriting department of Woodman Life Insurance Company in Omaha, Nebraska when I returned home. It is strange, while I cannot remember names; I am able to associate people with the car they drive, where they work, etc. The only reason I remember Dave and Heidi names is that they were caught on videotape. I easily found the address for the life insurance company she worked for because they were rated in the same book as Early American Life Insurance, for whom I worked.

Right after dropping off the couple, I broke the viewfinder on the newly purchased camcorder, with the rest of my videotaping all aimed high.

Needing gas, I stopped at a restaurant visible from the river around Rulo. Nebraska. I asked the first waitress I saw how far away a gas station might be, explaining I was in a boat. She said I could buy gas at 'Franks.' She offered the use of her pickup and warned me, "You better not have an accident, and you better bring it back!" In driving through the very small town and only seeing a closed two pump station reminiscent of the forty's, I returned to the restaurant and thanked her for the use of the pickup. The highway 159 bridge that crossed the Missouri at Rulo was closed. The next logical place to buy gas was at Island Marina, thirty-six miles downriver. Arriving there, I concentrated on safely maneuvering the swift current to a rickety dock behind a small spit of land. In climbing the steps and looking up for the first time, I found Island Marina devastated! It was obvious that buying gas there was not an option. Seeing a group of people working on a flood damaged house about ¼ mile down river I decided to stop and talk to them.

I idled the boat from the destroyed marina and close to the workers where I tied up to a tree. They were just finishing up for the day, eating a meal provided by the Red Cross. Coincidentally one of the workers was the owner of Island Marina, and it was his father-in-laws house, which had had seven foot of water in it. He volunteered to drive me the three miles to town in his pickup, so I grabbed six six-gallon containers. During the round trip he related the following: besides the damage done to the marina, as a farmer he had lost a major part of his crop, and just the day before an engine had blown on one of his three over the road trucks! So much for diversification! He'd been to the start of the Missouri River at Three Forks, Montana and had taken his pontoon boat all the way down river from Yankton, South Dakota. He would not accept money for helping me out. I had been down to three gallons of gas.

I continued on 100 miles to where the Kansas River enters the Missouri at Kansas City, Kansas where I spent the night tied to the bank.

SUNDAY, AUGUST 22ND, 1993

With Debbie not onboard, few notes and pictures were taken since I was not planning to write a book at this point. It was a major job just for me to stay out of trouble.

10:40 – I stopped at Missouri City to find gas. It was only after walking over the railroad tracks that I got the first good view of the town. It was devastated! I asked a bulldozer operator pushing down a house where a gas station might be. With him saying it was about three blocks away, I moved the boat about three blocks back upstream and tied it securely to the bank. While carrying two gas cans, I asked further directions of a guy passing by on a riding lawnmower. His answer was that that gas station was still two blocks away and that the owner was sitting on his back steps. When I got to the gas station it was locked, with the owner sitting on the back steps of the house next door, who then opened it up for me. I filled the two containers and said I had four more to fill. He said I could pay for them all at once. Taking the shortest possible route to the riverbank, I left the two containers there and then moved the boat up to where I'd left the gas containers. When I returned carrying the other four containers, a son and his elderly father were visiting with the station owner. Having once lived in the area, they were there to check out the flood damage. The son helped me carry the four gas containers back to the boat. It was HOT! I pulled away from Missouri City at 11:20.

2:00 – Mile 293.5 Since most navigation markers were gone I was using bridges to determine location. Stopping underneath the Hwy 65 Bridge at Waverly, Missouri, I climbed the steep bank carrying a six-gallon gas container. Finding a restaurant/bar close to the bridge, I entered and immediately the owner waved me over to the booth where he was sitting. He asked if I needed gas, as he had seen me through the window. I said I was boating the river and was trying to find gas, ice, and some beer. We went in his Cadillac to a local gas station, filled the gas container, and then returned to his place where I bought beer and ice. Wanting to see my boat, he drove us partway down the hill via a dirt road and offered to carry the beer and ice the rest of the way. Thinking it was too rough for him, I politely declined the offer. The bridge over the river was once again closed due to concerns about possible damage to its supports.

I could feel the boat rise and fall as it passed over wing dams in the still fast and high river. I saw everything from a bulk propane tank atop twists of driftwood, to massive cottonwood trees left stranded in farm fields, to broken levees, to severely damaged riverfront towns. I'm sure what I couldn't see was even worse as evidenced by the damage done to Missouri City, seen only after climbing the bank and crossing the railroad tracks.

If not obvious yet, my trip became a cycle of finding gas, a safe place to overnight, and trying to keep out of dangerous situations.

Mile 226.3 – I tied up to the Army Corps of Engineers dock at the town of Glasgow, Missouri and grabbed two gas containers for the ½-block walk to Hwy 87.

Upon getting to the highway, and without trying to hitch a ride, a farmer immediately stopped and picked me up. He took me six blocks to a gas station, waited while I filled, took me back to the dock, and even carried one container to the boat. He said that over 7,000 acres of local farmland had been flooded, with some people losing everything – houses, buildings, machinery, and crops.

Mile 130.0 – Dave Dickerson, the mechanic who had installed the auxiliary motor mount, recommended staying overnight up the Osage River, having done so last year. Passing many destroyed cabins and mobile homes during the three-mile upstream trip, I spent the night tied between trees about forty feet from shore. I used the Coleman stove to heat up meatballs and chili. Hot food was now a luxury since Debbie was not around to force me to stop.

MONDAY, AUGUST 23RD, 1993

12:00 Mile 98 – I bought thirty gallons of gas and two bags of ice at Hermann, Missouri, carrying it 1 ½ blocks in 90 degree heat back to the boat. While the exterior of the brick/limestone buildings that line the waterfront looked OK, I'm sure the interior damage was extensive.

4:30 – My arrival to the juncture of the Missouri to the Mississippi was like that of entering a big lake. There were many push boats waiting to head north. I called the Melvin Price Lock at Alton, Illinois (#26 Mile 200.8) on VHF channel 16 first, then on 14 when there was no answer. I never got a response, even though I could hear communication between them and push boats. I attempted to cross over the top of the dam, with less than eight inches separating the upside and downside elevations. The normal lift for this lock is twenty-three feet. Water was flowing just fast enough over its entire width to need to be under power and the prop would have hit. I ended up following a push boat without any barges into the lock.

While in the lock, I asked an attendant about the status of boating on the Mississippi and Illinois. He said he didn't know but thought they were both closed to recreational boating.

Lock 26, now called Melvin Price, was two miles further south than when Debbie and I passed through in 1988.

We saw construction work in progress, not knowing it was for a new lock.

I went 3.7 miles to Harbor Point Yacht Club, the first marina heading north on the Missouri side. When I arrived, they were busily preparing for a storm that was rolling in. "We don't have food, gas, or water, but your welcome to stay", and directed me to a sixty foot covered slip next to some very large and expensive boats. I asked the status of recreational boating on the Mississippi and the Illinois. They did not know, with the consensus being they thought that the Illinois was a No Wake Zone. They would check and get back to me.

The dock complex was surrounded by water, with the marina employees getting around by boat. I'd just finished eating warmed up canned goods when a major wind and lightning storm rolled through, dropping about two inches of rain. Much thanks much for the covered slip.

Since getting to shore was not an option, I roamed the dock and thought about what it would be like to cruise 'in style'.

About 9:00, the marina operator boated by, informing me the Mississippi and Illinois Rivers had opened to traffic at 12:00 noon. What timing, I had reached the Mississippi at 4:30!

I did not put the heavy mooring cover up due to the heat and humidity and being in a covered slip. The gnats and mosquitoes were looking for blood, and being the only target I suffered accordingly. Another heavy rain rolled through at 5:50 AM. I slept well from 6 to 7:30.

TUESDAY, AUGUST 24TH, 1993

Upon leaving at 9:15, I cruised the marina trying to find someone to pay for the covered slip. "No Charge, Good Luck".

Even though I did not have charts of the Illinois River, I decided to head up it.

At 10:07, I arrived at the junction of the Illinois and the Mississippi; Mile marker 217.9, 22.5 miles above the junction of the Missouri.

Shortly after entering the Illinois River, and directly across from the town of Grafton, Illinois, a Sheriffs boat stopped and informed me that the river was closed to recreational boaters. In my telling the Sheriff that restrictions were removed as of 12:00 noon yesterday, he got on the radio to Coast Guard officials who confirmed that the river was indeed open to recreational traffic. Hearing that, he allowed me to proceed.

The town of Grafton sustained major damage. The many sand bags that had been placed did not help, with the river simply flowing over them.

Seeing a gas pump, I stopped at the River Boat Trading Company, Mile 65. Two children playing outside the office found their mother, who sold me gas. They hadn't had any business for some time. She had not heard the news about the river being open. Their business was dependent on summer recreational boat traffic, and the river had been closed for six weeks. Having problems with the motor cutting out intermittently for the rest of the trip, I initially blamed it on water in the fuel bought there.

She said the houseboat moored to shore had arrived just as the river closed, and was prevented from proceeding ever since. Its occupants were moving to some place around New Orleans and their young children needed to be there in time to start school. Just the day before a helicopter had landed and showed them a video of how bad the Mississippi was heading south.

While passing under swivel railroad bridges and going by barge facilities I saw people flagging their hands, trying to slow me down. I continued without slowing, thinking they were unaware of the new river regulations.

As I cautiously approached La Grange Lock & Dam, Mile 80.2, I noticed a small boat occupied by two men tied to the lock structure. The actual lock was not staffed because its operation was unnecessary due to the high water. They motioned for me to come over. 'They' turned out to be a Conservation Officer and an Army Corp of Engineer employee 'lying in wait'.

The Conservation Officer said I was violating a 'NO WAKE ZONE'. The bottom line as it turns out is that while the river was open to barge and recreational traffic, it was only supposed to be used at very low speeds.

Saying I had talked to the marina operator at Harbor Point, the Sheriff at Grafton, and was operating using the best information available, asked for lenience. I also explained that I had made NUMEROUS telephone inquires to various agencies/bureaucrats/marinas prior to starting. Nobody would give me a definitive answer, YES/NO, as to whether the various rivers were or would be open to recreational traffic.

The Conservation Officer, who physically/vocally reminded me of Norman Schwarzkopf from the Desert Storm Operation in 1991, said he had been instructed to stop and issue me a ticket. 'Norman' would allow me to proceed as long as I did so in No Wake fashion and post $75 cash. I said going upstream in the swift current without leaving a wake was impossible. He said that if I continued to proceed upstream at the same speed used in my approach to the dam, it would be acceptable. The law could be interpreted to mean 'Least Disturbance', and the barge rule was **2 MPH Upstream and 4 MPH Downstream.**

As far as why I had not been able to get clear concise information from authorities, 'Norman' said that it was probably due to the implications of giving permission to proceed. If another dike had broken or additional damage was done due to my wake, serious financial consequences would have resulted.

One of the principal things that most recreational boaters do not know, or chose to ignore, is that you are responsible for problems caused by your wake. The law is vague and subject to interpretation. Here is how it reads in Minnesota's boating guide, "It's against the law to operate a watercraft so that its wash or wake endangers, harasses, or interferes with any person or property".

As 'Norman' wrote the ticket, we actually had a nice conversation. He told me what it had been like because of the flood. The thing that stood out the most in his mind was the many calls he had received to break up domestic violence since many people had lost everything.

In watching my wake at slow speed, I found out that even though it initially is higher at slow speed, it either did not carry all the way to shore/or it did so with less force as it would have at higher speed.

Four hours and twenty-eight miles later, I arrived at Mile 118, the end of the No Wake Zone. It was 7:30 and just starting to get dark. I tied up between trees on the still high river and ate cold food right out of the can. The boat had really sucked gas due to not being up on plane and plowing against the current.

It was hot and muggy, but I still put up the mooring cover to ward off bugs and mosquitoes. At 11:00, I lifted off part of the cover to get fresh air and slept well until 6:00.

WEDNESDAY, AUGUST 25TH, 1993

When I turned the key to get started at 6:30, all I got was a click. After six or seven turns of the key and getting the same click, it started. Then when I put the boat in forward gear, it would not engage. After playing around for a while, I found it would engage forward only after raising the lower unit to shallow water position. It would then stay in gear after being lowered to normal operating position. I had to do this for the rest of the trip, whenever going to neutral or back to forward.

The lock at Mile 157.7 Peoria Lock & Dam, East Peoria, Illinois, is a 'wicket' dam that does not require locking through when sufficient water depth exists, which there was. This is because they lower the dam to the river bottom. La Grange Lock & Dam, where 'Norman' had awaited my arrival, is also a wicket dam. Mile 231.0 – Starved Rock Lock & Dam, Ottawa, Illinois, – Lift 18' 7".

After returning home I went next door to invite George, who was renting the cabin next door, over for dinner. He asked why I was sprouting a beard. I started telling about the trip and that I don't shave while boating. When I mentioned the Illinois River, he interrupted and said his high school overlooked the Illinois River at Ottawa. More than once his teachers had had to call his attention back to class and off the river view.

He also mentioned that his father had taught there. When I told Debbie about George's father being a teacher at Ottawa High School, I found out she had student taught there. Small world!

Mile 244.6 – Marseilles Lock and Dam – Lift 18' 7"

Mile 271.5 – Dresden Island Lock and Dam – Lift 21' 7"

The Des Plains and Kankakee Rivers meet at mile 272.9, forming the Illinois River.

Mile 286.0 – Brandon Road Lock & Dam – Lift 34'

I bought just enough gas at Brandon Harbor – River Club to make it to Chicago, thinking that is where I would end the trip.

Mile 291.1 – Lockport Lock & Dam – Lift 30' to 42'

At 7:30, I arrived at Lockport, the last lock before downtown Chicago. Having encountered very little river traffic, and with just thirty-six miles left to reach 'downtown', I envisioned being there by dark.

WRONG!

As the lock doors opened, the change of view was as dramatic as that of Dorothy, the Scarecrow, the Lion, the Tin Man, and Toto's first view of Emerald City. Instead of being in awe, I was dismayed! Instead of a wide river with dirt banks, I faced a narrow concrete channel. The shooting flames from venting refinery stacks were reminiscent of when the Great Oz scared them.

The section between Lockport and Chicago Harbor Lock, known as the Chicago Sanitary and Ship Canal, is heavily industrialized the first fifteen miles or so.

Due to the narrow confines of the concrete channel, passing a string of barges ahead was not an option, keeping me at slow speed. I felt like a toy duck in a bathtub.

The only working lights I was able to display, which is all that is required, for a boat my size was the red/green on the bow and the white stern light. Realize The Boat sits low, with the high point of the windshield less than four feet above the water. I doubt the barge ahead was even aware of my presence. I listened to the heavy VHF radio traffic on channel 16, and heard no mention of a small boat. My thinking was to stay off the radio as long as I was not in danger. Just prior to starting the trip, I had installed a 12-volt cigarette type adapter to power a handheld searchlight. It worked fine at home, but now blew fuses for no apparent reason, resulting in my being unable to use it.

As I followed the barge string, and figuring the captain could not see me, called on VHF channel 16 letting him know I was behind. He radioed back, telling me to pass on his right after he eased over. With little extra space between the string of barges and the high concrete wall, I passed as quickly as possible. This was a scary move, being 9:30 and dark. I had never been that close to a barge before, and even a 'big boat' would be toast if squeezed between a barge and a solid concrete wall.

I passed OK and got out ahead. Using a strip of moonlight to navigate, I passed numerous floating objects, recognizable in size from a pop can to a 55-gallon drum while running at 30 mph. Wait, a 55-gallon drum, Yes, True! At that point, I decided to find a spot to spend the night. Besides the real possibility of crashing into something, where was I going to stay once reaching downtown? With normal marina office hours now well past closing time, I was concerned about being mugged within sight of the Sears Tower. I looked for the first best place to stop. As they say, any port in a storm.

I found an extra wide isolated spot underneath what I guessed to be an Interstate Bridge, which gave me a margin of safety from passing barges and far enough away from city streets to feel safe from being mugged. It was a six or seven foot reach to tie up to overhanging trees.

With the boat facing downstream and me in the bow to better hear the barge I knew was coming, I tried to nap. The proper thing for me to have done was leave the white mooring light on. Having only a single battery, I was concerned about draining it due to leaving a light on for an extended period. The last thing I wanted was a dead battery.

While sleeping very lightly, I listened for the sound of an approaching barge, up or down stream. It was hard to sort out the different sounds. There was the constant overhead bridge traffic, local traffic, rail traffic, occasional jet noise, and the general noise inherent of any large city.

At 11:30, I awoke to see a searchlight criss-crossing the river ahead of an oncoming barge. I shined a flashlight back towards the approaching barge so they would know that I was there.

The response I got back from a loudspeaker was, "You had better get your damn ass out of there or you will get hit!"

Not having a loudspeaker or an appropriate response, I kept quiet. As the barge slid by with fifteen feet to spare, the pilot commented, "You had better get some lights on. Not everybody is as careful as I am."

Taking his statement to heart, I decided to sleep on land so if the boat were hit at least I would not be in it. Using a rope wrapped around a small tree, I pulled myself up.

In settling down, I took the added precaution of tying myself to a tree. That way I would not inadvertently roll down the steep bank and over the ledge in my sleep. What sleep? The insects were terrible, and have you ever tried sleeping sitting up tied to a tree?

THURSDAY, AUGUST 26TH, 1993

Thinking the sky was getting lighter, I got back in the boat to check my watch. It was only 3:30, so I sat in the boat until 6:00. With all the portable cans empty and the gas gauge on E, I decided to cross over to the other side of the canal where I saw a road.

I again had to wrap a rope around a tree to get out, and used a second one to haul up two gas cans. For some unknown reason I wrapped one rope around my neck, and carried a gas can in each hand. I took a young woman unloading a bicycle from a van by surprise. Evidently she was going to take an early morning ride in the isolated area. I must have been a sight! Can you imagine seeing a man in dirty clothes with a week old beard carrying two gas cans with a rope dangling around his neck at 6:00 AM? Especially in Chicago!

I told her I was looking for a gas station and wondered if she knew where and how far away one was. She said yes there was, pointing the way, adding that a police station was also nearby. I walked about six blocks before realizing that she had just steered me away from her and that no gas or police station was imminent. Not blaming her, I decided to return to the boat.

Not knowing how far I had gone since hitting E on the gas gauge due to concentrating my effort navigating in the dark, I opted to make the run to downtown without looking any further for gas. Coming into Chicago by river was interesting. There were many dilapidated structures, and some kept up nicely along the riverfront.

It was 7:30 when I arrived at Marina City Marina, 300 North State Street, having truly arrived at Emerald City. Imagine the contrast of being tied to a tree with bugs swarming about to that of observing the well-dressed men and women on their way to work amidst the skyscrapers.

Marina City Marina is underneath a skyscraper and did not open until 8:00. I used an outside payphone to call Debbie, reaching her just before leaving home for the last day of teacher workshops. She was surprised I was in Chicago, this being the first time we'd talked since leaving Sioux City. I said I would call tonight to let her know where to pick me up.

While waiting for the marina to open, I observed this strange looking specially designed boat zigzagging back and forth on the river. It picked up floating debris on a wide conveyer belt and dropped it in a hopper.

The Chicago River used to flow directly into Lake Michigan until 1900. With Chicago drawing its water supply via water intake cribs from Lake Michigan and dumping untreated sewage into the Chicago River, they were polluting their own water supply. Disease from water pollution caused by human waste caused thousands of deaths. The solution to their problem was to redirect the flow of the Chicago River so that it flowed south, joining the Des Plaines River, eventually emptying into the Gulf of Mexico. That was part of reason for building the Chicago Ship and Sanitary Canal.

After buying gas, I went through the Chicago Harbor Lock into Lake Michigan. There was only a two-foot lock difference between Lake Michigan and the Chicago side, with the lake being higher.

I stopped at Lincoln Park – Montrose Wilson public marina to check out transient moorage. While waiting for the Harbor Master, I chatted with two men fishing for perch. Finding out that transient dockage was available, I weighed options; Stay here in the already hot day, or proceed north on relatively calm Lake Michigan?

It was only 9:00, and since Debbie would have to drive south out of Wisconsin to pick me up, I decided to head north, thinking I'd stop at Waukegan, Illinois.

Keeping The Boat about a mile offshore, the two to three foot swells experienced were far enough apart to make whatever bounce I received enjoyable. The water was clear and the offshore temperature was perfect. The view of Chicago and its skyline is awesome. Does it get any better than this? I cruised by Evanston, where Debbie spent her childhood.

I stopped to buy gas at Great Lakes Naval Training Station, just south of Waukegan. In talking with them, I decided to push on to Racine, Wisconsin, which they said had excellent harbor facilities. Arriving at Racine at 2:20, I checked out the public marina first, but liked the quiet of Racine Yacht Club better. To go from one to the other you have to go outside a breakwater.

Even though I didn't see a single powerboat in the Racine Yacht Club harbor, which was filled with large sailboats, they did not hold my being a stink (power) boater against me, allowing me to stay. By paying a $10 deposit for a night pass card, I had off-hour access to the bathrooms and showers.

I'd traveled approximately 1200 miles in my six days on the water.

It took quite a while to clean up the inside and outside of the filthy boat. I called Debbie to let her know where to pick me up, with her telling me it would be some time tomorrow afternoon before she would arrive.

After taking a much-needed shower, I walked to a nearby nightspot to eat. It sure was nice to order off a menu instead of eating out of a can. I was asleep by 9:00.

FRIDAY, AUGUST 27TH, 1993

Having a very restful nights sleep; I had coffee with two brothers aboard the sailing vessel named the 'Bublitchka'. Ukrainian for 'Little Cookie' named after its owners wife while still alive. They told stories about sailing Lake Michigan and their adventures in the Pacific during WW II. They did not like John Wayne, with one having met him. They grew up within three blocks of the harbor, and both lived within walking distance of each other.

Maybe after my power boating adventures are over, I will try sailing.

Debbie arrived at 1:30, and in hearing that she had never been on Lake Michigan, I naturally had to take her. It was a different day from yesterday. We took water over the bow during our brief venture into the lake. With the Yacht Club not having a boat ramp I returned Debbie to the dock and once again went outside the breakwater to reach the public dock to load.

We arrived back in Lakeville just before midnight.

Notes: While troubleshooting why the motor cut out intermittently, I found that in pulling one spark plug wire it had no effect on engine performance. I replaced the spark plug wire set, which resolved the problem and I now carry extra spark plug wires.

The reason the boat could not be shifted into forward without the lower unit first being raised to shallow water drive required a professional mechanic. The problem was due to excessive wear on a part called a shift spool that was caused by an incorrect factory setup. Long since out of warranty, the comment made by the mechanic was that most boaters would never have used their boat enough to realize this situation. The repair bill came to $216.62.

yesterday. We took water over the bow during our brief venture into the lake. With the Yacht Club not having a boat ramp I returned Debbie to the dock and once again went outside the breakwater to reach the public dock to load.

We arrived back in Lakeville just before midnight.

Notes: While troubleshooting why the motor cut out intermittently, I found that in pulling one spark plug wire it had no effect on engine performance. I replaced the spark plug wire set, which resolved the problem and I now carry extra spark plug wires.

The reason the boat could not be shifted into forward without the lower unit first being raised to shallow water drive required a professional mechanic. The problem was due to excessive wear on a part called a shift spool that was caused by an incorrect factory setup. Long since out of warranty, the comment made by the mechanic was that most boaters would never have used their boat enough to realize this situation. The repair bill came to $216.62.

enjoyable. The water was clear and the offshore temperature was perfect. The view of Chicago and its skyline is awesome. Does it get any better than this? I cruised by Evanston, where Debbie spent her childhood.

I stopped to buy gas at Great Lakes Naval Training Station, just south of Waukegan. In talking with them, I decided to push on to Racine, Wisconsin, which they said had excellent harbor facilities. Arriving at Racine at 2:20, I checked out the public marina first, but liked the quiet of Racine Yacht Club better. To go from one to the other you have to go outside a breakwater.

Even though I didn't see a single powerboat in the Racine Yacht Club harbor, which was filled with large sailboats, they did not hold my being a stink (power) boater against me, allowing me to stay. By paying a $10 deposit for a night pass card, I had off-hour access to the bathrooms and showers.

I'd traveled approximately 1200 miles in my six days on the water.

It took quite a while to clean up the inside and outside of the filthy boat. I called Debbie to let her know where to pick me up, with her telling me it would be some time tomorrow afternoon before she would arrive.

After taking a much-needed shower, I walked to a nearby nightspot to eat. It sure was nice to order off a menu instead of eating out of a can. I was asleep by 9:00.

FRIDAY, AUGUST 27TH, 1993

Having a very restful nights sleep; I had coffee with two brothers aboard the sailing vessel named the 'Bublitchka'. Ukrainian for 'Little Cookie' named after its owners wife while still alive. They told stories about sailing Lake Michigan and their adventures in the Pacific during WW II. They did not like John Wayne, with one having met him. They grew up within three blocks of the harbor, and both lived within walking distance of each other.

Maybe after my power boating adventures are over, I will try sailing.

Debbie arrived at 1:30, and in hearing that she had never been on Lake Michigan, I naturally had to take her. It was a different day from

1994 OHIO, MONOGAHELA, ALLEGHENY, MUSKINGUM, TENNESSEE, KENTUCKY

One of the things that long Minnesota winters cause me to do is to reflect on past boating adventures and get antsy about going on another one. While I enjoy winter, going snowmobiling, and downhill skiing, my primary passion is boating. So where else could I go? Having traveled the river systems close to home, my goal became the Ohio, the closest with lock and dams. I sent off for the three-chart set produced by the Army Corps of Engineers that covers its length, and in conjunction with the latest Quimby's, made cheat sheets showing lock locations, marinas, etc.

While returning from spending Christmas in Iowa, I pulled off the four lane limited access highway in Rochester, Minnesota looking for a used camper van. Wouldn't you know the first place we drove by had one? It was late at night and the place was closed, so I called the next day. Long story, short, we bought an 89 Ford E-150 camper van with a raised fiberglass roof, extended length, dual gas tanks, combination roof A/C and heat unit, microwave, and able to sleep four. We added a 12 volt/110 refrigerator, TV/VCR, Porta-Potti, sink, and a portable Coleman stove. With the 85 Nissan pickup now having over 100,000 miles, the camper van would prove its worth over the coming years.

I had to get Debbie onboard the idea of boating the Ohio. Her concern was what to do with the boys during the allotted two-week period I figured it would take. Her parents, who had retired to South Bend, Indiana, said they would be more than glad to take care of them. I arranged for time off, leaving shortly after Debbie and the boys got out of school.

Because the trip route is complicated, I'll explain it up front. From Saturday, June 11, to Saturday, June 25, we boated all or parts of the Ohio, Allegheny, Monogahela, Muskingum, Kanawa, Tennessee, Cumberland, & Kentucky Rivers travelling 2650 miles and locking 86 times in the process. I will also note times.

We started at mile 486 on the Ohio and headed to Pittsburgh, Pa, went up the Monogahela 130 miles, back to Pittsburgh, up the Allegheny 62 miles, back to Pittsburgh, then to mile 172 on the Ohio, up the Muskingum through the first lock(wooden doors) and back to the Ohio, then to mile 266 on the Ohio, up the Great Kanawa 90 miles and back to the Ohio, then to mile 933 on the Ohio, up the Tennessee through the first lock, across the Barkley Canal to the Cumberland River, and back to the Ohio at mile 923, then to the Kentucky River confluence at Ohio mile marker 545, up the Kentucky 82 miles, and then back to the Ohio, finally arriving back to mile 486 where we had started using The Boat.

SATURDAY, JUNE 11TH, 1994

10:00 AM – We left the boys with Grandma & Grandpa May in South Bend Indiana and headed east.

2:30 PM – We stopped in North Bend, Ohio and bought gas for The Boat, auxiliary tanks, and the van. In trying to find block ice, since it lasts longer, we happened to see an ice delivery truck. The driver did not have any, maybe the plant would. We drove about two miles up highway 50 and checked their outside ice machine, but no block ice, so I went in. The kid inside said, "We don't sell blocks anymore. Try Pfissers, as they have 40 pound bags." I dropped Debbie off and circled around the block since I couldn't find a parking spot for the van and trailer. When Debbie came out of Pfissers, she had the carryout guy leave the ice at the street edge where she waited. The only reason I relate this story is that we had left Lakeville less than 24 hours ago and already I'd abandoned the wife.

When I refer to Debbie as 'the wife', it is not meant to be impersonal. A car dealer by the name Elmer Witte from the Chicago area came with his wife to their seasonal cabin next door to our resort every summer. While he was very friendly, coming over often to buy pop and socialize, you never saw her, as she evidently was a more private person. Anyway, he always referred to her as 'the wife.' It wasn't until I saw a Christmas card they sent that I found out her name was Lillian. It was obvious when he referred to her as 'the wife' it was with the deepest respect, as is true with me to Debbie when I use it.

3:00 PM – We pulled into Presidents Boat Club, just west of Cincinnati on the Ohio River, where I had arranged to leave the camper van and trailer. We packed the boat, unloaded it off the trailer, and parked the van and trailer on a freshly bulldozed area overlooking the river. I was a little concerned about it being vandalized or being stuck if it rained. We were off by 4:30.

The riverbanks became more heavily populated as we neared Cincinnati. The Ohio was very busy with small boat traffic, including many jet skis. Cincinnati has a very nice riverfront, (skyline- riverboat, restaurants, parks, and docks for boats).

Mile 436.2 – Captain Anthony Meldahl Locks & Dam – Lift 30' – Locks 1200 x 110, 600 x 110 – Felicity, Ohio. We talked with some men in a very nice boat while waiting to lock through. While telling of prior trips and our plans for this one, the "I'd like to do that someday" is heard once again. Many of the twenty dams on the 981-mile length of the Ohio have two locks of different size. This allows for better recreational and commercial traffic flow.

The lock cycle ran slowly.

7:00 PM – A transient boat slip facing the river was found at White Oak Creek Marina. I was happy about being back on a river trip! A very fast red Donzi pulled into a slip close to us. The driver was a dead ringer for Rod Stewart. I admired his boat and called him Rod. He didn't appreciate the humor, while his friends did. We went to the marina restaurant to eat after setting up the boat. The cooks were giving a customer a hard time for ordering so late, and then we come in.

SUNDAY, JUNE 12TH, 1994

I woke very early as boats for a Bass tournament were taking off. As a boat number was called out over a bullhorn, it would scream off, thirty-two in all. Debbie didn't hear a thing. We had breakfast, showered, packed, and were back on the river at 8:45.

It was calm, with the sun just burning off the misty clouds. The area is very scenic as the river passed between hills with Ohio on the left bank and Kentucky on the right. There was lots of haze in the hollers.

The word 'hollers' is purposely used here. Debbie's father was born and raised in the hills close to Salyersville, Kentucky and that is how he, and consequently Debbie, refer to narrow deep valleys.

Mile 341.1 – Greenup Locks & Dam – Lift 30' – Greenup, Kentucky.

We had lunch in the boat while waiting for a downriver group to lock through.

12:30 We stopped at Holiday Point Marina for gas, buying 24 ½ gallons.

Mile 279.2 – R. C. Byrd Locks & Dam Lift 23 – Gallipolis Ferry, W Virginia.

The two locks have the same width at 110' but one is twice the length as the other at 1200' and had just opened in 1993. They are accessed via a two-mile long channel dug to help barges have a straight shot, eliminating the bend previously required to navigate past Gallipolis Dam and its single lock.

Somebody didn't plan very well as an exiting downriver string of barges got hung up on the bottom coming out. Its towboat struggled as it tried to clear the lock exit. Fortunately a towboat without barges was coming down behind and helped push the grounded tow on through to deeper water. We heard over the VHF radio that this wasn't the first time this had happened.

Mile 237.3 – Racine Lock & Dam – Lift 22' – New Haven, W Virginia.

Sometime after leaving the lock, I had a feeling that something was wrong. The motor didn't sound the same, having just a slight variation in pitch than normal. Remembering breaking the alternator belt on our first trip, I looked at the charging rate on the gauge. It was higher than normal. I lifted the motor hood and found the bracket that holds the alternator had broken, allowing it to drop and bend the cooling fins. The bracket broke right at the point where the bolt holds the belt at the correct tension. I reattached it just short of where it should be, resulting in the belt being thrown off. I used a pair of Vise Grips to hold the alternator in place until I could replace the bracket. You would think that if the alternator wasn't working the gauge would show a low or no charging rate, with the opposite being true.

Mile 203.9 – Belleville Locks and Dam – Lift 22' – Reedsville, Ohio.

At 8:00, we arrived at Eddies Marina, located at the mouth of the Big Hocking River. Eddie got to talking about historical river conditions and said this years spring floods were the worst he'd seen in fifty-seven years, leaving three inches of mud next to his buildings.

MONDAY, JUNE 13TH, 1994

Knowing the alternator bracket was broken, Eddie volunteered us the use of his golf cart to drive to a marine repair shop a short distance away. They didn't have one, saying Dave's Marine might. Returning Eddie's golf cart, he wouldn't take money for its use or the overnight dockage.

We hustled off to Dave's Marina, fifteen miles upriver. There were lots of nice houses on either bank. Sun is HOT! Dave's had the bracket so I immediately put it on. We hardly got out of sight when I heard a loud 'snap.' A bent fin had flown off the alternator, cutting off the belt. Back to Dave's for a new alternator belt. They didn't have one so I put on the only spare.

Mile 172 – In stopping at the mouth of the Muskingum River at the town of Marietta to buy gas, I found belt # 2 cut off. I walked into town to an auto parts store and bought two belts and bolts to hold the alternator to the bracket. By now I had stripped the machine threads on the alternator and was using a bolt to hold the alternator in place. I put on a new belt, fastening with a new bolt, and was off again. We got upriver one mile and 'snap' went belt # 3. Between replacing belts and the HOT sun, I was really starting to get ticked off! I put on another belt and back to town we went. The auto parts store suggested I buy a better quality belt than they had on hand. They ordered several from their warehouse and would have them in 45 minutes.

2:00 PM – While waiting, we followed the Muskingum River walk and learned that Marietta was the first city established after the Northwest Ordinance of 1787 making it legal to settle north of the Ohio River. It is a nice town with big older buildings. We picked up the belts and returned to the dock. The city was building a cement platform for a monument, which the young gas attendant was against because girls sunbathe there.

Mile 161.7 – Willow Island Locks & Dam – Lift 20' – Newport, Ohio.

#4 & #5 belts had now been cut off due to bent fins flying off the alternator. When the RPM approached 5000, '*Snap*', another belt gone. I had had enough! While replacing #6, I used a vice-grip to break off the remaining cooling fins and went the rest of the trip without another belt related problem.

I have since learned a quick way to change a belt in the boat. While each boat is different, I had to remove an engine mount to replace a belt. If you slip another belt in at the same time and cable tie it out of the way it is a much quicker process.

Mile 126.4 – Hannibal Locks & Dam – Lift 17'8" – Hannibal, Ohio.

The last sixty miles of the day were tough! We faced strong head winds between the high hills, causing constant whitecaps.

Mile 84.3 – Pike Island Locks & Dam – Lift 17' 8" – Wheeling, W Virginia. Mile 54.4 – New Cumberland Locks & Dam – Lift 20' 5" – Stratton, Ohio.

Mile 43 – In trying to check in at Holiday Yacht Club, the only people we could find were two guys working on a boat. I asked about staying, while keeping my distance since one was smoking while working in the bilge. They said to just pull into any slip and if no one finds us before we leave, then move on out. We found an empty slip close to the bathrooms and were just getting settled in when Mike Pusateri, owner/manager?, came by. I asked about buying gas, and learned they didn't have pumps. Mike took me to a gas station to fill the four six gallon belt and back to town we went. The auto parts store suggested I buy a better quality belt than they had on hand. They ordered several from their warehouse and would have them in 45 minutes.

2:00 PM – While waiting, we followed the Muskingum River walk and learned that Marietta was the first city established after the Northwest Ordinance of 1787 making it legal to settle north of the Ohio River. It is a nice town with big older buildings. We picked up the belts and returned to the dock. The city was building a cement platform for a monument, which the young gas attendant was against because girls sunbathe there.

Mile 161.7 – Willow Island Locks & Dam – Lift 20' – Newport, Ohio.

#4 & #5 belts had now been cut off due to bent fins flying off the alternator. When the RPM approached 5000, *'Snap'*, another belt gone. I had had enough! While replacing #6, I used a vice-grip to break off the remaining cooling fins and went the rest of the trip without another belt related problem.

I have since learned a quick way to change a belt in the boat. While each boat is different, I had to remove an engine mount to replace a belt. If you slip another belt in at the same time and cable tie it out of the way it is a much quicker process.

Mile 126.4 – Hannibal Locks & Dam – Lift 17'8" – Hannibal, Ohio.

The last sixty miles of the day were tough! We faced strong head winds between the high hills, causing constant whitecaps.

Mile 84.3 – Pike Island Locks & Dam – Lift 17' 8" – Wheeling, W Virginia. Mile 54.4 – New Cumberland Locks & Dam – Lift 20' 5" – Stratton, Ohio.

Mile 43 – In trying to check in at Holiday Yacht Club, the only people we could find were two guys working on a boat. I asked about staying, while keeping my distance since one was smoking while working in the bilge. They said to just pull into any slip and if no one finds us before we leave, then move on out. We found an empty slip close to the bathrooms and were just getting settled in when Mike Pusateri, owner/manager?, came by. I asked about buying gas, and learned they didn't have pumps. Mike took me to a gas station to fill the four six gallon first trip, I looked at the charging rate on the gauge. It was higher than normal. I lifted the motor hood and found the bracket that holds the alternator had broken, allowing it to drop and bend the cooling fins. The bracket broke right at the point where the bolt holds the belt at the correct tension. I reattached it just short of where it should be, resulting in the belt being thrown off. I used a pair of Vise Grips to hold the alternator in place until I could replace the bracket. You would think that if the alternator wasn't working the gauge would show a low or no charging rate, with the opposite being true.

Mile 203.9 – Belleville Locks and Dam – Lift 22' – Reedsville, Ohio.

At 8:00, we arrived at Eddies Marina, located at the mouth of the Big Hocking River. Eddie got to talking about historical river conditions and said this years spring floods were the worst he'd seen in fifty-seven years, leaving three inches of mud next to his buildings.

MONDAY, JUNE 13TH, 1994

Knowing the alternator bracket was broken, Eddie volunteered us the use of his golf cart to drive to a marine repair shop a short distance away. They didn't have one, saying Dave's Marine might. Returning Eddie's golf cart, he wouldn't take money for its use or the overnight dockage.

We hustled off to Dave's Marina, fifteen miles upriver. There were lots of nice houses on either bank. Sun is HOT! Dave's had the bracket so I immediately put it on. We hardly got out of sight when I heard a loud 'snap.' A bent fin had flown off the alternator, cutting off the belt. Back to Dave's for a new alternator belt. They didn't have one so I put on the only spare.

Mile 172 – In stopping at the mouth of the Muskingum River at the town of Marietta to buy gas, I found belt # 2 cut off. I walked into town to an auto parts store and bought two belts and bolts to hold the alternator to the bracket. By now I had stripped the machine threads on the alternator and was using a bolt to hold the alternator in place. I put on a new belt, fastening with a new bolt, and was off again. We got upriver one mile and 'snap' went belt # 3. Between replacing belts and the HOT sun, I was really starting to get ticked off! I put on another cans carried and gave us the combination to the bathroom locks. We weren't asked to register or pay a transient dockage fee.

TUESDAY, JUNE 14TH, 1994

Our arrival at Holiday Yacht Club was with only three gallons left. I wanted to start the day off with the full 39 gallons I could carry, and walked to the now known gas station location for cheap gas ($1.069). Debbie walked to the IGA for milk and ice and we were back on the river at 8:00 to calm water.

Mile 31.7 – Montgomery Locks & Dam – Lift 17' 5" – Industry, Pennsylvania.

Debbie, the designated VHF radio operator, had a confusing conversation with the lockmaster. Then *after* pulling into the lock chamber, we were told to get our 100-foot rope out. I had read that 100' of line was required for some of the Ohio locks, with this being the first one asking for its use. In preparation, I had carefully coiled a ¼" line in a coffee can with the end sticking out the plastic top so it would not tangle. It was a mad scramble to find where we had stashed it. It uncoiled without a kink and the rest of the lockage went smoothly.

Mile 13.3 – Dashields Locks & Dam – Lift 10' – Glenwillard, Pennsylvania.

Mile 6.2 – Emsworth Locks & Dam – Lift 18' – Emsworth, Pennsylvania.

We tied up to await a double length barge, since the smaller chamber was unavailable due to maintenance. We tried to feed breadcrumbs to ducks while waiting.

Mile 0.0 is known locally as Three Rivers, the point at which the Allegheny and Monogahela join to form the Ohio, at Pittsburgh, Pennsylvania.

The Lock and Dam #'s above the Ohio no longer follow a numerical sequence due to being replaced by higher dams, reducing the total number needed. A current copy of Quimby's is well worth the purchase price as they update changes to multiple river systems annually.

Taking the right fork, we headed up the 128-mile navigable length of the Monongahela River.

I will mention all the Lock location Mile and lift #'s once. With the exception of the Kentucky and Cumberland

Rivers, we locked through the rest both up and downstream.

Mile 11.2 – Locks & Dam #2 – Lift 8' 7" – Braddock, Pennsylvania.

Mile 23.8 – Locks & Dam #3 – Lift 8' 2" – Elizabeth, Pennsylvania.

A pilot referred to as "Junior" hardly slowed down upon lock approach, while stopping precisely. His crew quickly lassoed the mooring bits and tied down the barge.

Mile 41.5 – Locks &Dam #4 – Lift 16' 6" – Monessen, Pennsylvania.

Mile 61.2 – Maxwell Locks & Dam – Lift 19' 5" – LaBelle, Pennsylvania.

Mile 85.0 – Lock & Dam #7 – Lift 15' – Greensboro, Pennsylvania.

The lock was busy letting a loaded barge down and taking an empty one up.

While waiting and tied to a branch in the river with the top up we played gin rummy. I won 25 - 98, Mile 90.8 – Point Marion Lock & Dam – Lift 19' Point Marion, Pennsylvania. Mile 102.0 – Morgantown Lock & Dam – Lift 17' Morgantown, Pennsylvania.

The final two locks on the Monogahela were only open from 8:00 to 4:00. The friendly lockmaster at Morgantown Lock said the new owner of Uffington marina didn't accept transients. We stopped anyway, and in finding no one around and gas at $1.64 a gallon decided to camp in The Boat under trees on the right bank at Mile 104. The day's run had gone well, with the locks being the controlling factor in the distance covered.

WEDNESDAY, JUNE 15TH, 1994

With the boat barely moving during the night, we slept very well, leaving at 7:00.

Mile 108.0 – Hildebrand Lock & Dam – Lift 21' – Laurel Point, West Virginia.

The Lockmaster at Hildebrand said there is no gas available at Six & Plum Marina, even though Quimby's had them listed as selling it.

Uh, Oh, Now what? We made it to just below Opekisli L&D and added the mixed gas from the auxiliary motor tank.

Mile 115.4 – Opekiski Lock & Dam – Lift 22' – Catawba, West Virginia.

The 2.5 gallons from the auxiliary tank gets us through the lock and up river seven miles to Rivesville. We parked at a private dock, where I walked one block to a gas station. Debbie filled the boat tank from the first two six gallon cans, while I made two additional trips, buying thirty-six gallons at $1.089 a gallon. Debbie then went to buy ice and groceries, having a goose chase her. We had gone 166 miles since last buying gas, averaging just over 4 mpg going upstream.

While heading to Fairmont, West Virginia, the uppermost town on the navigable portion of the Monogahela, I saw a houseboat being worked on with 'Port of St Louis' painted on the stern. I asked the old man if he had been there and we began talking river travelling. He said we should check out the Taggert River coming in from the right bank as we continued upstream. We took him up on his suggestion.

9:45 – The Taggert River was narrow, with trees growing flush to the bank. Per his instructions, we stopped going upstream upon seeing a railroad bridge with a broken walkway dangling from its side. There were lots of small old rusted barges from an earlier era lining the banks. I wondered if they had been used to keep the bank from washing or just abandoned there.

Mile 130 – Back on the Monogahela, we turned to go back down river immediately after crossing under a railroad bridge and seeing the channel narrow drastically.

10:36 – Opekisli L&D – Just Cruis'n and listening to blue grass.

11:00 – Hildebrand L&D.

11:30 – Morgantown L&D.

12:00 – Point Marion L&D.

1:00 – L&D #7

While waiting for a double lockage, we ate lunch, played cards, and watched a boat full of females ages, 4 - 30.

Some were rather large, with their swimsuits barely able to contain them as they played in the water.

2:40 – Maxwell L&D, 3:35 L&D #4.
4:30 – L&D #3.
5:30 – L&D #2.

Back at Three Rivers, and having made the Monogahela round trip, we headed up the Allegheny. There were more boats out, with many anchored close to the beautiful fountain that is the focal point of the three river junction.

6:00 – We stopped at North Shore Marina and bought forty gallons at $1.409, which included refilling the auxiliary motor tank, about a 30% markup over yesterday's price at the roadside gas station. Our theoretical maximum fuel capacity was 41 ½ gallons. There is a markup on the price of on the water gas and I don't begrudge them for it. Growing up in the resort business, I understand why charges are higher for on water services. There is the high cost of real estate, additional regulations, and the fact that business is seasonal by nature. Being cheap and on a budget, I still bought gas at automotive stations wherever possible.

The current was fast, with major water churning from the open upstream control gates of the first lock on Allegheny. (Posted Small Craft Warning) Hearing thunder and feeling raindrops, we decided to find overnight moorage after locking through.

Mile 6.7 L& D #2 – Lift 11' – Pittsburgh, Pennsylvania (No Lock #1)

Mile 12.1 – We inquired at Oakmont Yacht Club about overnight dockage. First saying they didn't take transients, then upon noticing our MN registration, asked if we were really from Minnesota. Confirming we were, and after telling where we had put in and our goals for this trip, their attitude changed. Just as quickly as we'd been turned down, Vern & Sheri, the Club Commodores, said it was OK to pull into an unused slip next to them.

While seeing just a small part of Oakmont during our six-block walk to a Subway sandwich shop, we found it to be a very nice town. After showering and readying The Boat for rain, we talked to Vern & Sheri. They gave us a local magazine with information about the locks on the Allegheny, whose hours and days of operation vary widely depending on the time of year.

THURSDAY, JUNE 16TH, 1994

Up at 6:30, we got another quick shower, had breakfast, and arranged The Boat for another day on the water.

Three men in full dress uniform and fancy ties stood on the dock while a black and gold trimmed Cadillac limousine waited at the clubhouse. While Debbie videoed the clubhouse, the chauffeur asked if she knew about any sea planes landing on the river, which of course she didn't. As we left somebody in uniform and tie said to have a good day and we should stay again, with a floatplane landing almost immediately after we cleared the area.

Mile 14.5 L&D #3 – Lift 13' 5" – Barling, Pennsylvania

While keeping the motor in slow forward due to fast and rough water against the lock wall, we waited for a barge doing a double lockage. The Lockmaster wouldn't acknowledge us on the VHF radio.

I should address the issue of maybe why lock operators wouldn't return calls during various trips, and yet talk to barges and other boats. A recreational VHF radio license first wasn't required, and then was required, then not required for recreational boats. I had one costing $100 for ten years. There is a procedure to identify your license # and boat name. Rather than go through the BS of saying Lock #, this is 'boat name' and license #, we chose to call the lock and only identify ourselves as a 'recreational boat' awaiting lockage. I suspect that most small recreational boats with VHF radios do it the same way.

Mile 24.2 L&D #4 – Lift 10'5" – Natrona, Pennsylvania

The upstream dams were releasing a lot of water causing three foot choppy waves close to the locks. Mile 30.4 L&D #5 – Lift 11' 8" – Freeport, Pennsylvania

Each lock (5, 6, 7 & 8) got progressively calmer, while still running fast.

Mile 36.3 L&D #6 – Lift 12' 2" – Freeport, Pennsylvania

Mile 45.7 L&D #7 – Lift 13' 1" – Kittanning, Pennsylvania Mile 52.6 L&D #8 – Lift 17' 9" – Tempeleton, Pennsylvania Mile 62.2 L&D #9 – Lift 22' – Rimer, Pennsylvania

This is the last lock heading upstream, and at the time was only open Friday-Monday from 12:30 to 8:30. There is only ten miles of navigable water past the lock, and being 12:35 and Thursday, we headed back downriver.

Mile 60.2 – Just below Lock #9 at the Spot Marina we bought - gas, milk, bread - from a friendly young lady. The temperature was 97.

Upon seeing a waterside lounge, we stopped only to find it not open. I asked a man at a repair business next door where a guy could get a beer. He grabbed one out of the fridge and gave it to me. Only after opening and taking a swig, I found out he didn't work there and that it was his nephews business.

3:30 – L&D #4 – The Boat was not running right so I sprayed carburetor cleaner into it, which seemed to help. This is not as simple a process as it sounds, requiring moving about half the boat's contents just to lift the motor cover. A beaver swam into the lock chamber as we left.

4:40 – L&D #3 – Our first inclination that there was a US Open Golf Tournament being held in the area was seeing a blimp overhead. The Lockmaster said that four golfers had dropped out of today's round due to heat, and that it was 100 - 107 degrees at the lock.

The discharge from the last lock was substantially less than in the morning.

6:00 – Emsworth L&D We're now back on the Ohio amongst lots of traffic. The lock will not talk to us on the VHF radio, but talks about us. They kept the red light on, barring entry to the open lock gates. A tugboat pushing a barge with a crane idled by, parking right next to the lift gates. While awaiting instructions and keeping the boat at the lock wall, we ate sandwiches and played cards.

7:30 – The lock finally let us through. The Lockmaster said they had answered, but we never heard any conversation directed towards us. They probably thought we were day-trippers who would lock right back up and were waiting us out.

Finding C & E Marina closed; we went around the tip of Neville Island and upriver one mile to the Greater Pittsburgh Aquatic Club. We met two couples at the private marina who invited us to stay and told us where the bathroom key was hidden. As Debbie cooked dinner, a lightning storm approached. We saw, then heard several cloud to ground lightning strikes, some maybe less than a mile away. Then just as we were falling asleep, rain came. The mooring canvas allowed some water in, but fortunately it was just dribbles.

FRIDAY, JUNE 17TH, 1994

We were up at 6:00, with the neighbors inviting us over for coffee at 7:00. We'd already had ours and were preparing to shove off. I regret not socializing more with the many wonderful people met along the way, but doing these trips within an allotted vacation time doesn't allow much down time. We called South Bend and talked with the boys who weren't very awake.

Mile 58.1 – We bought twenty-eight gallons of gas and some ice at River Mist Marina. The motor was not running right so I sprayed Gum Out in the carburetor.

12:00 Noon – We lucked out at Pike Island L&D. A barge had just locked through, with the lockmaster holding the doors open for us. To be able to run forty miles between locks and slip in without having a wait is unusual.

2:00 – Hannibal L&D I talked Debbie into making lunch while waiting for a gray houseboat to come around the bend and lock up with us.

3:00 – I wanted Debbie to drive because I was getting eye weary. This was the second time of only four she would be at the helm this trip, and never on the rest. It's not that I won't let her, she prefers not to. As we changed places while maintaining throttle, we both lost our hats! Mine landed in the boat while Debbie's went in the river. She drove for ½ hour while I slept in the bow. Looking directly into a western sun is difficult on the eyes, even with sunglasses. Not only is a sharp eye needed to stay in the marked channel while traveling at 32 mph, there was also a fair amount of driftwood to dodge.

Mile 156 – We stopped at Newport, Ohio to buy gas, milk, and ice. We saw an off river gas station and took advantage of the low bank to refuel, buying twenty-four gallons at 1.069.

6:00 – Mile 172 Ohio River/Muskingum River Junction. Town of Marietta, Ohio.

I'd been mulling over Marietta's place in history since buying the alternator belts. Having an interest in history, we slowly cruised up through the No wake Zone to the first lock on the Muskingum at mile 5.8. We pulled the boat up on shore and walked to the information house. The lock was small and the gates wooden.

I asked the lockmaster how it worked, with him saying, "It worked good." He offered to put us through, so we did. The lock controls are ran using hand cranks. After locking up & down, we returned to the Ohio and raced downstream to Eddie's Marina. The sun was still high, but it was really cloudy so it got dark fast. We saw a speedboat called 'Frustration' being towed.

8:30 – Eddie was very busy. He was supposed to be in town cooking pork chops for a Lion's fundraiser at 8:00. Eddie's does not have shower facilities, but he drove us to the nearby Athens Boat Club in his golf cart and assured us it was OK to use theirs. He used to own the land now occupied by the Athens Boat Club, keeping the corner having dockage on the Hocking River, off the Ohio

While walking back to Eddie's we saw a boat called 'Wet Dream', a 28 - 30 footer with five bladed stainless steel props on twin outdrives. I talked to the owner who said it could run 90 MPH. When opened up it used 2 ½ gallons per mile from its 150 gallon gas tank, giving it a range of 60 miles at full throttle. That same 150 gallons would take my boat 600 miles running about 32 MPH. He didn't offer and I didn't ask for a ride. I would love to be in a boat running at that speed just one time to feel what its like.

We bought gas and again asked Eddie what we owed for dockage -still saying "nothing" even though it was our second stay with him.

SATURDAY, JUNE 18TH, 1994

We arrived at Belleville L&D at 7:00 just as the doors were closing. Debbie radioed and they waited for us.

8:30 – Mile 237.3 – Racine L&D – Nice day, sunny, hazy, calm river, cool when running.

10:00 – Mile 250 – We stopped at the town of Pomeroy, Ohio to buy gas, ice, & milk.

10:30 – Mile 265.7 – Great Kanawa /Ohio River junction Figuring we'd never be this way again turned and headed up the Kanawa's 90-mile navigation limit and into West Virginia.

11:00 – Mile 20 – Bass fishermen are serious about their sport. Trying to be friendly, we'd wave while they passed by. They didn't wave back, although one guy did nod. The land was level to either side, with hills rising off in the distance.

11:30 – Mile 31.1 – Winfield Locks & Dam Lift 28' (2) 360' X 56' Locks.

With four barges waiting outside the lock and a barge in each of the twin chambers, we slipped through with only a 15-minute wait. I barely had time to add gas. We heard the Lockmaster say 109 lockage's were stacked below Marmet Lock. The bottleneck was due to Marmet having one chamber being worked on. According to Quimby's, pleasure and tour boats get priority.

The shoreline area below Winfield Lock was undeveloped, above Winfield Lock is Money! There were big houses with nice boats at their docks for miles.

I bought twelve gallons of gas at an Exxon station, having to go through a hole in a security fence at the top of a hill to reach it. The West Virginia capitol at Charleston is just off the river and its shimmering gold dome was beautiful. The river was very busy, with people skiing through barge wakes!

1:30 – Mile 67.7 – Marmet Locks & Dam Lift 24' (2) 360' X 56' Locks Debbie used the VHF radio to politely ask about lockage. The lockmaster comes right back and says we're next! As we waited for the Lillian M to exit the lock, we had a sausage and cheese lunch. We locked through before 2:30, with the Lockmaster saying having a VHF radio is the key to being worked in. The heavily populated stretch of river above the lock wasn't as rich looking, while still very nice with the hills becoming more like you would expect West Virginia to be.

3:00 – Mile 82.8 – London Locks & Dam Lift 24' (2) 360' X 56' Locks.

The chamber was ready for us to lock up so we figured we might just as well keep going. The friendly lady lockmaster tells us it is 91 degrees today and that she has individual names for the flock of crows that hang around. In hearing our story of travelling rivers, she said not to tie up to the lock wall upon returning since she knew we could handle our boat.

3:30 – Mile 92 – or so Immediately after passing under a long steel railroad bridge held up by six massive concrete pillars and seeing the unmarked channel narrow, I decided to head back downstream. The upstream and downstream views are worthy of a National Geographic photograph.

4:00 – London L&D Since the lockmaster was expecting us, we locked right back through.

5:00 – Hearing it'd be an hour to lock back down at Marmet and spying an Exxon sign up the steep bank, I decided to refuel. Two round trips and twenty-four gallons later we were ready to roll. With time still left we cleaned the boat and I duct taped my canvas shoes back together as best I could. Climbing the steep and often rocky banks were taking their toll.

6:00 – Marmet let us float without tying up. As we left the lock Debbie made a little speech on the VHF radio, thanking the barge traffic for their patience as we locked through ahead of them. One towboat captain replied by saying, "Fine Little Woman".

7:25 – It was starting to get dark when we arrived back at Winfield L&D. We had peanut butter sandwiches for dinner during the half hour wait for lockage.

8:00 – The lockmaster radioed to tell us that we will lock through with the gas barge just ahead of us and to pull in first. Evidently I didn't move fast enough as the towboats captain said to hurry. "I'm about to pull these gas barges forward and, well, you'll get run over." As we free floated at the far end, I had to keep the boat in forward gear since the barge was drawing water out as it entered.

8:30 – It was dark as we left the lock. I followed the wake of a fishing boat while Debbie used the search light. She found a spot between a tree and a stump to tie up. Since last year's trip experience of blowing fuses, I'd hooked the spotlight directly to the battery with its own fused connection. Shortly after tying up, two barges met directly across from us, coming much closer than we'd expected.

SUNDAY, JUNE 19TH, 1994

5:15 – Well we stayed in our spot. Debbie slept well while I did not.

7:15 – RC Byrd L&D Mile 279 – Back on the Ohio, it took a while to get an answer from the Lockmaster working in an area without a radio.

Mile 304 – We stopped at Huntington West Virginia to add gas, and tighten the alternator bolt.

10:15 – Geenup L&D – After locking through with a gas barge and two bass boats we searched for a roadside gas stop.

11:00 – I spotted a BP gas station about 1 ½ blocks off the river in Sciotoville, Ohio with a decent tie off spot close to a refinery. We got the OK from a refinery worker to use the stairs that came down to the river. Carrying four gas cans, we went around the refinery, across train tracks and a four-lane highway – separated by a 3 ½ foot concrete divider – to the BP. Debbie helped by carrying two back. While climbing over the concrete divider, we heard a train whistle. I quickly picked up two gas containers and got across the track ahead of the train. Debbie, not as fast, waited for the coal train to pass. That gave me time to carry the two gas cans to the boat and meet her halfway between the bank and the RR tracks. While Debbie put in one can of gas, I brought down the last two. She waded in the river while I put a second one in.

All this work to buy gas at automotive stations instead of marinas might seem a little ridiculous. Many marinas have a long no wake zone, then you have to find an attendant, maybe to find out they didn't sell gas. Depending on how much gas they pump, there can be water contamination. With modern gas stations also selling bread, milk, ice, lunchmeats, etc, it makes it a one-stop deal. Then, besides the obvious cost saving, when you spend all day in a small boat a little forced exercise is good for the body.

Debbie fell asleep partway through the stretch of Mile 349 - 396. Upon waking, she commented that the scenery was just as beautiful as before she fell asleep.

Mile 397 – Stopping just downstream from Manchester Island to add gas, we cooled off by taking a swim. There were lots of families in smaller boats out for a Sunday afternoon of skiing, and tubing.

Mile 436 – Meldahl L&D – While waiting to lock through we put the boat top up to ward off the hot sun. Leaving the lock, Debbie drove while I made a nest amongst the gear in the bow and took a much-needed nap.

Mile 449.5 – Stopping at Port Tacoma Harbor Marina for gas, we bought T-shirts that said in bold blue JUST DO IT, with *On The Ohio River* superimposed in bright pink. I tried to fall sleep again, with the boat traffic around Cincinnati making it a wild choppy ride! Telling Debbie I'd break my back if I couldn't see the wakes coming, I took over driving. About five miles from Presidents Boat Park, our point of origin, we saw lightning hit land and rain pouring down. By the time we tied up, it had stopped.

While Debbie restocked the boat from supplies in the van, I started it up, turned on the A/C, and had a really good nap.

Mile 492 – With Indiana on the right bank, it seemed as if the almost constant hills seen since our start had melted to become farmland.

Mile 529 – Looking to find a quiet spot off the Ohio, we headed up Turtle Creek to Cast-a-ways Yacht Club. It was very nice, and off the bounce of the river. Juanita, the manager, was very talkative while not being a very good listener.

MONDAY, JUNE 20TH, 1994

5:30 – Up and at'em. When Debbie used the women's restroom, she noticed the tank top on the toilet was broken.

contamination. With modern gas stations also selling bread, milk, ice, lunchmeats, etc, it makes it a one-stop deal. Then, besides the obvious cost saving, when you spend all day in a small boat a little forced exercise is good for the body.

Debbie fell asleep partway through the stretch of Mile 349 - 396. Upon waking, she commented that the scenery was just as beautiful as before she fell asleep.

Mile 397 – Stopping just downstream from Manchester Island to add gas, we cooled off by taking a swim. There were lots of families in smaller boats out for a Sunday afternoon of skiing, and tubing.

Mile 436 – Meldahl L&D – While waiting to lock through we put the boat top up to ward off the hot sun. Leaving the lock, Debbie drove while I made a nest amongst the gear in the bow and took a much-needed nap.

Mile 449.5 – Stopping at Port Tacoma Harbor Marina for gas, we bought T-shirts that said in bold blue JUST DO IT, with *On The Ohio River* superimposed in bright pink. I tried to fall sleep again, with the boat traffic around Cincinnati making it a wild choppy ride! Telling Debbie I'd break my back if I couldn't see the wakes coming, I took over driving. About five miles from Presidents Boat Park, our point of origin, we saw lightning hit land and rain pouring down. By the time we tied up, it had stopped.

While Debbie restocked the boat from supplies in the van, I started it up, turned on the A/C, and had a really good nap.

Mile 492 – With Indiana on the right bank, it seemed as if the almost constant hills seen since our start had melted to become farmland.

Mile 529 – Looking to find a quiet spot off the Ohio, we headed up Turtle Creek to Cast-a-ways Yacht Club. It was very nice, and off the bounce of the river. Juanita, the manager, was very talkative while not being a very good listener.

MONDAY, JUNE 20TH, 1994

5:30 – Up and at'em. When Debbie used the women's restroom, she noticed the tank top on the toilet was broken.

pull these gas barges forward and, well, you'll get run over." As we free floated at the far end, I had to keep the boat in forward gear since the barge was drawing water out as it entered.

8:30 – It was dark as we left the lock. I followed the wake of a fishing boat while Debbie used the search light. She found a spot between a tree and a stump to tie up. Since last year's trip experience of blowing fuses, I'd hooked the spotlight directly to the battery with its own fused connection. Shortly after tying up, two barges met directly across from us, coming much closer than we'd expected.

SUNDAY, JUNE 19TH, 1994

5:15 – Well we stayed in our spot. Debbie slept well while I did not.

7:15 – RC Byrd L&D Mile 279 – Back on the Ohio, it took a while to get an answer from the Lockmaster working in an area without a radio.

Mile 304 – We stopped at Huntington West Virginia to add gas, and tighten the alternator bolt.

10:15 – Geenup L&D – After locking through with a gas barge and two bass boats we searched for a roadside gas stop.

11:00 – I spotted a BP gas station about 1 ½ blocks off the river in Sciotoville, Ohio with a decent tie off spot close to a refinery. We got the OK from a refinery worker to use the stairs that came down to the river. Carrying four gas cans, we went around the refinery, across train tracks and a four-lane highway – separated by a 3 ½ foot concrete divider – to the BP. Debbie helped by carrying two back. While climbing over the concrete divider, we heard a train whistle. I quickly picked up two gas containers and got across the track ahead of the train. Debbie, not as fast, waited for the coal train to pass. That gave me time to carry the two gas cans to the boat and meet her halfway between the bank and the RR tracks. While Debbie put in one can of gas, I brought down the last two. She waded in the river while I put a second one in.

All this work to buy gas at automotive stations instead of marinas might seem a little ridiculous. Many marinas have a long no wake zone, then you have to find an attendant, maybe to find out they didn't sell gas. Depending on how much gas they pump, there can be water

She reported it to Juanita so she wouldn't think it was us.

Mile 531.5 – Markland Locks & Dam – Lift 35' – Warsaw, Kentucky At 8:30 we encountered bad fog.

Mile 545 – While floating by Carrollton, Kentucky in fog, I sprayed the carburetor with Gum Out.

Mile 600 – Kayrouz Marina did a quick tune up, changing out the points, plugs, and condenser. It was a typical Southern Indiana day – high heat and humidity – with us sweating even in the shade. We fueled up and were off again.

Mile 606.8 – McAlpine Locks & Dam. Lift 34' – Louisville, Kentucky.

While waiting for a down bound barge and the lock to refill, we refueled the boat tank from cans and took a swim. During the extended wait, we cleaned the outside of the boat, taking advantage of how good it felt to be in the cool water.

Mile 711 – 5:20 – The town of Cloverport, Kentucky looked like a good place to buy gas off the water. I first tried a station close to the low bank, finding it closed. I then carried four six-gallon containers up a steep road to the next visible station. I read two historical markers along the way stating that Cloverport had started out as a coal town, declining in prosperity when people started using petroleum.

Just after filling the gas cans, a gentlemen in a pickup pulling a flat bottom boat offered me a ride back to the ramp. He'd seen me leave the ramp carrying the cans, and Debbie moving downstream to where I would have clambered down the bank. The video camera cut off his name; He is from Ledbetter, Kentucky and was a commercial net fisherman who doesn't like fluctuating water levels because it required resetting nets. A recovering alcoholic and pastor of a church with a dock on a creek just up from the Kentucky River; he'd committed himself to preach to other recovering alcoholics. He baptizes people in the creek next to the dock. We thanked him for his help. He said river people help each other, just a code of ethics, without expecting anything back. Land lovers, if they do something for you, expect something back.

Mile 720.7 – Cannelton Locks & Dam Lift 26' Cannelton, Indiana the setting sun was obscured by haze, making channel navigation more difficult.

Mile 768 – 7:30 – It was getting dark quickly, with the next marina shown in Quimby's twenty-three miles away. I thought about stopping behind either French or Ellis Island at mile 768 to spend the night. Debbie suggested French Island Marina & Boat Club at Mile 765, noted on the river chart but not in Quimby's. Not seeing it heading downstream, and against one of my cardinal rules to not backtrack, we headed back upstream. We found it, and in stopping once again met the nicest people. Two men were working on a boat tied to the outside of the dock. Its owner said we could have his more protected spot on the inside of the dock, if we got the OK of Don or Annie who operate the marina.

We talked to Don for a while. He pointed out a houseboat that had been to New York, and said their trip had been very expensive. They had blown an engine, had a fire, and had to have it rewired.

Don told of his favorite club member. This guy works all week at a regular job and is a volunteer firefighter so is on call 24 hours a day. He comes to the river and runs night and day. Says that is what he comes for and does not care what anyone else thinks. Don likes him because he can spend $2000 a weekend on gas. The first time he was at the marina he left $500 and said let me know when it's gone. In a very short period he'd filled up twice, and spent the $500.

TUESDAY, JUNE 21ST, 1994

6:30 – Now back on Central Time we slept 'late.' Don said he had checked the dock at 3:00 and heard us snoring loudly. We went on shore and enjoyed coffee with some club members. I told Debbie to get the 'chattiness' out of her system. Other than when we stop for locks or add gas, we cannot hear each other over the sound of the motor and usually loud cassette deck. She did talk a lot, saying later that it didn't help. We visited with a couple, who through remarriage had seven kids, and were living at the marina for the summer.

8:00 – Got gassed up and headed down the channel between French Island #2 and Indiana. The twenty-year-old gas barge used at the marina had come from the Wabash River, costing $30,000.

Mile 776 – 8:45 Newburgh Locks & Dam Lift 18' Newburgh, Indiana It was humid and hazy with heavy barge traffic.

Mile 846 – 11:30 Uniontown Locks & Dam Lift 28' – Mount Vernon, Indiana

Mile 889 – 1:15 Elizabethtown, Illinois – Thunder & lightning were off in the distance.

1:45 – Heavy rain, accompanied by thunder, & lightning, forced us to put the top up and drive close to shore since we couldn't see far enough ahead to see other boat or barge traffic.

Mile 918.5 – 2:15 Smithland Locks & Dam Lift 22' – Hamletsburg, Illinois We locked through with a barge behind us in the chamber. Mile 934.2 – 3:30 – Tennessee River Confluence

Just two years prior, we'd bypassed the last 22.4 miles of the Tennessee crossing over to the Cumberland in favor of a lesser lock wait. Now that we were back, I was determined to go through the last lock of the Tennessee River, which we'd earlier been discouraged from doing.

We headed up the Tennessee, having boated the last 46.6 miles of the Ohio three years ago.

Mile 22.4 – Kentucky Lock & Dam Lift 57' – Gilbertsville, Kentucky Upon arriving at 4:40 they once again tried to discourage us from locking through by saying it would be at least three hours. We occupied our time playing cards, watching birds, and a raccoon, locking through at 7:45.

Mile 24.1 – 8:00 – Looking for transient dockage, we stopped at Lighthouse Landing where we bought gas two years ago. The office had closed at 6:00, so we found an open slip and set up for the night. I was able to get a shower because someone had propped open the otherwise locked door. Debbie wasn't so lucky and was now on her third day without a shower.

WEDNESDAY, JUNE 22ND, 1994

Being in a hurry to get moving I left a note at the gas dock with my name and address so they could send a bill for the slip. (Never heard from them) Two big old turtles surfaced right next to the slip.

Mile 25 – We crossed over to the Cumberland River via the Barkley Canal.

Barkley Lock &Dam Lift 57' Grand River, Kentucky With major maintenance work in progress we were forced to wait an hour and a half to lock through. We kept cool in the shade of the lock wall approach. A string of empty barges came grinding to a halt just twenty feet from us. They were pretty imposing being so much taller than us. Since we'd been there first we were able to lock through ahead of them.

10:30 – A mussel fisherman was just bringing in his lines, so we videotaped the process. He said 80 pounds of the large size sold for $50 and showed us a gauge that if a mussel could pass through must be tossed back.

11:00 – Cumberland/Ohio River Confluence – Mile 923

Mile 902 – 1:00 – Golconda Marina – We bought food, ice, & thirty-two gallons of gas. It wasn't as hot today but thunderstorm clouds were gathering over the calm river. The Boat still won't come up to speed, even after the tune up. I stopped and tried to figure out what the problem was to no avail.

Mile 881 – 2:00 – Cave-In-Rock has an infamous spot in history. From here many flatbed boats en route to New Orleans were waylaid, with their crew murdered and replaced by their killers. We stopped to check it out. The muddy narrow entrance opened up into two chambers, one larger than the other with a hole to vent smoke.

Mile 797 – 6:00 – Dogtown Marina for gas 11.2 gallons

Mile 765 – 8:00 – Were back at French Island Marina. Debbie must have acquired a distinct odor as she was offered the use of a shower at Don & Annie's house. We bought 33.8 gallons at $1.379.

THURSDAY, JUNE 23RD, 1994

Getting up at 6:40, we left French Island at 8:00. The Boat is still not running right. The day is sunny, humid and hazy, with very little breeze.

Mile 720.7 9:40 – Cannelton Locks & Dam – While waiting to lock we cleaned the boat, checked again why the engine was cutting out, and played cards.

Mile 718.9 – 11:30 Rocky Point Marina Stopped for twelve gallons of gas and groceries.

Mile 656 – or so. 2:00 – We headed into the seemingly routine daily rain and put the top up.

Mile 642 – 2:30 What wimps! After just a few sprinkles, we stopped and Debbie took the top down while I added gas. Debbie heard a Bobwhite in the Kentucky woods. I know the difference between a cow mooing, a pig oinking, and a rooster crowing, beyond that I'm at a loss to recognize animal and bird sounds.

Mile 606 – McAlpine Locks & Dam I'd pushed our gas limit range to the max, and waxed Debbie at cards while waiting to lock through.

Mile 600 – 5:15 – It took 42.2 gallons of gas at Kayrouz Marina to fill the 15 gallon tank and four auxiliary six gallon cans Theoretically, this is 3.2 gallon over capacity. Either their meter was off, the containers were filled past recommended capacity, or a combination of both. In any case, I came in on empty. Having the backup motor with its 2 ½-gallon tank made me feel more comfortable when pushing fuel limits.

Mile 545 – 7 7:00 – Kentucky/Ohio River Confluence

Other than going the maximum possible distance on previously untraveled waters within the finite period of a two-week vacation and the round trip 1500 highway miles to get there, the plan stopped. I had really pushed us. Now being just Thursday and only sixty miles from the van, I decided to head up the Kentucky's 220 miles of navigable water and still operable 11 locks. There are three more above #11 no longer operated or maintained.

Mile 2 on Kentucky River 7:30 – Admirals Landing supposedly had showers, bathrooms, and a restaurant. We found just the shell of a building on the river. There was a nice houseboat tied to the dock and a motor home up the hill, but no people, just seven dogs running around loose. A local rainstorm must have just passed through since the docks were wet.

With no better place to go, we stayed overnight. For once, Debbie was able to cook in daylight. Admirals Landing was the only place I ever told her to, "Be sure to boil the water". It came out gray with white specs still floating even after settling down.

Some time in the night (3 or 4 AM), there was a group of four to six people who arrived to party across the river. Shouting and hollering (not the nicest language), they swung and dropped into the river from a rope swing. Ellen & Dave were two names heard. "We're just going down to underwear, Right?" a female voice says. When the racket got to be too much, I shined our 12-volt halogen spotlight on them. At first they yelled "Turn it off!" Then when I turned it off, they switched to, "Turn it back on, We'll show you something!" I didn't shine them any more and they left soon after.

FRIDAY, JUNE 24TH, 1994

It was only after finishing breakfast that a man came down to the dock. He said that the restaurant, restrooms, and docks were broken off in February by a passing barge. The restaurant sank, and the dock floated fifteen miles to Madison, Indiana, taking seven hours to tow it back. No barge ever admitted to hitting them. We bought gas and were off.

Mile 4 – 8:00 Lock & Dam #1 Lift 8'3"

Not getting an answer on the VHF radio, I got out and found the Lockmaster working in a garage. Mile 31 – 9:30 Lock & Dam #2 Lift 14'

It started to rain, but we didn't put the top up because I had to fight fast water being released from the chamber and it was sunny upon leaving.

Mile 42 – 10:15 Lock & Dam #3 Lift 13'2"

Mile 65 – Lock & Dam #4 Lift 13'2"

Bought gas right after exiting the lock at Frankfort, Kentucky.

Mile 82.2 – 1:00 L&D #5 – Not getting a response from the lockmaster, we didn't lock through. Locks 5 through 11 are exclusively operated by the Kentucky Water Patrol for recreational traffic. Hours of operation were from 1 to 9 PM on Fridays and 10 AM to 9 PM on Saturdays and Sundays. I've since learned that some are now totally closed due to lack of funding for operation and maintenance. Locks 12, 13, & 14 had already been closed.

It was probably fortunate that we didn't lock through as I would have kept going through the final six, adding another 277 miles to the trip. It was Friday afternoon and we had 140 miles of river, and five lockage's before getting back to the van. Then we had to pick up the boys in South Bend and return to Lakeville in time for me to get back to work Monday morning. We headed back downstream.

Mile 65 – 2:00 L&D #4 – Due to a threatening storm we stopped to buy gas and tried calling South Bend, getting no answer.

Mile 42 – 3:00 L&D #3

Mile 31 – 4:00 L&D #2 The Lockmaster said a barge was headed to #1 and guessed it would arrive about 6:00. Mile 4 – 5:15 L&D #1 We passed the barge about 10 minutes above the lock. The lockmaster again didn't answer

so I climbed the ladder and found him mowing the lawn this time. Due to time zones and the sometime discrepancies on who does and does not go on daylight saving time we miscalculated our arrival ahead of the barge.

On arriving back at the mouth of the Kentucky and turning upstream on the Ohio we encountered major chop. We encountered a downstream tow taking spray clear over the front of the foremost barges as it hit the white caps generated by the westerly wind. You'd think that with the wind mostly at our back, the going would be easy. We took two or three waves over the windshield and onto our heads. Debbie told me later that I had done a good job of piloting us through. I said the only thing I did differently was to grit my teeth.

Markland Locks & Dam 6:00

Mile 529 – Along with gas, we bought cheesy souvenir T-shirts for the boys at Turtle Creek Marina.

Mile 529 – Continuing up Turtle Creek, we again stopped at Castaways Yacht Club, which does not sell gas. In trying to tell Juanita's son about where we'd tied up the boat, I said it's hidden from view by the motor home. As we walked onto the dock, a 26 - 27 foot cruiser came into view. Juanita's son said, "Boy, that's a nice boat!" "It sure is, but that's not mine." The only visible sign of The Boat was the VHF antenna sticking above the high dock.

When Debbie asked Juanita if they sold milk, she went to a local store and bought some for us. Juanita also said that a raccoon probably had knocked off the toilet bowl cover during our prior stay. A friend had given her a matching cover.

Two couples, who both belonged to the same boat club and were on a destination cruise, gave us tours of their houseboats. The couples used to have the same type of houseboat, until a big tree fell on one of them during a big storm while tied to shore.

His wife was monitoring waves washing up at the stern and he was in the pilot area when the tree fell. It broke off the top deck overhang, folding it right down over the front windows without breaking them. He shouted when it happened and she came running up. He said, "Half the boat is gone!" She said, "Raise the blinds so you can see out". He said, "That's the upper deck you're seeing, not the blinds!" While a tugboat was pulling them back to a marina he said, "I'll never buy another boat – I'm Done!" Somebody handed him a business card when they pulled into the marina, and they bought a slightly bigger boat within two weeks. Originally from Kentucky and West Virginia, they said the correct pronunciation of the Kanawa River is 'Ka-naw.'

In traveling upriver from Louisville to the Cast-A-Way's, someone in their boat club destination cruise lost a ladder, and what normally takes seven-hours took ten against the wind.

During the night, I had my typical nightmarish dreams that occur towards the end of all day on the water minimum sleep trips. I woke Debbie up twice. The first, because I wanted help entering a lock in the dark, and the second because I thought she'd fallen overboard when I didn't hear an answer to my question of asking when the burgers would be ready.

SATURDAY, JUNE 25TH, 1994

With me thinking it was 5:45 Central Time, I tried to get Debbie up by saying it was 6:45 Eastern Standard Time, not actually knowing local time. After showering, having breakfast, and packing, we shot the breeze with an untypical 'young house boater' using his father's houseboat for a family vacation.

Being just three miles below Markland Locks and Dam, we coordinated lockage availability, leaving at 7:50.

We're headed home, missing the boys and can't wait to see them.

Our arrival back at President's Boat Park completed the circuitous route started 14 days, 86 lockages and 2650 miles prior. As we cleaned the boat on the trailer, I saw only one additional nick in the original aluminum prop.

We talked to four or five people while cleaning and loading the boat. One gentleman said, while shaking his head after telling him of the distance just traveled, "I thought I was a boater. I Guess I'm Not!"

10:15 – As we drove out of Presidents, the river folks were still helping us out. The guy who said that he thought he was a boater got on a golf cart, and without saying a word, followed us out. At a steep difficult uncontrolled obscured turn onto the highway as you exit the marina, he pulled the golf cart out onto the highway and stopped an oncoming semi so we could leave safely.

Addendum: We sent Thank You letters to all of the marinas and transient spots we stayed at along the way with a brief synopsis of the trip.

The problem with the motor turned out to be another bad spark plug wire.

1994 BIG STONE LAKE TO RENVILLE CO PARK #2 MINNESOTA

With Debbie and the boy's summer vacation quickly ending, we decided to combine family time and a boat trip by finishing the rest of the Minnesota River.

WEDNESDAY, AUGUST 17TH, 1994

The Minnesota River's official start is the outlet of Big Stone Lake, close to Ortonville at the Minnesota/South Dakota border. Using the camper van to pull The Boat trailer hauling a 12ft Alumacraft boat resting on the rollers with the canoe tied to the top of it, we arrived at the Minnesota River outlet.

Just below the railroad bridge that crosses over the Big Stone Lake outlet south of Ortonville, Minnesota, the northerly flow of the Whetstone River joins Big Stone Lakes southerly flow, forming the 'Official Headwaters of the Minnesota River'. The Whetstone River had many places where steel posts had been driven into the river bottom with barriers attached between them to prevent dead wood from floating over a dam, just below and around the bend from the railroad bridge. There was a lot of dead wood floating behind the barrier, and a big pile on shore where it had been drug out.

While heading north trying to find an access as close to the upper portion of the Minnesota River as possible, we also checked out a park in Ortonville as a potential meeting spot.

We found an access at the upper end of Big Stone Lake State Park, unloaded the Alumacraft, put on the 7 ½ HP Mercury, then the four of us headed north. About four miles later, we found ourselves amidst reeds in shallow water and no visible channel. The view looking north closed off to a solid tree line mile about a mile away. While returning to the access point, Nate said that he'd never been in South Dakota. We pulled over to the west bank and took pictures of the boys on the South Dakota shore.

By the time we returned to the access it was too late to start the sixteen-mile trip to the dam. We asked day users of the area if we would get in trouble sleeping in the van overnight. The access was posted as no camping. They said the ranger that patrolled the area didn't have defined times, and was more concerned about weekend activity. Since it was Wednesday and having a current State Park sticker, I felt justified in staying over since we would be leaving first thing in the morning.

THURSDAY, AUGUST 18TH, 1994

The boys and I set out on Big Stone Lake, agreeing to meet Debbie at the City of Ortonville Park. She would now be the 'chase vehicle', meeting us at points along the way. We had a nice comfortable ride, thoroughly enjoying the run down the lake.

After a quick hello at the park, we took off to meet right above the dam that controls the headwaters of the Minnesota River a short distance away. I barreled underneath the railroad bridge that had a DO NOT ENTER sign posted, striking an invisible under water concrete shelf that probably maintains a certain water level for the lake separate from the dam. The only damage done was a small dent to the leading edge of the lower unit.

A sign at the dam stated that this is the Minnesota River Headwaters, Elevation 967 ft., Gulf of Mexico - 2130 miles, Big Stone Lake – 1.1 mile.

Due to my normal rush to get started and keep going, I made a dumb decision. Instead of switching over to the canoe, we dragged the Alumacraft around the dam and continued. Sort of! Almost immediately we were hitting bottom with the motor and encountering logjams. It was five miles to our next planned meeting spot. One particular logjam took the three of us to get over. With Kevin and me mired knee deep in river mud pushing the boat up, Nate climbed the three boat seats, like steps on a ladder, successfully tipping the balance of the boat over the logjam.

Debbie found a local road three miles from the dam, and happened to wait for us there. The place was too brushy to exchange the boat for the canoe, but we did swap the 7 ½ horse Mercury for the 4 horse Johnson since it operates better in shallow water.

We met again at another local road where we exchanged the Alumacraft and motor for the canoe and paddle power. I should have heeded the warning on the canoe map stating, 'There are many log-jams blocking the river between Big Stone Lake and Marsh Lake.' It took us three hours and a lot of physical effort to travel the first five miles. There was seventeen miles yet to go before reaching Marsh Lake.

The next meeting with Debbie was at an access just outside of Odessa.

We boys portaged across a dike and back into the old riverbed. Two miles of clogged river paddling could have been bypassed by portaging around a dam less than a mile south. The dam basically bypassed two miles of winding river – in the interest of covering 'true' miles I elected to cover the original river channel.

After we'd portaged, Debbie saw us pass under the Hwy 75 bridge at 7:00 and watched and waited for us to come up to the bottom side of the dam to meet her. On a turn close to Hwy 75, we talked to a DNR officer who told us that Debbie was waiting at the dam outlet. As we rounded the final turn about 8:30, and barely able to see the dam off to the West, it required a last burst of energy to paddle upstream against the current.

At 8:00 Debbie had began to worry that we had missed the turn to go back upriver. Noticing a change in the darkness, she realized it was us. What Relief! Debbie's concern was of us not being dressed or packed right for a night on the river. The DNR officer had not gone back and told Debbie that he'd seen us. So while we were not concerned about finding her, she worried about us.

After finding a private campground and eating Dinty Moore stew, we went to bed. It had been a tiring day.

FRIDAY, AUGUST 19TH, 1994

Hoping for more open water, I put the four horse on the canoe. Returning to the dam at Hwy 75, we covered the seven miles to Cement Bridge access in 80 minutes. There were several places that I 'jumped' trees blocking the river. Not telling the boys before I jumped the first one, keeping the throttle at full power on and tilting the motor up while passing over the tree. They were impressed!

We portaged across Marsh Lake Dam, which is earthen filled, 11,800 feet in length, 19.5 feet high and not accessible by road. Less than three miles put us into the backwater of Lac Qui Parle Lake. Its French name was a translation from Dakota Indian and means 'talking water.'

The lake formed by Lac Qui Parle Dam heads pretty much straight southwest for twelve miles. Our first indication of motors not allowed in the upper area of Lac Qui Parle was a sign, which we honored by paddling through. In the latter portion, we had a following wind generating three-foot waves. As we approached the lower end of the lake, it was hard to find the outlet, causing us to frequently bottom out resulting in waves piling in. Not thinking a dip can necessary, we didn't have one. By the time we arrived at the dam, we'd taken on a fair amount of water.

Lac Qui Parle Dam is earthen filled, 4,100 feet in length, and 15.5 feet high. The fifteen-mile trip to Preins Landing was without trouble and done within fifteen minutes of my predicted time.

We continued sixteen more miles to a dam at Granite Falls, where Debbie picked us up. Being almost 8:00, we camped at War Memorial Park, one mile downstream.

SATURDAY, AUGUST 20TH, 1994

There was only thirty miles left to go before hooking up to where Kevin and I had left from four years ago. What a difference four years makes in the growth of a child. Nate was now just a year younger than Kevin had been at the time. They had been a joy to be with on this trip, nary a complaint, lots of shared laughter.

Since War Memorial Park is right on the river it made for an easy start. After covering the mile run to the upstream dam, we then had a three-mile stretch before having to portage around another one. There was not a road access to this one either.

Debbie videotaped as we flew by the Kinney Access with twenty-miles to go, covering it in 2 hours & 7 minutes. Debbie had positioned herself upstream and videotaped our arrival to Renville County Park No. 2, where I whipped the canoe in a tight turn and totally beached it. A fitting end to a varied trip.

I pushed the canoe back in a little bit so I could run the gas out of the motor. In leaning over to disconnect the gas line I lost my balance and fell in, getting my last set of clean clothes wet.

The town of Butterfield, seventy-five miles southeast, has an annual Old Time Threshers celebration featuring steam engines, old tractors, and generally showed how farming was done in the early 20th century. It was this weekend, so we drove there. We spent the rest of the day there, camped, and saw more on Sunday before returning home.

We'd traveled 115 water miles, and portaged 7 times in our 2-½ days on river.

1995 ARKANSAS, TENNESSEE, & CUMBERLAND RIVERS

An unwanted early Christmas present from the life insurance company that we had merged with three years earlier was that they were closing our office. I don't have any lasting hard feelings as I was one of the few offered a transfer, which I declined. In order to receive 12 months of severance pay, based on longevity, I had to stay on until the office closed on February 28, 1995.

I stayed on, but was so burnt out that I didn't seriously look for a job, deciding to vacation instead. Experiencing an especially harsh winter and never having been in Florida, that's where I decided to go. I bought a Zodiac Fastroller 380 inflatable boat and a 25HP Johnson outboard, picking them up in Florida a week after the office closed.

At Key Largo I went about eight miles offshore with the Zodiac to a reef, snorkeling for the first time amidst the colorful fish and coral. Other than spending a day in the Everglades with the Zodiac, I generally spent the next month relaxing and touring the Southeast.

The main reason for buying the Zodiac was not to play in Florida, but to boat southern rivers without having to pull The Boat all the way to Key West. So when temperatures somewhat warmed, I drove to Fort Loudoun Marina, located on the Tennessee River 602.5 miles above its junction with the Ohio. I packed as if not returning to Fort Loudoun, intending to use the 100 mile round trip to the source of the Tennessee as a test run. The load included eighteen gallons of gas, sleeping bag, tent, food, Coleman stove, cooler, clothes, attachable wheels, VHF radio, battery, etc.

The Zodiac started to get 'floppy,' towards the end of where I figured the confluence of the French and Broad Rivers was before I investigated why. In pulling back the cover that fastens to the rub rail, I found that one of the two attachable wheel legs had worn a hole in the inflatable floor. Since the high-pressure inflatable floor provides most of the internal stabilization, my return trip to Fort Loudoun Marina was less than pleasant, with every boat wake causing a rippling effect.

I did my best to patch the hole. Before turning in for the night, I socialized with Jim Peters and his wife aboard their houseboat moored at Fort Loudoun. While bringing the Zodiac floor up to pressure the following morning the patch bubbled up and would probably have blown upon hitting the first big wave. Now what?

I spent another week in the South. While dining at a place in Louisiana where entire families were dancing to zydeco music, I felt homesick and decided to try to get home for Easter Sunday. While heading north on I-45 in Texas in the wee hours of the morning, I saw a tall white angel framed by light standing in the middle of the road. Was it a real angel? And if so, why was it there? Was it waiting for me to 'come home'? If I pulled over could I avoid judgment day? I continued on figuring if it was 'my day,' it was my day. Then the interstate curved and I saw that the 'angel' was actually a flood lit white statue of Sam Houston. I made it in time for the Easter Sunday evening dinner meal.

After Easter, restless, money in the bank, and not wanting to waste my new found freedom sitting around home while the rest of the family went to school, I geared up for another river adventure.

WEDNESDAY, APRIL 26TH, 1995

I left Lakeville packed very differently from the aborted Tennessee River attempt; No bike, no backpack, and no winter coat; but with the professionally repaired Zodiac, 25 HP Johnson, and towing The Boat. My next stop was at Don McCusker's townhouse in Urbandale, Iowa, where we rehashed 'old times' experienced while living in Cedar Rapids, Iowa and working for Network Data.

THURSDAY, APRIL 27TH, 1995

Before leaving Don's, I called Jim Hanson in Indianola to arrange a stop. Jim works out of a garage on his acreage doing car repair. The first thing he *had* to show off was the new stereo system. We were roommates when I bought a Quad system (Four channel) in 1973, and I was best man in his wedding. He demonstrated the TV/VCR/CD/AMP/PRE AMP/ and six speaker remote capable system. This turned out to be an expensive visit as four years later I bought a similar type system and added a satellite receiver and DVD player to it. We also shared woodworking as a hobby and talked tools and recent projects completed.

I passed through Branson, Missouri, an evolving center of entertainment, and into scenic and hilly Arkansas. Even though it was April, pulling the boat with the fully loaded camper van caused the heat gauge to reach hot, so I'd occasionally stop and enjoy the view while letting it cool off.

Using Don Wright's 'Guide to FREE Campgrounds', I found Riverview Park just outside of Dardanelle, Arkansas. The river view is that of the Arkansas River and was an excellent spot with a picnic table, fire pit, and water and electrical hookups. Best of all it was free due to being off-season.

Water was boiling out of the Dardanelle Lock and Dam outlets due to high water. Having traveled in floodwaters before, I felt experienced enough to travel the Arkansas River in such conditions.

FRIDAY, APRIL 28TH, 1995

Since there is not a boat ramp at Riverview Park, I went in search of a ramp and a place to leave the van. Along the way I loaded up on perishable food such as milk, cheese, sausage, and bread; Debbie had sent me off with enough canned goods to supply the D-day invasion force for a week. I also filled The Boat and four auxiliary gas cans.

I hadn't bought navigation charts for the Arkansas River for two reasons. First, this was a 'seat of the pants' trip, with the duty of helping shutting down our office primarily occupying my mind. Secondly, I'd been on enough charted navigable rivers to know that I did not look at them anyway.

While Quimby's uses the disclaimer, 'Maps are for general reference only and are not meant to be used for navigation' the information they provided was all that I needed.

I checked out two possible launch areas; the first was isolated, with the van subject to vandalism, and the other being an Army Corps of Engineer Park, where you are not allowed to leave a vehicle unattended. At the 2nd place, and a mile from the river, I found a business that sells minnows, ice, and stores travel trailers that would take me back to the river after unloading The Boat. It took an hour to pack and then unload The Boat off the trailer. The guy who gave me a ride back to the water also gave me a beer to drink along the way.

In order to reach the navigational channel of the Arkansas, Mile 222, four miles from the boat ramp, I had to ask directions from a passing boat. From there I headed west to Lock & Dam #12 at Ozark, Arkansas, Mile 256.5. Upon turning the key to start the motor and exit the lock, the starter would only click. I started the 7 ½ Mercury motor and precariously made my way out of the lock against the fast spring runoff current and tied up to trees just upstream to spend the night. Due to being bounced around by the current and concerned about the motor not starting, I did not sleep well.

SATURDAY, APRIL 29TH, 1995

Awaking at 7:00, and after tightening a loose nut that connected a wire from the solenoid to the starter, I was off. As I went through Lock 13, Mile 292.8 at Burling, Arkansas, Lift of 20' there was a lot of lightning off to the Northeast.

After exiting Lock 14 at Mile 319.6 at Spiro, Oklahoma, Lift of 20' and with the lightning closer, I stopped and put up the top. Within a minute, a heavy rain started to fall and continued to do so for a ½ hour with the temperature also turning colder.

I stopped at Applegate Cove Marina to fuel up, buying thirty-five gallons.

The pool formed by Webber's Falls Lock and Dam #16 Mile 368.9 is known as Lake Kerr and is pretty good size with a lot of floating wood at the time. It must have been shallow as the marked channel meandered through it.

At 4:22, I arrived at Mile 397.2, where the Verdigris River joins the Arkansas. Now fifteen miles from Tulsa, Oklahoma and with the Arkansas not considered navigable past this point, I decided not to go any further. I'd been hitting small pieces of driftwood in the swift narrow channel as it was.

About ten miles downstream I heard a sudden terrible clatter accompanied by a severe vibration from the stern. I was 165 river miles from the van, 47 miles from the closest marina, no other recreational boats were on the river, and no roads close. Now What? While I had plenty of gas to run the main engine, and 2 ½ gallons of oil/gas mix for the 7 ½ Mercury outboard emergency motor, what I did **not** have, and had never crossed my mind that I would need, is more oil to mix for the outboard. There was no way that the 7 ½ could push the boat 47 miles on just 2 ½ gallons of gas.

What a **conundrum**! I happened to hear this word once and like the way it sounds. The second definition given to it in The American Heritage Dictionary is "A problem admitting of no satisfactory solution." I suppose I could have used the VHF radio to call for help or ask for help at Webber's Falls Lock, but that is against my nature.

After experimenting running the engine at different rpm's, I settled on 1500 rpm. That reduced the vibration and clacking sound to a more acceptable level while still providing headway. I covered twenty miles in three hours, including the time required to pass through Webber's Falls Lock. At 8:00, one mile south of the lock, I tied up in an out of the way area next to a grain barge loading area to spend the night.

I slept fairly well until dreaming that raccoons were trying to get into the cooler in the front of the boat, which turned out to be the boat bouncing off the bottom.

SUNDAY, APRIL 30TH, 1995

When I got back underway at 7:00, the vibration and clacking almost immediately doubled with the engine still running at 1500 rpm. There was twenty-five miles still to go before arriving back at Applegate Cove Marina.

By running I/O engine at less than 1000 RPM and the 7 ½ together, I managed to maintain control and go faster than just drifting downstream. Maintaining control was very important since I met two barges and was able to steer out of harms way. Initially I tied the steering wheel in a fixed position and sat on the stern using the 7 ½ to steer, which got old quick.

Upon reaching a spot close enough to Applegate to make it using the 7 ½, I locked its steering into a straightforward position with the throttle wide open. I then shut off the I/O motor, and set the lower unit just deep enough to create drag so I could steer from the helm.

It was 1:00 when I arrived at Applegate Cove, experiencing a choppy ride back across shallow Lake Kerr. I averaged 6 mph going **downstream** after experiencing the problem, a far cry from the 30-mph running **upstream**. Pat, the operator of Applegate, set me up in a 50 foot covered slip and said a mechanic would check the problem "First thing tomorrow."

With a feast of cheese, crackers, sausage, and milk making me sleepy and having no place to go, I laid down for a nap. A short time later I awoke to what I can best describe as the sound of someone driving over a wooden bridge. RAIN, Hard Rain! It dumped for a full ½ hour making me so ever glad to be in a covered slip and not on the river.

By 7:30 I was back fast asleep, hoping The Boat could be fixed relatively quickly. Another major rainstorm rolled through during the middle of night, making me again grateful for the covered slip.

MONDAY, MAY 1ST, 1995

The mechanic arrived at 8:45, and after listening to the motor idle and in slow forward believed it to be a motor problem. Being a 'traveling in water mechanic', he did not have the capability to do the kind of work that the symptoms suggested.

I asked Pat if he knew of anyone who could take me back to the van and trailer, being compensated for time and gas money. Pat suggested Roy Morris, the father in law of an employee. When Roy got back from town 1 ½ hours later he readily agreed to take me.

Roy, a military pilot in WW II and a commercial pilot until needing glasses, was a colorful character. It was a very enjoyable two hour ride as he related stories; such as the one of uncovering a major scandal while working security at a race track and finding double cashing of winning numbers. Roy would only accept ten dollars for the 100 mile one way trip, saying he felt like it was still too much.

Upon returning to Applegate, Pat gave me a ride between the boat ramp and covered boat slip. When asking what I owed for slip rental and his help, the answer was 'Nothing.' I thanked him, and said how much the covered slip was appreciated.

Ending up back at Riverview Park, I hooked a water hose to a muff around the water intake of the lower unit and listened intently to the clatter. Not hearing noise at the front of the motor or from the lower unit led me to believe the problem might be in the gear transfer between them.

While not a motor head, I still found it hard to believe that it was an engine problem.

TUESDAY, MAY 2ND, 1995

Across the river from the campground is Russellville where I stopped at a Mercury dealer and described what I perceived to be the problem. Without actually listening to the motor, they made an educated guess that the problem could be the 'gimbal bearing.' This is where the drive shaft passes between the motor and the lower unit. They were booked for a solid week and would not work me in. I offered to pay extra, thinking it could be done off-hours, with both mechanics declining. Nice people, just busy.

I called another place in Russellville, and upon hearing the same story, I drove to Little Rock, stopping at the I-40 visitor center. The friendly young lady behind the counter called three Mercury repair shops; with the first two saying they were busy for the next two weeks, and the third, while busy, said that my being on vacation changed things. She handed me the phone and I talked to John Kozak and said that possibly the gimbal bearing needed replacing. John said that if that were the only problem they would do it.

Upon arriving at River Valley Marina at 10:30 the cashier said it would be a little bit before the mechanic could look at it. I poured a cup of coffee and before it even cooled enough to take a sip they directed me to back the boat up to the shop.

Without attempting to start the motor, John pulled the out drive, inspected the gimbal bearing, not finding it bad. While working, he conversationally said that he'd reserved a small plane for an afternoon of flying. I would not have blamed him one bit if he had quit working on it right then and there, but he didn't. John then hooked a water line up to an internal water intake and went to start the motor. Click, Click, Click, etc.

Now I really felt bad! Not only was the problem not the gimbal bearing as I'd suggested, now it wouldn't even start. After replacing the starter, it fired right up with the severe vibration and clacking still there. This was with the out drive totally removed. Now what?

As John, Randy, an assistant mechanic and Kevin, part's manager/mechanic, worked on the boat, I told them of where I'd been with The Boat and where I planned to go. We had become friends!

The consensus of the group was to pull the engine and see if the flywheel was loose, which it wasn't. John thought that the crankshaft might be broke. Kevin said to drop the oil pan and take a look at it. The crankshaft turned out to broken in two places towards the back of the engine. This explains why the clacking doubled, due to breaking a second time.

John commented that my options were; return home, repair the crankshaft, or replace the motor. While contemplating, they offered a lifeline.

Over winter they'd replaced the original four-cylinder engine on an under powered 1992 20 foot boat with a six cylinder. The removed motor with less than 100 hours on it was sitting in their showroom.

OK! I thought this is one of those deals where you don't ask how much, but how soon. I still asked how much. The answer, while not cheap, was more than reasonable. For $1500 total they would install it, taking my motor in on trade. I didn't hesitate, Just Do It!

Morning had become afternoon so I asked John about his plan to go flying. He'd already cancelled, without guilt tripping me about ruining his planned time off.

In addition to swapping engines, they also installed a new water pump, changed the lower unit grease, put in new plugs, rotor, condenser, and allowed me to keep the old starter and alternator at no additional charge.

Upon finishing the installation of the engine and lower unit, a simple turn of the key resulted in an instant start.

They then set the timing, and doubled checked everything, finishing at 5:00.

I have to thank John, Kevin, Randy, and cashier Susie for going the extra mile and coming to my assistance, even though the problem ended up being much more involved than initially thought. They even allowed me to overnight in the van plugged into an outlet next to the shop.

Comments: In the process of switching engines, I asked that a compression test be done to both engines, the result being interesting. You would suspect that an older motor would have variances between cylinders and the compression less on the old motor. The actual test result showed compression of 140 on all four cylinders on the old motor and 125 on the newer engine. We surmised the lower compression on the newer motor might be due to engineering changes Mercury made due to the change over from leaded to unleaded gas.

It is unusual to break a crankshaft. I've heard two reasons why this might have happened; One is that I'd put an abnormally high number of hours running at least 4200 rpm and at typical speed of 32 mph. While 32 mph is not fast, a constant 4200-rpm on a production inboard/outboard engine is not normal. The second reason an inboard/outboard motor crankshaft is more susceptible to breakage than an automobile engine is because of the inconstant resistance of water that less back loads it. The small and minute variations of rpm flux variations take their toll.

It seems like I have a guardian angel sitting on my shoulder because the right things seem to happen at the right time. Maybe the fact that I have a deceased uncle that was a priest and two aunts that are nuns is working for me.

WEDNESDAY, MAY 3RD, 1995

I awoke in time to catch Good Morning America with Joan London and Charlie Gibson. While drinking coffee and watching TV in the light rain, I decided to resume my trip on the Arkansas by starting from River Valley Marina. At 10:30 I was ready, with Randy using a Case tractor to back the boat down the ramp into a closed side channel of the Arkansas. The motor *almost* started on the first turn of the key, then went back to the same click, click, experienced off/on for five years. But this time I had a totally different starter, motor, etc.

Randy pulled the boat back to the shop where John and Kevin tried to figure out what the problem might be. Kevin noticed that the main power cable assembly that plugs into the motor from the battery did not have a clamp to secure it from slipping out. He'd read a service bulletin that said this could cause the problem. They added a clamp, and I have never experienced exactly the same problem since.

The engine had to taken out two weeks after buying the boat new to replace a cracked oil pan. Obviously you can't hit anything in a boat to cause such a crack unless you break through the bottom of the boat. I've often wondered since if they'd neglected to reinstall the clamp, or whether it was a design feature added later to help alleviate a poor connection point. If you remember back in 1992 the Alabama Star towboat stopped on the Tenn-Tom to help while I'd been experiencing the same problem. That was the only time that I received any on water help. I wonder if while looking at the motor they almost automatically put a hand on the connection point, possibly reestablishing the necessary electrical connection to start the motor.

Just as I entered the main channel of the Arkansas at 12:00 and headed west/northwest to rejoin my original starting point, the light rain stopped. While powering up the new motor under load, there was a vibration at about 1300 rpm, but once beyond that point ran just like the old motor.

I went about 100 miles upstream through the fast, wooden debris strewn current, passing through four locks in the process.

While in Lock 9 at Morrilton, Arkansas I was asked if I was passing through to Dardanelle Lock, another twenty-eight plus miles, saying yes. Then over the VHF radio I heard the lock operator talking to Dardanelle saying to ready the lock, "There is a small craft on the way and he is boogien."

At 6:30, I checked in at the Shoal Bay Boat Marina mobile home office, Mile 222, almost directly across from my starting point five days ago. They gave me a covered slip.

THURSDAY, MAY 4TH, 1995

With a light rain falling on the roof of the covered slip and insects strangely absent, I had an especially restful night. I awoke at 7:00, showered at the park across from the marina, and was generally awaking to the day when the owner stopped by with a fresh cup of coffee in hand. We had a nice conversation, with him explaining how the husband/wife team had left the Denver area two years ago to run the marina. I left at 9:00 after buying gas, ice, and paying the modest $7.50 transient dockage fee.

After covering 185 miles going back downstream, I stopped at Pendleton Bridge Marina for the night. It had been a cool day so the top was up the entire time to help stay warm, and I was the only boat out.

I'd passed through eight locks along the way; with at least two of them having zero drop. They would simply open the upper gates, and upon me entering, close them, then open the downstream side to let me exit. I assume this allows them to maintain control and not damage the lock gates during a period of unpredictable flow.

All eight locks were 600' long x 110' wide and their maximum lift/drop is as follows; Note there is no Lock & Dam #11

Mile 205.5 Dardanelle Lock & Dam #10, Russellville, Arkansas – Max Lift 54'

Mile 176.9 Lock & Dam #9, Morrilton, Arkansas – Max Lift 19'

Mile 155.9 Toad Suck Ferry Lock & Dam #8, Conway, Arkansas – Max Lift 16'

Mile 125.4 Murray Lock & Dam #7, Little Rock, Arkansas – Max Lift 18'

Mile 108.1 David R, Terry Lock & Dam #6, Scott, Arkansas – Max Lift 18'

Mile 86.3 Lock & Dam #5, Tucker, Arkansas – Max Lift 17'

Mile 65 Lock & Dam #4, Pine Bluff, Arkansas – Max Lift 14'

Mile 50.2 Lock and Dam #3, DeWitt, Arkansas – Max Lift 20'

Pendleton Bridge Marina put me in covered slip immediately adjacent to the floating bar where I drank beer with the locals; discussing the level of the Arkansas River, the state of the State of Arkansas, the Kennedy Assassination, etc. After setting up for the night, calling home, and eating Dinty Moore stew, I played pool and drank more beer than was necessary. I drifted off to a deep sleep, awakening very briefly upon hearing rain hitting the tin roof.

FRIDAY, MAY 5TH, 1995

Around 7:30 I awoke to find that 'wild animals' had gotten into the cooler left on the dock. It was kind of funny since the only thing taken was beer. I fueled up, paid the cheap $6.00 transient dockage fee, and was on my way by 8:30.

The area between Lock 1 & 2 is unique. The Arkansas and the White River used to enter the Mississippi at different places. Due to flood control reasons they were artificially merged so they both join the Mississippi where the White naturally entered. To accomplish this, a canal was dug to direct the Arkansas northeast into the White, and a blocking levee built to stop it from following its natural path.

There is only three miles separating Lock & Dam 1 & 2, each visible from the other due to the straight canal joining them.

Ten miles after leaving Norrell, Lock & Dam #1, Lift 30', and dropping only about five feet, I entered the Mississippi River about 600 miles above mile Zero. The current was fast with a lot of sand mounds exposed.

While videotaping the junction of the White and Arkansas, I almost ran aground! It is hard to drive, videotape, and hold a position in the fast current at the same time. I saw a very large black snake swimming across the river. I hate snakes!

I made my way back to River Valley Marina, arriving about 5:30. I'd only seen two different barges on the river during my 5-½ days on the water, and no pleasure boats. While idling past the almost 100 slips of River Valley Marina on the way to the boat ramp, I received numerous invitations to join the weekend crowd on their houseboats.

That evening has to be in the top ten of my most enjoyable memories! First, I had just completed another section of navigable river. Second, I was back at a marina that had helped me in my time of need. Third, they were a group that liked to party!

I went aboard more than one houseboat for food, beverage, and conversation. The late evening was spent around a fire with two couples who were fifties music lovers. Besides singing, we swapped stories while melting beer bottles over the well-fed fire. They soon had me singing along at the top of my lungs to the lyrics. The women did 80% of the vocals while the husbands came in with the background, Do, WA, Do WA's, and provided the appropriate body movement. One of the women also played a guitar. It made for a passably good sound and an especially good time. I didn't get back to the van until 1:00.

I'd traveled 678 water miles, and locked through 26 times in my 5-½ days on the water.

SATURDAY, MAY 6TH, 1995

I slept in until 10:00, loading the boat at 11:00. While John Kozak checked out the vibration that I'd continued experiencing, I cleaned and unpacked it. He found a bolt missing on a plate cover and some loose screws.

By 12:30 The Boat was ready, but I waited for the mail to arrive since Debbie had sent some important papers relative to options for my 401k and pension. I opened a can of fruit cocktail and was only half finished when the mail truck arrived with the package. Perfect!

After again thanking the marina crew, I headed southwest on Interstate 30 to check out the Red River. Upon finding the Red, I jumped back and forth from main to side roads attempting to see it and to get a feel for what boating it would be like. The only information I had about the Red River was from a one page foldout pamphlet titled 'The Red River Waterway Project put out by the US Army Corps of Engineers Vicksburg District dated January 1990, which provided no user access details. I followed the roads along the Red into Louisiana.

Again using the Guide to Free Campgrounds guide, I found a spot at Kisatchie National Forest in Louisiana to spend the night, with me being the only one there.

SUNDAY, MAY 7TH, 1995

I was out by 8:30, after using my small portable generator to make coffee, and continued investigating the Red River. I found public access points few and far between. I didn't find any overnight facilities on the river, although my research method was haphazard at best. I followed the Red River southeast, ending up where it is separated from the Mississippi by a lock. After talking to a local sheriff while on LA 15, I decided not to travel the Red River for the following reasons;

It really didn't flow into the Mississippi. At the time I was there you had to lock UP at Lock and Dam #1 to get to the Mississippi. A paragraph taken from The Red River Waterway Project is as follows:

> *From its source in the arid plains of eastern New Mexico, the Red River travels through Texas, forms the southern border of Oklahoma, dips into southwest Arkansas, and cuts a swath through Louisiana's agricultural heartland. Seven miles west of the Mississippi River the Red joins the Atchafalaya and Old Rivers in route to the Gulf of Mexico via the Atchafalaya Basin.*

Also;
1. I had not found any place to leave the van beside the day use public access areas. I must confess that while I don't believe myself to be prejudice, I was uncomfortable being in an area that was overwhelmingly black and poor.
2. No marinas or gas places.
3. No charts and not mentioned in Quimby's.
4. Possibly still under construction.

I headed north on LA 15, most of which is built on a levee designed to contain the Mississippi from breaking through to the Red. If this ever happened, which it almost did once, the Mississippi would have set a new course, bypassing Baton Rouge seventy-five miles to the south, creating economic havoc to all of the established port facilities.

Being Sunday, and in passing several small well-attended black churches along back roads, I was very tempted to stop and attend service since I truly love lively black gospel choir music. I didn't.

I camped at a private campground and talked to two couples from Germany touring the US in a rented a motor home.

MONDAY, MAY 8TH, 1995

While waiting for the Tallulah, LA Post Office to open after lunch to send a certified letter, I talked with a nice old guy and told him of my trip thus far. He said that he was too old now, but he'd wanted to travel by water from Vicksburg to the Tombigbee Waterway. Upon telling him that I'd already covered that stretch he said that I was a "fine young man from Minnesota."

Louisiana had a lot of real rundown houses, especially in the smaller towns. A lot of farmland is irrigated by plowing furrows in the very flat ground.

I camped at Great River Road State Park, just outside of Rosedale, Mississippi, and read information picked up along the way about Mississippi's involvement in the Civil War.

TUESDAY, MAY 9TH, 1995

Now heading towards the Tennessee River, my planned route included a stop to tour Mud Island Mississippi Museum at Memphis, Tennessee. The museum, just across from the marina where Debbie and I'd spent the night in 1992, has a huge scale model of the Mississippi River and its tributaries. At 7:30, I arrived at Eastport Marina on the Tennessee River, ten miles upstream from the Tenn-Tom Waterway. The only person in the office was a late working accountant who pointed out a spot on a side hill overlooking the marina as an OK place to spend the night. I reviewed the charts of the Tennessee, bought from Grand Mariner Marina on the Dog River in Mobile Bay three years ago.

WEDNESDAY, MAY 10TH, 1995

At 8:30, I saw the marina office door being unlocked. Fortunately the accountant communicated that he'd given permission for me to park overnight, another free site.

I told of my plan to travel the Tennessee from its junction with the Tombigbee to its official beginning and asked if I could leave the van and trailer there for five to seven days. For the very modest fee of two dollars a day I could leave the van and trailer in 'dry storage' behind a locked and fenced area about a mile away.

As I got ready for the river run I decided to check the lower unit gear lubrication. When I pulled the lower screw to check the oil condition, it ran out **pure** water for a little bit, and then changed to normal looking oil. This is highly unusual in that if you ever have water in the lower unit it usually mixes with the oil and comes out milky. It must be that the jarring of trailering the boat for five days caused the natural viscosity difference between the oil and water to separate.

I unscrewed both the upper and lower plugs to drain the lower unit and couldn't find one of the fabric washers that seals out water when ready to fill with new gear lube. Whether it never got put back when the lower units lube was replaced at Riverview or if it dropped out and

I then couldn't find it when I drained the oil, I don't know. In any case I needed another washer before refilling the gear case.

Eastport Marina didn't have one so I headed towards town, stopping at 'Ledbetter's' which had a lot of boats in 'perpetual storage.' At first it didn't appear anyone was around, then I saw an old man asleep on a couch in the junky shop. I didn't know what to do, so I just stood there for a little bit.

He woke up and started to tell me of his 'Ills'. Normally I love chatting with older people, but I was in a hurry to get on the river. He finally got around to asking what he could do for me. I tried to explain that I needed the fiber washer for a Mercury lower unit, and due to being very of hard of hearing, I just showed him the screw that it fit on so he could better understand. After searching through three shelves of glass jars containing miscellaneous parts, one was found. But he kept looking. I tried to tell him that he needn't look anymore, while he continued searching through his jars. I gave up trying to talk to him, and he finally stopped searching. He gave me the washer.

Back at Eastport while buying lower unit grease from the part's guy, I mentioned I was still using the original aluminum prop, which now had over 10,000 miles of use. He was impressed, and also surprised at how nice that Ledbetter had been to me, having a reputation as a mean old man known to send people out of his shop without helping them.

After finishing putting grease in the lower unit, I put the boat in the water and paid a $3 launch fee. I then drove the van and boat trailer to a locked chain link fenced storage area followed by an employee in a pickup truck, who then gave me a ride back to the marina. I told him of my plan to boat the area between where the Tenn-Tom Waterway joins the Tennessee and the junction of the French and Broad River, the official beginning of the Tennessee, saying I'd be back in five to seven days. He said, "I'll see you in two weeks."

My original intent upon leaving the marina was to head downstream ten miles to the Tenn-Tom junction, then go upstream. Upon arriving at the marked channel from the back water of the marina, I did some videotaping and last minute rearranging before heading off. It wasn't until I'd gone five or six miles that I realized I was heading upstream, not down! This is true to form because of my typical hurry to get going and doing dumb things because of it. While rearranging the boat, it must have done a 180-degree turn. Oh well, the water was rough, and I was going with the waves making for a smoother ride.

With Wilson Lock, Mile 259.4, visible in the far background, I couldn't proceed because of two barges cabled together lengthwise spanning the entire bank to bank distance. Thinking I'd taken the wrong channel, I retraced my route. After going up another channel and passing under a low non-swinging railroad bridge against the swift current of the hydro-electric plant, I realized that barges couldn't clear the bridge so this couldn't be the right channel either.

I radioed the lock to find out what was going on, not receiving a reply. There was one more river channel, which turned out to lead to a barge loading/unloading area. So I went back up the center channel and eased up to the blocking barges where two men were standing and asked how to get to the lock. They said to drop my VHF antenna and slip through underneath the lip of the barge that was to my right.

I fit, but just barely. What happens when a barge passes through? The blocking barges were being used as a road to drive equipment from the mainland to an island for some construction project.

Just outside the downstream lock doors, I radioed Wilson Lock & Dam to arrange passage. They finally acknowledged me, saying the wait would be about two hours.

The sun was hot so I pulled into the shade of the high lock wall. Wilson Lock is the highest on the Tennessee and was in the top ten in the world at the time with a lift of 93'. There are actually two locks, the primary being 600 x 110' and an auxiliary measuring 400 x 60'. While being the highest dam on the Tennessee it has the shortest pool, with a length of only 15 ½ miles.

My wait turned out to be 3 ½ hours. Sitting in the lock as it filled, I debated with myself on how the exit structure worked. It did not have the typical upper two doors that open outward, and instead was a solid continuous structure spanning the entire 110' width. After equalizing the water height, the lock gate structure initially rose about one foot, then lowered out of sight.

Just to explain to non-boaters or those who haven't locked through such a tall lock, I'll explain how the upper and lower end of a lock can differ. There only needs to be enough movable structure at the upper end to allow entry for a nine foot channel depth. The lower end lock doors must be at least as tall as the entire vertical drop, plus leave enough water in the lock to exit into the nine foot channel. So for example, the downstream lock doors at Wilson were at least 100 foot tall, while the upper blocking structure, normally doors, were probably less than fifteen feet in height.

It was getting dark when I pulled into Lucy's Branch Marina, after locking through Wheeler Lock & Dam Mile 274.9 Lift 48'. Finding the office closed, I docked next to an occupied houseboat and asked where I could spend the night. The friendly couple said the covered slip I'd pulled into would be okay for me to spend the night since they knew their 'neighbors' were spending the night on the river.

Within five minutes of arriving, it rained and continued to do so off and on during the night. My seemingly innate ability to get off the river just in time to avoid most rainfalls is not due to cutting the day short, simply good fortune.

THURSDAY, MAY 11TH, 1995

I left at 6:30, and while locking through Guntersville Lock & Dam, Mile 349 Lift 39', the lock attendant told me told me about 'Old Bill', a local who traveled rivers in a boat even smaller than mine. Bill lived just a couple of blocks off the river from Guntersville Marina nine miles upriver. I felt it worthwhile to look him up.

While fueling at Guntersville Marina, I asked directions to his house. He wasn't home, but his wife said that he was probably at the Rexall Drug store two blocks away. I found Bill there, already fired up since he and two of his river traveling buddies were in the process of exchanging trip pictures. I introduced myself by saying that I was also a river tripper.

Bill said he'd traveled about 53,000 river miles, having been on some of the same stretches multiple times. These included the Mississippi, Tennessee, Cumberland, Ohio, Missouri, and the Tenn-Tom Waterway.

He bought me a hamburger with sauerkraut, and fries. The only reason I mention what I ate is that this was the first meal I'd eaten out since leaving home two weeks ago. After all, I was unemployed.

We went back to his house where he showed me the small aluminum boat housed in the garage with each trips duration and year stenciled on the side.

Bill, 83, short, weighing 135 lbs. tops, told me his 'running rules' not open to negotiation were as follows: 1 gas stop a day, No food stops, No 'pee' stops- a can must be used while underway, they never go to the riverbank-staying at marinas, tied to a dock, or to an over hanging tree, wide open throttle using a 25hp motor and the 24 gallons of gas they carried, 12 to 18 hour days, music at all times, and the locks need to be ready.

Sponsored by a local radio station, he used to call in from wherever he was at for an on-air update. After the trip was over, he'd send thanks to all the locks and anybody else who'd help speed up the trip.

We then walked to the marina where I showed him The Boat. Bill danced a little jig when I turned on my also ever present music. He said he'd like to go with me. I did not offer since it was obvious that he was used to being in charge and there can only be one captain.

It was 1:30 as I locked through Nickajack Lock & Dam at Mile 424.7, lift of 39', followed by Chickamauga Lock & Dam at Mile 471, lift of 48'.

7:30 found me at Mile 504.4 tied up to the gas dock at Blue Water Campground, where I took a shower before turning in for the night. Don't knock the simple pleasures of taking a shower or eating in a restaurant unless you've experienced what it's like to not have them.

FRIDAY, MAY 12TH, 1995

Back on the river by 6:00, I inadvertently took a 'wrong turn' at Mile 567.6 and headed up the Clinch River. I didn't notice my mistake until seeing a Mile Marker sign of 4.5, obviously wrong, but I continued on another mile and a half since the scenery was so beautiful.

Then upon returning to Mile 4.5, I made another wrong turn going four miles up another channel. I was obviously not paying particular attention to navigation markers. This being a vacation with no time limit in mind, I figured that as long as there is enough depth under the keel, enough gas in the tank, and sufficient daylight, I was having fun.

I got straightened out, continuing up the Tennessee, arriving at Fort Loudon Lock & Dam at 11:30. It took only fifteen minutes to gain access, with the 72' ascent being extremely slow, taking 40 minutes. I heard over the radio that the lock was undergoing maintenance.

Just outside the lock is Fort Loudon Marina, Mile 602.5 where I'd stayed overnight less than two months ago. I fueled up there, and made the 100 mile round trip to the source of the Tennessee.

Yes, I'd already been on this stretch in the Zodiac, while not feeling comfortable that I had actually reached the 'official' beginning of the Tennessee. It turned out that I had not, being just ¼ mile and the next bend short of actually reaching the junction of the French Broad and the Holston Rivers that form the Tennessee.

Shortly after returning to Fort Loudon Marina, I once again talked to Jim Peters and his wife aboard their houseboat. They suggested that since it was still early I should travel the Little Tennessee's twenty-nine mile navigable distance. Hearing how scenic the trip is, and with them offering the use of their charts and giving me a sweater since I'd overlooked putting a jacket in the boat, I decided to go.

The Little Tennessee, now renamed Tellico Lake, is connected to the Tennessee by a canal just above Fort Loudon Dam. It is a very scenic trip, and even with charts I still ended getting up getting lost due to 'crane necking' and not paying attention.

I got pretty close to Chilhowie Dam, 33.7 miles upstream, but due to quickly gathering darkness amidst the hills I turned back someplace short of traveling the last four unmarked miles considered navigable only by small boats. Back at the marina by 7:30, I returned the charts, talked with other boaters, called home to say Hi to Kevin on his 14th birthday, and was asleep by 10:00.

SATURDAY, MAY 13TH, 1995

By 8:00 I'd organized, talked, showered, fueled, and then waited out a possible storm. It was 12:20 before the storm clouds cleared, whereupon I contacted Fort Loudon Lock to schedule lockage.

The 103 mile downstream trip to the junction of the Hiwassee River at Mile 499.4 was uneventful. I went thirteen miles upstream to B & B Marina, arriving at 8:00. With no covered slips available, I slept in the canvassed boat.

SUNDAY, MAY 14TH, 1995

Still used to waking up early and going off to work, I did so at 6:00. Seeing heavily overcast skies, I easily fell back to sleep. About 8:00, it started to rain and continued to do so for another three hours. I slept very soundly while rain pelted the canvas.

When the rain eased, I went for a walk and met a 48 year old retired man. Over coffee in his pontoon converted to a houseboat, I found out that he'd been forced out of his job. Hmm! Company closed, he retired, his wife didn't! I wonder if Debbie would go for that. Considering that I was only 45 with two young kids at home, retirement was not an option.

I reconnected with the Tennessee and headed downstream, arriving back at Guntersville Marina about 8:00. They recognized me from when I'd stopped to find 'Old Bill' on the way upriver and put me in a covered slip saying, 'No Charge'.

While visiting 'Old Bill' and his wife, I called home and had Bill talk to Debbie about his trips and the boat used. For some reason he insisted on calling Debbie, 'Betty', even after I corrected him several times. Oh well, I had come to realize that listening was not one of his strong traits.

MONDAY, MAY 15TH, 1995

Almost immediately after leaving the marina at 6:30 I ran into heavy fog. I sat under a highway bridge and updated my journal while waiting for it to clear. Started again at 7:00, Stopped, Fog, Started, Fog, Stopped, and Started arriving at Guntersville Lock at 8:45 taking 2 1/4 hours to travel less than ten miles.

While passing a public boat ramp and noticing a boat with the motor lid lifted, I stopped to render assistance. A young couple taking their boat out for the first time this season had heard strange sounds coming from the engine compartment. They found four baby kittens in the engine compartment, meowing as loudly as they could.

My arrival back at Wilson Lock was to windy, stormy conditions and an estimated 1 ½ hour wait while a barge locked through ahead of me. I'd just pulled into a protected area and opened a cold can of beans when the lock radioed back. Due to high wind the barge was holding back, and I could enter immediately. Good Break!

The construction barges still blocked the channel as I exited the lock, except this time they utilized a winch system to pivot so I had plenty of room to get through.

I continued onto Mile 215, the junction of the Tennessee-Tombigbee Waterway where Debbie and I had passed through on the 1992 trip, making another connection.

Arriving back at Eastport at 4:40, and after retrieving the van and trailer from 'dry storage', I loaded and cleaned the boat. Not much cleaning needed to be done since the Tennessee is a pretty clean river. I checked the lower unit grease, finding it milky and only 2/3 full. I again drained and refilled it, deciding to have it serviced when I got home.

I'd traveled 914 water miles, and locked through 14 times in my six days on the water.

I could have slept at Eastport Marina 'rent free', but wanting a place free of traffic and lights shining 24 hours a day, continued on and found a TVA (Tennessee Valley Authority) campground called Goat Island. entering the previously unoccupied and unlit campground, I drew the attention of the husband/wife resident managers. They were going to turn the campground lights on, except upon hearing that I'd been looking for a quiet, unlit area, left them off.

I fell asleep watching the tail end of my video recording of the Tennessee.

TUESDAY, MAY 16TH, 1995

Over morning coffee I planned a scenic drive using roads not previously traveled to reach the midpoint of the Cumberland River.

I fueled and restocked in Savannah, Tennessee, arriving at Merriweather Campground on the Natchez Trace at 3:00.

It was about 90 degrees, and with no electricity to run the roof A/C making it hard to take a nap, I updated my journal and made plans for the Cumberland.

A retired gentleman who lived about fifty miles north of Pittsburgh stopped by to chat and offer firewood for the coming evening chill. The ash and oak wood pieces offered have a story behind them.

Seven or eight years ago, he and others built a raft to float down the Allegheny, Ohio, and Mississippi. They did so to recreate the early days. Once the pre-steamboat era rafts reached their destination, the cargo was sold, and the rafts broken up and sold for firewood. The rafters would either buy horses or walk back home. This is how the Natchez Trace Trail came to be. It was not a wagon route, rather an old Indian trail that became a well-worn foot and horse path with various places along the way to stay. The Trace was also dangerous, with many of the returning travelers robbed and murdered for the money they were carrying.

The retired gentleman's trip ended up stopping someplace on the southern bank of the Ohio River in Kentucky due to crew quarrels. They broke the raft up and the wood he gave me came from it.

WEDNESDAY, MAY 17TH, 1995

The first place I checked out to start the Cumberland from was at Rock Creek Harbor Marina in Nashville. They didn't have a boat ramp, only a 30-ton lift out, and it was not the best place to leave a vehicle unattended so I drove to Henderson, Tennessee, forty-seven river miles upstream. Stopping at City Hall for directions, I arrived at Drakes Creek Marina. The two women in the office didn't offer much hope of being able to leave the van and trailer, saying parking space was limited.

They didn't outright say No, only that I had to talk to Don, who was away from the marina.

While walking to the launch ramp I met a young man named Chris, Don's son. Telling Chris of my plan to travel the Cumberland and that I was looking for a place to leave the van and trailer he said, "No problem," and gave permission to park on the grass next to the office. Now 3:00, I decided to hold up since it was 87 degrees and the weather predictions heard from my 12volt/110 TV and VHF radio did not sound good.

While waiting the weather out I toured their facilities. There was a large building with boats on 'shelves' stacked three and four high on either side of the wide alleyway. They used a large forklift to slip under a boat hull, and then drive it to the harbor and gently lower it to the water. Sometimes they had to use two 55-gallon barrels of water on the back of the forklift to offset the boat weight. It amazed me how many boats were in the building. Instead of renting a slip, people paid a smaller fee to store it, and then called ahead to have the boat placed in the water. This was my first exposure to the concept of 'dry storage' which is now common.

THURSDAY, MAY 18TH, 1995

It rained heavily from 8:00 to 10:00 AM. I watched local TV from 11:00 to 1:00. With the weather worsening and grateful to be on land, I popped the movie 'Tootsie' into the TV/VCR.

During a brief storm lull I walked to the office, finding out that a tornado had touched down just two or three miles away, and that the marina had lost power. I took a hasty circuitous walk through the immediate neighborhood, returning to watch TV coverage of the damage. They reported sixty injuries, with only two or three serious, and baseball size hail in Decatur County where I had been just two days ago.

Most of the Tennessee River Valley/Cumberland River areas were under tornado watch or warning until 9:00 PM. As I monitored the TV, there were;

- 11 tornado touch down downs in Tennessee as of 4:00 PM
- 28 tornado touch down downs in Tennessee as of 6:00 PM
- 43 tornado touch down downs in Tennessee as of 8:15 PM
- 48 tornado touch down downs in Tennessee as of 8:45 PM
- It was the worst since 1974.

FRIDAY MAY 19TH, 1995

I awoke to an overcast sky, leaving Drakes Creek Marina at 11:45. At Mile Marker 222, the junction of Drakes Creek and the Cumberland, I headed downstream 190 miles, arriving at Green Turtle Bay Marina at 8:00.

I'd avoided damage from the enormous amount of floating wood encountered along the way. Some places had so much wood that you'd think a logging company was doing a log drive.

I'd locked through Old Hickory Lock, Mile 216.2, Maximum lift 60', and Cheatham Lock, Mile 148.7, with a Maximum lift of 26'

Green Turtle Bay Marina is thirty-one miles above where the Cumberland joins the Mississippi, having passed through here in 92 and 94. I was a little taken back given my dock assignment, placed in an area referred to as the Dinghy Dock. While I realize that my excursions are unusual, I don't know if I should be classified as dingy, meaning being a little unbalanced.

SATURDAY, MAY 20TH, 1995

I was out early and headed back upstream, arriving at Cordell Hull Lock & Dam, Mile 313, Maximum lift of 59', at 7:30 PM covering 282 miles.

I'd bought twenty-four gallons of gas at Clarkesville, Tennessee from an Amoco station for $1.19 a gallon as opposed to paying a $1.59 at a marina stop. Not getting a response on the VHF radio from Cordell Hull, I crept closer and saw a sign indicating they were only open by appointment. Nothing had been noted in Quimby's about limited locking availability. I tied up to the lock wall ladder and climbed up to videotape and view the opposite side. Fuel was now an issue as I had planned to lock through and gas up at Defeated Creek Marina, less than four miles upstream. I went about twenty miles back downstream and found a side channel with overhanging trees to tie up to for the night.

SUNDAY, MAY 21ST, 1995

I awoke to such a clatter! There were geese honking, ducks quacking, fish flopping, birds singing, and an occasional cow mooing off in the distance. At first I thought the mooing was just my stomach demanding attention, with the feeling in my stomach and the sound out of synchronization.

Fifty miles needed to be covered before gas was available at Mile 240, Cherokee Resort. I used the 7 ½ HP for 46 minutes, then switched to the I/O, running it out of gas. With only three miles to go, I dumped the rest of the mixed gas from the outboard into the I/O tank and made it to Cherokee Resort.

I only bought eight gallons since I was within twenty miles of Drakes Creek, arriving there at noon. After loading up, I checked into the office to see what I owed. The only charge was for the use of the boat ramp, nothing for the four days parked there.

I'd traveled 563 water miles, and locked through four times in my two days on the water.

On my way out of town I surveyed the not all that far away tornado damage done to major buildings, with lots of trees also blown down.

Crossing the Ohio, Mississippi, and the Missouri on my way home, I noticed they were all high and running fast.

MONDAY, MAY 22ND, 1995

It was 1:30 AM when I arrived at my parent's small acreage outside of Washington, Iowa, so I slept in the van until 7:30. I totally surprised them when I walked in as they hadn't looked outside and seen the van and boat.

TUESDAY, MAY 23ND, 1995

I made it back to Lakeville and the family. Two weeks later we set off for an 'Out East' family vacation trip lasting almost six weeks. Some of the places visited include; Washington DC, Atlantic City, Philadelphia, New York City, Boston, Acadia National Park in Maine, and Niagara Falls.

When I took The Boat in for servicing the following was done; lower unit seal kit, U-joint, water pump assembly, impeller, and gimbal bearings at a cost of $569.41.

I finally acceded to replacing the prop, which had developed a noticeable bend in one of the three blades. Even a slight bend can cause vibration, not necessarily noticeable, that will take out seals and wear gears unnecessarily. I asked about having the prop rebuilt, to which I got a hearty laugh. They held my prop up next to a new one with the same pitch and diameter with the result being that mine appeared to have shrunk by about 20 % all the way around.

1996 MISSOURI RIVER FROM FORT BUFORD, NORTH DAKOTA TO SIOUX CITY, NEBRASKA

Still burnt out with computers I found a 'three month job' through a temporary agency last October, which I held for almost three years installing patient monitoring equipment for the medical division of Hewlett Packard. I worked a five-state area, spending most of my time at the Mayo Clinic in Rochester, Minnesota since it was undergoing a major upgrade.

Buying the Zodiac opened up the ability to go fast in shallow water while still being portable.

I ordered the eight Army Corps of Engineers charts that cover the Missouri River from eastern Montana to Sioux City, Iowa and planned a trip with the intent to start at the Montana/North Dakota border and go to Sioux City, Nebraska. The Lake Francis Case chart did not arrive until three years later due to its being under development.

SATURDAY, AUGUST 10TH, 1996

We left Lakeville at 4:15 PM, after Kevin returned from Boy Scout Camp and me from an every other Saturday morning computer operations job taken only to keep my skills 'fresh.' On the way out of town, I bought a water-resistant Casio watch at Sam's Club, which became the Zodiac speedometer for the trip.

At 2:00 AM we stopped at an Interstate 94 rest area just outside Dickerson, North Dakota, sleeping in the camper van.

SUNDAY, AUGUST 11TH, 1996

We arrived at Fort Buford, located less than a mile from the junction of the Yellowstone and Missouri Rivers, and took a quick tour of the Fort. From there we went to the boat access and organized to run the Missouri River from river mile 1578, to mile 732.

Debbie would drive the camper van to prearranged spots, acting as both a chase vehicle and a place to sleep. We carried the inflated Zodiac with the 25 hp Johnson mounted on the transom on a sixteen-foot aluminum snowmobile trailer, bought to haul our snowmobiles three years ago. To keep gas smell out of the van, I devised a way to haul four six-gallon gas cans on the front of the trailer.

Onboard the Zodiac we carried the following: five boat cushions, *it bounces you around a lot,* 3 life jackets, 2 six gallon gas tanks, sometimes an additional 6 gallon gas can, four 20' nylon lines, a waterproof bag containing: flashlight, rain suits, two-man tent, emergency food, camcorder, binoculars, and jackets; an orange dry box containing: state highway map, knife, mirror, lighter, $100 cash, driver's license, AT & T calling card, flares, and sun tan lotion. Using see through waterproof plastic I carried maps and notes showing the approximate locations of; boat ramps, bridges, marinas, cities, dams, stump fields, sand bars, & hazard areas. Also carried in the Zodiac stern storage area was a pair of two-piece paddles, inflation pump, and a repair kit.

After rolling the Zodiac down the ramp, loading all the gear, and with Kevin and Nate aboard, I hit the throttle to start another adventure. The Zodiac struggled to accelerate. I had been into too much of a hurry again, forgetting to remove the attached wheels.

The scenery was very different from Minnesota. The almost treeless river bluffs were scenic in their own way, with a wide variety of colorful hues. We met Debbie for brunch underneath the Lewis and Clark

Memorial Bridge on Highway 85, about twenty-five miles downstream from Fort Buford. It took almost exactly an hour, using three gallons of gas. So I now knew that I could run about twenty-five mph fully loaded with the gas consumption being a little over eight miles per gallon based on heading downstream in calm conditions. Using the stopwatch feature on my Casio, I was able figure fuel usage and distance traveled at any one point with a surprising degree of accuracy.

We met Debbie at the beach of Four Bears Recreation area, Mile 1480, a public access located within the Fort Berthold Indian Reservation. During a very quick lunch and refuel, we had a major misunderstanding about where we would meet next.

Kevin stayed with the van, while Nate and I set off at 4:45 for the ninety mile run to Garrison Dam. No problem, Right? **Wrong!** Nate and I were going to experience how rough a large body of water can get in a seemingly slight wind. With no trees on the high bluffs to block the wind sweeping down the long expanse of the lake formed by the dam, we were in for a ride.

Lake Sakakawea is named after the female Shoshoni Indian who joined the Lewis and Clark Expedition in present day North Dakota. It is one of the largest man-made lakes in the United States, extending 178 miles from Garrison Dam northwest to Williston, North Dakota. The lake averages between two and three miles in width, and is six miles wide at its widest point. The maximum depth of the lake is 180 feet at the face of the dam. When at normal operating pool (1850 feet mean sea level), the lake covers 368,000 acres, and has 1,300 miles of shoreline.

The river was relatively calm until a 90-degree turn forced us to run due east in four-foot white caps for five hours. I slowed somewhat, but due to oncoming darkness I had to maintain a good pace while also making sure to follow a course that would take us to the dam and not shoot us off into one of the large bays.

Nate was a trooper, joking, and saying that it was OK for me to curse. He was getting the worst of the ride, with waves constantly breaking over the bow and dowsing him. In working at the Mayo Clinic with Felix Olivares, who was from Venezuela, I'd learned some prime Spanish phrases that I'd rattle off as we hit especially hard waves. This cheered both of us up until one wave visibly whip-lashed his neck. Nate, just ten, expressed his desire for the trip to be over and be on land with his mother.

The Zodiac Fastroller 380 inflatable has totally different characteristics from that of a traditional boat. Due to its weight of just one hundred five pounds and short length of twelve-foot six inches it goes over, and not through, waves. So you experience the full up and down motion of the water, much like a fishing bobber. The Zodiac has three main inflation chambers, an inflatable floor, with two additional chambers called sponsons that provide lift at higher speeds.

Along the way I stopped and asked two different fishing boats how far it was to the dam, getting differing answers. I crossed to the south bank, hoping to not miss the dam in the dark. If we happened to overshoot it, there is fifteen more miles of water before hitting the eastern end of the lake.

While we had rain gear, it was dumb that neither of us thought of stopping to put it on. As day turned into moon lit darkness, I think I started to hallucinate due to being cold and exhausted. The white caps either turned into rocks over which water was breaking, or white birds skimming or sitting in shallow water. Nate was worried that Debbie was worried about him.

While approaching Garrison dam, I tried to figure out which side Debbie might be. I went to the east side where the spillway passes excess water around the dam during periods of high water. While cautiously approaching the bank, I told Nate to jump out with the rope when we hit shore so that we would not be swept through. He did, and then I jumped out. Instead of my legs responding to the command of forward, the first four steps ended up being in reverse, cramped due to being cold, wet and in the same position for so long.

We did a quick survey of our surroundings. Not seeing anywhere Debbie might be, I decided to make a night of it right where we were. Pulling the Zodiac all of the way on shore, we then used it as a bed and the tent as a blanket, having beef jerky for dinner.

It was a long cold mostly sleepless night, I thought about Debbie worrying about us. The stars seemed so friendly, almost close enough to touch. Some time during the night, Nate woke up and said he **was** going to change sides, rolling out in the process.

MONDAY, AUGUST 12TH, 1996

The view of our surroundings at 7:30 showed no boat ramp in sight. I'd given the river chart set to Debbie since it showed greater detail of the local roads to access points than the highway map and it was all 'downriver' for me. I was using notes and highway maps to keep track of our progress, with bridges being the key. Now in the light of day it was obvious there wasn't a boat ramp close to the dam as I'd anticipated. Now what?

Nate, barefoot, having left all footwear in the van, and I, wearing water shoes, walked to an overlook, and in seeing campground facilities below the dam, headed there. A passing government vehicle offered us a ride, so we hopped in the pickup bed. Not finding the van at the campground facilities, we continued onto the hydroelectric generating plant where they were originally headed. I used a calling card to telephone our next-door neighbors, who had agreed to be an emergency contact, and left a message on their answering machine telling of where we were.

While waiting for a ride back to the Zodiac, we checked out the displays in the visitor lobby. There were models, interesting exhibits, and brochures giving information about dams on the Missouri. After being dropped off close to the Zodiac, we ate a breakfast of jerky, beef sticks, potato chips, and Ritz crackers.

About twenty minutes later a guy from Arkansas walked down and asked how the fishing was. Explaining the situation, he said about the only place Debbie could be was at a boat ramp about two miles away and volunteered to drive us there. I left Nate posted at the small park/overlook in case Debbie drove by, and rode with him to the ramp, finding Debbie parked in an out of the way spot casually reading a book. I thanked 'Arkansas' for the ride. When Nate saw Debbie, he was happy once again.

The following is Debbie and Kevin's story about what happened during the time we'd last parted at Four Bears until we met almost seventeen hours later.

First of all she said that we'd agreed to meet at the boat ramp to the northeast of the dam, to which I don't disagree. I tend to get 'tunnel vision,' thinking of the closest water connection and not of the closest vehicle access point.

They'd maintained a vigil from a hillside overlook, watching for any boats heading their way. While doing so, using a 12-volt spotlight, they signaled a small boat they thought was us. Debbie held the spotlight on a break in the bluff, behind which was the ramp, while Kevin ran the one-third mile there. It was not us, but two men who'd been out fishing all day. They were grateful for being signaled in, as they'd been lost in the dark.

Debbie said she was worried that Nate was worried that she was worried about our well being. She also professed not being particularly concerned, figuring rough water had slowed our progress, saying that I usually played it safe and figured we'd been forced to stay someplace on shore.

That morning she'd also left a message on the neighbor's answering machine, and drove across the earthen dam.

Not seeing the Zodiac, hidden by the steep bank, she'd returned to the boat ramp where we finally hooked up.

It was too steep and rocky to load from where we had stayed the night. Nate, still a trooper, rode with me to the ramp. The boat ramp is on a dogleg behind a high bluff, and even with seeing Debbie parked on the hill, I still overshot the entrance since the ramp can't be seen in passing.

We loaded the Zodiac to portage around the dam, ate, and then unloaded on the downstream side. Noticing three cushions missing, Debbie went back to where Nate and I spent the night while the boys and I headed downriver.

When Debbie walked down the hill looking for the cushions, she found an older fisherman sitting on one, with the other two lying next to a log. The fisherman readily gave it up and just as Debbie topped

The following is Debbie and Kevin's story about what happened during the time we'd last parted at Four Bears until we met almost seventeen hours later.

First of all she said that we'd agreed to meet at the boat ramp to the northeast of the dam, to which I don't disagree. I tend to get 'tunnel vision,' thinking of the closest water connection and not of the closest vehicle access point.

They'd maintained a vigil from a hillside overlook, watching for any boats heading their way. While doing so, using a 12-volt spotlight, they signaled a small boat they thought was us. Debbie held the spotlight on a break in the bluff, behind which was the ramp, while Kevin ran the one-third mile there. It was not us, but two men who'd been out fishing all day. They were grateful for being signaled in, as they'd been lost in the dark.

Debbie said she was worried that Nate was worried that she was worried about our well being. She also professed not being particularly concerned, figuring rough water had slowed our progress, saying that I usually played it safe and figured we'd been forced to stay someplace on shore.

That morning she'd also left a message on the neighbor's answering machine, and drove across the earthen dam.

Not seeing the Zodiac, hidden by the steep bank, she'd returned to the boat ramp where we finally hooked up.

It was too steep and rocky to load from where we had stayed the night. Nate, still a trooper, rode with me to the ramp. The boat ramp is on a dogleg behind a high bluff, and even with seeing Debbie parked on the hill, I still overshot the entrance since the ramp can't be seen in passing.

We loaded the Zodiac to portage around the dam, ate, and then unloaded on the downstream side. Noticing three cushions missing, Debbie went back to where Nate and I spent the night while the boys and I headed downriver.

When Debbie walked down the hill looking for the cushions, she found an older fisherman sitting on one, with the other two lying next to a log. The fisherman readily gave it up and just as Debbie topped to touch. Some time during the night, Nate woke up and said he **was** going to change sides, rolling out in the process.

MONDAY, AUGUST 12TH, 1996

The view of our surroundings at 7:30 showed no boat ramp in sight. I'd given the river chart set to Debbie since it showed greater detail of the local roads to access points than the highway map and it was all 'downriver' for me. I was using notes and highway maps to keep track of our progress, with bridges being the key. Now in the light of day it was obvious there wasn't a boat ramp close to the dam as I'd anticipated. Now what?

Nate, barefoot, having left all footwear in the van, and I, wearing water shoes, walked to an overlook, and in seeing campground facilities below the dam, headed there. A passing government vehicle offered us a ride, so we hopped in the pickup bed. Not finding the van at the campground facilities, we continued onto the hydroelectric generating plant where they were originally headed. I used a calling card to telephone our next-door neighbors, who had agreed to be an emergency contact, and left a message on their answering machine telling of where we were.

While waiting for a ride back to the Zodiac, we checked out the displays in the visitor lobby. There were models, interesting exhibits, and brochures giving information about dams on the Missouri. After being dropped off close to the Zodiac, we ate a breakfast of jerky, beef sticks, potato chips, and Ritz crackers.

About twenty minutes later a guy from Arkansas walked down and asked how the fishing was. Explaining the situation, he said about the only place Debbie could be was at a boat ramp about two miles away and volunteered to drive us there. I left Nate posted at the small park/overlook in case Debbie drove by, and rode with him to the ramp, finding Debbie parked in an out of the way spot casually reading a book. I thanked 'Arkansas' for the ride. When Nate saw Debbie, he was happy once again.

the bank, a black truck drove by and slowed. It was 'Arkansas.' Debbie yelled that all was OK and we were already on our way downriver.

Between mile 1390 & 1315, a dam does not back the river into a pool. The level is somewhat controlled by the release from Garrison Dam upstream, and by how much is held back by Oahe Dam, Mile 1072.3 downstream. I couldn't find a map covering the seventy-five mile stretch above the uppermost reach of Lake Oahe.

Scenery varied between bare bluffs and treed banks as we followed the original unmarked channel, running aground once. At 2:30 we met Debbie underneath the Hensler/Washburn Bridge ND Highway 200A, the only natural stopping point before Bismarck, eating lunch and fueling up.

Between the Hensler/Washburn Bridge and Bismarck, I ran hard aground at least six times. I became more educated about where the shallow water was by observing birds. Since I don't know bird species names, my referral to them will be elementary at best. I noticed that the small white birds tended to stand on sandbars that were just below the surface, while the larger white birds liked to swim and eat in the deeper water closer to the channel. Therefore whenever I saw small birds on the water I immediately steered clear, and tended to stay the course upon seeing the larger ones.

While traveling the upper reaches of the Mississippi and Saint Croix rivers, there had been mostly rock bottom structure that defies the cutting of any particular channel pattern. Now being on a stretch of the Missouri with a mostly sand/dirt bottom, the channel was more predictable.

If there was a high bank and a low bank, the channel was always towards the high bank. However, you should not necessarily hug the high bank due to trees that drop and are silted in. When that happens eddies and backwashes can develop from 'holes' washed into the bottom. For example, while you might expect a depth of three feet, it could be more than five times that with the swirling action causing you to be sucked closer to the semi-submerged trees. This wasn't a cause of concern for me since the Zodiac is very stable, but it could cause an inexperienced canoeist some anxiety.

I also learned to somewhat ignore the visible obstructions; downed trees, sand bars, etc and instead concentrate on looking for the more hidden dangerous obstructions revealed only by the occasional flutter or riffle of the water surface.

As we approached the outskirts of Bismarck, there was an increasing amount of new housing built along the river. I selected what I figured to be the best route, only to end up in a shallow side channel. We encountered two *very large* people in a dinky rubber raft powered by a four-horse motor, who then stopped to talk to two equally large people firmly planted in the soft riverside mud.

While passing through the slew, people from shore yelled unsolicited advice on how to get to deeper water. Finding what I thought was deep water I opened the throttle and we ran the hardest aground that would happen the entire trip. Going from twenty-five mph to a dead stop within the length of the Zodiac, tossing one of the boys out the front, with the rest of us thrown forward. The kill switch cord attached to my life jacket stopped the motor. We dragged it back to the channel and continued onto Mile 1313 where we meet Debbie at a boat ramp.

Mile 1315 is about where Interstate 94 crosses over the Missouri and the Lake Oahe chart starts. Debbie and I discussed where to stay for the night and decided to meet at General Sibley Park, five miles downstream. While at the ramp we talked with a local boater who gave directions to the park, by land and water. By water it was through a maze of small islands and past a State Correctional Farm. If you see a houseboat moored, you went too far.

Just a short distance downstream, we saw a houseboat next to a side channel. The consensus was that it was too soon, so we continued. Shortly after, I asked directions of a Bayliner slowly heading upstream. Its occupants assured us that the park was still downstream, so we kept going. Stopping at a dock where a family was just getting into their fifty-hp Lund aluminum fishing boat, I once again asked directions to the 'Park.' After a futile attempt to comprehend their directions, they said to just follow them upstream about four miles. I lagged behind, unable to maintain their speed.

After many twists, turns, and passing the Bayliner still heading upstream, the Lund directed to us to enter the side channel we'd bypassed earlier. It was 7:00 and we'd traveled about thirteen miles to make what should have been a five-mile trip.

W loaded up, selected a campsite, and had a meal of burgers, beans, with peach cobbler for dessert. It was easier to settle in for a restful night's sleep with the family back together safely.

TUESDAY, AUGUST 13TH, 1996

Not in a particular hurry, we didn't leave the campground until 10:30, agreeing to meet at Mile 1251.

The water got rough, with the wind at our back. The boys enjoyed the ride for the first twenty-five miles, then admitted they had had their fill. Slowing for a tree field and spotting Debbie at a boat ramp on a straightaway, we made an unplanned stop. Being close to noon, and somewhat sore from being bounced around, we stopped to fuel up, taking sausage, cheese and crackers with us.

We continued on in three to four foot waves, with the wind still at our backs. During a group pee, Kevin and I both fell into the boat while whizzing, with Nate almost falling out the opposite side when a particularly large wave hit.

It was 2:15 when Kevin and I left Beaver Creek, Mile 1251, fueling up and eating the lunch carried with us on shore due to the rough water. Nate, who had had enough bouncing around the last three days, rode with Debbie.

The water got even rougher so I slowed down and we shifted around a lot trying to get comfortable. Major water was taken over the front three times, half filling the boat each time. It self bails through two drains fairly quickly with out any danger of sinking since the three main air chambers provide plenty of buoyancy.

In the process of creating the reservoirs backed up by the dams on the Missouri numerous issues needed to be addressed. I'm caught between being an environmentalist and a practical person who knows that for our modern society to exist certain issues need to be compromised. While I know that many thousands of acres were flooded, how many more thousand acres are now able to be more reliability planted? How do you calculate the effect of the electrical energy generated and increased state tourism created from fishing to the effects on the local economies?

When the reservoirs were flooded, trees were cut off at various heights to assist fish reproduction. While passing through areas marked as stump or submerged tree fields on the chart I always slowed down.

As the channel wound back and forth between areas shielded from the wind, we would alternately wear rain gear to protect ourselves from spray or take it off to stay cool in the sun's heat. Now in South Dakota, Kevin and I met Debbie and Nate at a ramp in Revheim Park/Indian Creek Area, close to Highway 12 and the town of Mobridge.

We found a campsite in the same general area as the ramp, getting two free bags of ice because of buying gas. As Debbie fixed goulash and things were hung out to dry, we discussed the day. I commented that I'd felt queasy for at least half of the last leg, only feeling better upon stopping to adjust my position.

Debbie related her days travel. Due to the van overheating, she had turned the air conditioner off and the heater on to help cool the engine. Grasshoppers were all over the road; jumping up as she drove, splattering the windshield, grill, high top camper shell and flying in through the open windows. Upon seeing a resort sign as a possible place to have the van looked at, she left the desolate main road. The dirt road she'd turned onto went through two open fence gates and kept going and going. Upon coming to the top of a rise and seeing the road split with no buildings still in sight, she decided to turn around since it was the widest, flattest, spot around. Finding seemingly rare trees to park under, she let the engine cool there and then continued back to the highway and onto Mobridge. The problem was that the radiator was low on anti-freeze, and after refilling, it didn't overheat the rest of the trip.

WEDNESDAY, AUGUST 14TH, 1996

Us 'boys' were back on the semi-calm river by 8:30, with the wind and waves picking up within the hour. We met Debbie at a boat ramp in Forest City, fueled, and grabbed food to go.

From Forest City to Oahe Dam, the water was calm so we were able to enjoy the scenery. The river was wide with major twists and bends; I had to watch carefully to not end up in a side bay.

Lake Oahe is 231 miles in length, when the pool formed by the 245-foot high dam is at full capacity. We portaged around the dam, dropping into Lake Sharpe below the tailrace of Oahe Dam. While it was fairly calm during the eighty-six mile run to Big Bend Dam, I had to be alert for submerged trees.

The only incident of note occurred around Mile 1000. While searching my way through a stump/tree field, Kevin's feet obscured my view so I slowed to have him change positions. While watching him, and not looking ahead, I tapped a tree stump three inches above the surface. Then just a ¼ mile later, still going slow, I hit another one six inches below the surface, throwing the motor up.

About seven miles as the crow flies from Big Bend Dam, we found out how it got its name. The Missouri makes an almost complete loop, flowing twenty-five miles easterly before returning to its 'neck,' which is only one and a half-mile wide.

Big Bend Dam, Mile 987.4, is constructed of rolled earth, as were the prior two we'd portaged around, with a height of ninety-five feet and eight generators.

We loaded up at 7:30 and found a nice campsite just downstream; feasting on barbecued chicken that Debbie had grilled at the ramp while awaiting our arrival.

THURSDAY, AUGUST 15TH, 1996

Nate and I left from just below Big Bend Dam at 9:00, after enjoying an egg, sausage, muffin sandwich that Debbie fixed for breakfast. Kevin stayed with Debbie and helped with house keeping chores.

With the chart for Lake Francis not yet published, I had to rely on a Public Recreation Facilities pamphlet put out by the US Army Corps of Engineers. Since overhead bridges are easy to spot from the water, and with Snake Creek Recreation area just above the third one, that became our next meeting spot.

After fueling up and eating a snack at Snake Creek, us 'boys' took off for Fort Randall Dam, Mile 880. The last ten miles of Lake Francis Case were pretty rough, and upon arriving there at 4:45 couldn't find Debbie. I dropped both boys off at the ramp that I thought she should have been at and went looking for her. With near empty gas tanks and just me in the Zodiac it really cruised. I found Debbie parked just around the next bend.

While loading the Zodiac to portage around the dam, the boys told of two characters they'd observed loading their boat while I was gone. The story was reminiscent of the movie, 'The Grumpy Old Men' starring Walter Mathau and Jack Lemmon.

We then tried to figure out the next thirty miles since it is not a pool backed up by a dam covered by an Army Corps chart. In talking to a local, he suggested a place to meet called Lazy River Acres, close to Verdel, Nebraska. Debbie got detailed road directions and we were both off at 5:45. With Fort Randall Dam releasing a lot of water, it appeared the downstream water level was about three feet higher than normal.

At one point, the motor started to throw up spray and bog down so I stopped to see what the problem was. As I tilted the motor up, Nate said it was probably just weeds. It turned out to be a three-foot long stick wedged underneath. Ever since, we jokingly refer to small pieces of driftwood as 'Missouri Weed,' keeping that stick as a souvenir.

Not knowing how far Lazy River Acres was, and with the river wider than you might think, I passed by. Something told me to turn around, and within a mile of travelling back upstream, we found Debbie sitting on a dock. Lazy River Acres had the basic essentials that we needed; a ramp, outhouse, water faucet, and a place to park. While not appearing to be an official campsite area, there weren't signs prohibiting camping so we did. Other than a friendly dog whose owners must live at a nearby house, we were the only ones there.

FRIDAY, AUGUST 16TH, 1996

Dreaming that I was part of a team laying wires in the riverbed, and while trying to find connectors, Debbie woke up. She asked why I was rolling around, so I explained it to her. At the time I was working on a major wiring project at the Mayo Clinic.

It was 9:00 by the time we left, after having oatmeal and my mandatory morning coffee. The first twenty miles of river were unpredictable, being highly braided with no discernable true channel to follow. It was very flat country; muddy and grassy in the riverbed. Meeting an oncoming boat that would not share the center point of the river, we went aground. Channel Hog! I picked a route through the 'delta,' and most of the time it worked.

Seventeen miles from Gavins Point Dam, and upon seeing the wide expanse of Lewis & Clark Lake, the motor started churning through mud and water only a foot deep. I had the boys move forward to help raise the prop. The twenty-five horse motor has minimal propulsion in shallow water drive. Just as I'd tell the boys to go back to their normal positions, we would hit bottom again.

We cleared the mud field only to hit three-foot waves. I found calmer water only to end up in an area with major tree debris. Nate was jumping up and down, so I yelled at him three times to stop so that if I hit something he wouldn't fly out. Within thirty seconds we hit mud, stopping abruptly. Fortunately he'd settled down and we all stayed in the boat.

With Lewis & Clark Lake being fairly wide, the depth was very unpredictable. It was best guess as to where the channel ran prior to being flooded.

Arriving at Gavins Point Dam around noon, we portaged around to travel the last seventy-eight miles of this trip.

With no more dams on the Missouri after Gavins Point, it flows 811 miles before joining the Mississippi.

About fifteen miles above Sioux City we saw a deer swimming across the river.

We arrived at Scenic Park River Access in South Sioux City, Nebraska at 5:00, the same park I'd left from with The Boat in August of 1993. We camped there, and returned to Lakeville the following day.

Length of trip – 843 miles – Six days
Order of dams and miles between

Lake Sakakawea – Fort Buford to Garrison Dam	1578-1390=188
Garrison Dam to Upper end of Lake Oahe	1390-1315=75
Upper end of Lake Oahe to Oahe Dam	1315-1073=242
Lake Sharpe to Big Bend Dam	1073-987=86
Lake Francis Case to Fort Randall Dam	987-880=107
Fort Randall Dam-Upper end Lewis & Clark Lake	880-850=30
Upper end Lewis & Clark Lake-Gavins Point Dam	850-811=39
Gavins Point Dam to Ponca Bend	811-750=60
Ponca Bend to Scenic Park River Access	750-732=16

Total Distance – 843 Miles

1997 JEFFERSON RIVER FROM TWIN BRIDGES TO THREE FORKS, MONTANA

Since we were going west to Durango, Colorado for a family reunion, doing a river trip from that part of the country was natural. Over the winter I'd seriously thought about being able to go North to South, and East to West by water and formed a vague plan to do so. I arranged to take four weeks vacation, half without pay, so we could attend the reunion, take a river trip, and allow time for sight seeing along the way.

While the camper van was in for some last minute brake work at Midas, they found the top of the front gas tank rusted through. Taking it to a local repair shop to have the gas tank replaced, they found out a self-contained fire caused a fuel gauge sensor to melt. What probably started the fire was heat from a worn out muffler about three feet away from the tank. After replacing the muffler system and not able to immediately get a replacement tank, they reinstalled the bad one without permission. In a hurry to get started, I figured that we could just run on the rear tank.

While heading northwest on I-94 and thinking the gas gauge on the rear tank was dropping too fast I pulled off on an exit ramp to make sure it wasn't leaking. Not finding a problem, I then realized we'd headed off in the wrong direction. With our initial destination being Colorado, we should have headed south on I-35 and picked up

I-90 going west. Talk about haste in getting started and making dumb mistakes! It caused a rethinking, resulting in us leaving home three days later with a new front gas tank and all known problems fixed.

Over the next two weeks we; stopped at the Corn Palace in Mitchell, South Dakota, viewed Mount Rushmore, visited my sister in Colorado Springs, toured the Air Force Academy where Kevin was thinking of applying, attempted to surf sand at the Great Sand Dunes and boated a small nearby lake, saw Gunnison Canyon, climbed through the Indian dwellings at Mesa Verde National Park, stayed at a nice resort on a small lake just outside of Durango, Colorado for the reunion, rode the Durango Silverton Narrow Gauge railroad, soaked in natural hot springs, spent two days in Yellowstone National Park, and then drove to Three Forks, Montana where the boating portion of the trip began.

WEDNESDAY, JULY 16TH, 1997

The main thrust of my vague plan to boat East to West was to have the least amount of land miles between an East to West connection, even if it maximized water miles. This meant boating seventy miles of the Jefferson River first, one of the three rivers that forms the Missouri River.

We stayed the night at mosquito-infested Three Forks State Park and agreed to meet back at a nearby parking spot after boating the Jefferson River from Twin Bridges.

Getting an early start, we arrived at 8:30 to a park on the west bank next to the east most bridge of Twin Bridges. This turned out to be the Beaverhead River, which ten miles upstream stream is joined by the Ruby River. You would think that after relating so many errors in my haste to get started I'd learn, *but no*. I overlooked the fact that two *different* rivers pass under the two bridges, which are a mile apart. This error would affect future planning since I would now have to continue past the other bridge to fully travel the Jefferson.

With both boys in the four hp powered canoe and at an elevation of 4627 feet we shoved off from the park, agreeing to meet twenty-eight miles downstream at Parrot Castle. The Beaverhead was a fast running narrow shallow stream until it joined the Big Hole 2.2 miles later, forming the Jefferson River. The river picked up volume and width while the depth did not immediately change.

Debbie videotaped while we passed under Ironwood Bridge, mile 63, stopping just long enough to touch base. There were places with sufficient depth across the entire width of the river, and places with visible 'high' spots as

the hydraulics of water became apparent. Hydraulics, as defined in The American Heritage Dictionary, is 'The physical science and technology of the static and dynamic behavior of fluids.' I can only explain this phenomenon by telling what I have since come to understand. What happens is, depending upon the drop, rate of flow, obstructions, curvature, and width of channel, a river dramatically changes character. This is especially true of rivers where the primary flow comes from winter snowfall and the rate that it melts.

As we looked for Parrot Castle, I thought back to the original settlers of this area and what they must have encountered. According to the 'Montana Afloat' map, available through the Department of Fish, Wildlife, and Parks, Parrot Castle was named for R. P. Parrot, who built a smelter to process ore from the mines in the foothills of the Tobacco Root Mountains. Their office in a large red brick building resembled a castle.

Just after passing rubble of red brick to our right, which I assumed to be Parrot Castle, and while going through the remains of bridge supports, I saw we were approaching a diversion dam.

The purpose of a diversion dam is to form a small backwater from which farmers can draw water for irrigation. Its design can be as simple as piling boulders across most of the rivers width causing the flow to temporality constrict. This temporary constriction causes the water to flow faster through the portion that isn't blocked.

Having explained that, the boys were primed for a more adventurous 'Western Experience' than they had thus far experienced. I asked if we should run through the opening or portage around. After twenty-eight miles of relatively small rapids/fast water, they wanted excitement, so we shot through the opening. Kevin was hunched in the front of the canoe facing me, while Nate was sitting in the center facing forward on an improvised seat.

As we started through, Kevin and I were like **"Oh Yeah! All Right!"**. Then the first wave came over the canoe.

With each succeeding wave washing over, Kevin said my facial expression changed from excitement to concern.

The canoe quickly filled with water!

We exited the chute of white water upright with the canoe full of water and the engine dead due to taking on water. Giving credit to ourselves, nobody had made any false moves causing us to capsize while going through. Then, while being swept downstream in the fast current, the canoe took a roll.

Kevin and I bailed out immediately, with Nate exiting last. I had been telling Nate to sit still so as not to tip the canoe. With the boys hanging onto the canoe, I grabbed the floating map case, seat cushions, and paddles, with most everything else being tied in. We worked our way out of the current and just as we reached the right bank Nate let loose thinking he could walk the rest of the way. The current swept him off his feet, with Kevin quickly grabbing him since I was on the opposite side. We were all wearing life jackets.

We dumped the water out, reloaded, with the only thing missing being a plastic dip bucket. The motor started, then died. We paddled off and on for thirty minutes while I tried to restart the previously submerged motor. When it fired up, I yelled out triumphantly, **"Hang out the sign Boy's, Were back in business!"**. This became a motto, spoken when overcoming major obstacles. While rounding a bend we spotted our missing dip bucket and retrieved it.

Encountering just a few small rapids after dumping, we arrived back at the Three Forks State Parks area about 7:00, dropping 427 foot of altitude over seventy-two miles.

Unknowingly I missed the channel that would have run us by the agreed upon meeting spot. Besides the Jefferson having braided channels, the Madison and Gallatin Rivers also join close by to form the headwater of the Missouri, making it a confusing situation at best.

By way of history, the rivers were named by Lewis and Clark in 1805 during their expedition to explore a possible water route to the West following the Louisiana Purchase. The west fork for President Thomas Jefferson, the middle fork for Secretary of State, James Madison, and the east fork for Secretary of Treasury, Albert Gallatin.

We stopped at a boat ramp and saw a sign confirming we were in Three Forks State Park. Not having explored it enough before, I still did not know where we were at. The mosquitoes were terrible, with the only refuge being in a foul smelling outhouse. I told the boys to wait at the ramp while I walked to a set of concrete storage elevators visible in the distance.

Arriving at a railhead called Trident; I stopped at the depot finding five or six men inside. One asked what I wanted, so I explained that we had come down the Jefferson and had missed connections with Debbie. He volunteered to drive me around to find her.

His name was Bob Todd, who was employed to help maintain local rail lines. The other men were travelling the rails, working wherever they were needed the most. Bob said they were called 'Gandy Dancer's.' I looked Gandy Dancer up in the dictionary. The primary definition means being a railroad worker. The origin of the term comes from the rhythmic movement of a railroad laborer working with tools produced by the now defunct *Gandy* Manufacturing Company.

Within a ¼ mile of driving back to the ramp, we saw Kevin running towards us. Kevin said that Debbie had driven by fifteen minutes after I left, not looking to the left where the boys were frantically waving from the boat ramp. We picked up Nate and backtracked the road that goes by Trident trying to find Debbie.

We took the left fork of the road five miles later since it follows the contour of what was now the Missouri River.

Finding one boat access blocked by a train, which Bob knew hadn't moved for a couple hours, we skipped it.

While checking out the right fork, we saw a Sheriff's car going the opposite direction. Concerned that Debbie may have contacted them; we caught up and explained the situation. The officer hadn't heard of anyone looking for us but took Bob's number in case.

Bob was a good conversationalist, entertaining us with local stories and his own perspective on life. His passion was golfing, saying he was not a particularly good player. He'd quit drinking in '83' and quit hating his job in '86'. When Bob volunteered us the use of his back yard pickup camper, I gladly accepted. We stopped by the canoe and loaded up what we could to avoid theft.

It was 10:30 as we headed to Bob's house; being engrossed in conversation I'd quit looking for Debbie. Fortunately Kevin was watching out the window and spotted the van parked right where we'd agreed to meet. We'd checked the area out once before, with Debbie not being there. I thanked Bob for his help and tried to give him gas money, which he wouldn't accept.

Debbie said she hadn't been particularly worried, knowing we had food and a tent with us; her main concern was not having sleeping bags. While the day had been sunny and hot, the night air was cold. She then told about her adventures.

We'd agreed to meet across from Parrot Castle if she could find the road, otherwise she would return to Three Forks to do laundry and then meet us at the headwaters' area. Following what she thought was the right dirt road; it came to a wash out. She got out, walked across a tilting bridge, and followed an overgrown path leading to the river. From there she saw the same bridge supports we had passed through, with no bridge. According to the map there should have been an access point and a primitive campground. It appeared that the channel had moved to the opposite side, and since the bridge was also down, the campground had been abandoned.

It took twenty minutes for her to turn the van and trailer around, bending in a rear panel on the van with the trailer by turning too short. There wasn't sufficient room to turnaround considering the unexpected washout. After completing the turn she noticed a sign that said 'Parrot Castle' hidden by a bush.

Careful not to end up in another dead end she followed more back roads, stopping at the first bridge crossing water. She stayed there for a half hour before realizing it was Fish Creek, a tributary of the Jefferson. Finding another bridge spanning the Jefferson, she waited there until

2:00. Needing to do laundry, she left for the city of Three Forks. After laundry, she went to the spot where we eventually found each other.

At 7:30, and tired of waiting, she decided to drive around to find us. Debbie, not seeing Kevin waving his arms from the poorly marked boat ramp, drove to Toston Dam on the Missouri. She thought maybe we'd overshot Three Forks State Park, and continued another twenty miles to the next logical stopping point. Not finding us there, she returned to our agreed upon spot and was just settling in to sleep when we arrived.

1989 Lake Itasca Mississippi River Headwater

1990 Minnesota River Kevin- Age 9 Nate Age- 4 wants to go

1991 St Croix River Debbie, Kevin, & Nate doing dishes

1992 Ron celebrating the arrival to the Gulf of Mexico

1993 Missouri River Leaving from South Sioux City, Nebraska

1994 MN River Headwaters sign Ron, Kevin (13) Nate (8)

1996 Missouri River Ron, Kevin, Nate

1997 Missouri River Leaving from Three Forks, Montana

1998 Big Hole River Kayaking

2001 Columbia River Loading the boat to go around a lock

1997 MISSOURI RIVER FROM THREE FORKS, MONTANA TO FORT BUFORD, NORTH DAKOTA

THURSDAY, JULY 17TH, 1997

Us boys left the Missouri Headwaters boat ramp at 8:30, still using the canoe and 4hp. The river width stayed pretty much the same, with the depth unpredictable.

Seeing a log cabin in an isolated area, we stopped and checked it out. While the log cabin was old, it was resting on a fairly new concrete foundation. The mosquitoes and gnats were terrible, which I understand was true of when the Lewis and Clark Expedition passed through here in 1805, also in the month of July.

The twenty mile run to Toston Dam, named for an early settler, occurred uneventfully. Originally built in 1940 for irrigation control, the dam has since had hydro-electric generating capacity added.

I switched to the Zodiac and 25 HP, encountering many shallow spots and 'touched' bottom three or four times, slightly dinging the prop. The channel constantly switched between banks and braided around islands, requiring quick decisions to stay in the deepest part of the swift current. I ran at wide open since that is when you draw the least amount of water. OK, OK, I was also going fast since that is when it is the most fun due to the challenge of 'reading' the river successfully.

Nate and I entered the twenty-five mile open water section of Canyon Ferry Lake just as a lightning storm caused heavy rain to fall. We laid up at a boat ramp on the left bank and waited out the worst of the storm. With the wind still up, we left and tacked across it's four mile width trying to find calmer water. I didn't like being bounced around, but Nate talked me into opening up the throttle. We flew from wave top to wave top, with the motor over revving as the prop came out of the water.

Upon arriving at the 225 foot high Canyon Ferry Dam, named after a river crossing before the dam was built in 1953, we found the ramp where Debbie and Kevin were waiting and portaged around.

The fifteen mile run to Hauser Dam, named after an early banker and stockman, started out in rough water and intermittent rain. There being no takeout next to the dam, 'we boys' made the round trip between it and Black Sandy, which is the closest access point above the dam.

Due to mountainous terrain, no access is immediately available below. Immediately below means that even though there is a hand launch area just one and ½ river miles below Hauser Dam called Beaver Creek, it's one of those places that you can't get there from here easily.

I still don't know how we found Beaver Creek, other than Debbie had become somewhat familiar with this area after getting lost trying to find Hauser Dam. This is a very scenic area, by road or water.

The view one sees upon entering the valley of Beaver Creek can be compared to that of the TV series Bonanza, except in color. For those too young to have seen the show or those not seeing reruns on cable, the scenery filmed is that of the Lake Tahoe area on the California/Nevada border. I guess that at least part of it was televised in color, but I never saw it that way until 1973 when I bought my first color TV.

To get the Zodiac in the water required a major group effort. We had to cross a foot bridge, carrying the Zodiac above hand rails, and beat a path through brush to reach the river. The short upstream run to Hauser Dam was through an especially scenic steep rock canyon wall.

Someday I'd like to take Debbie back to view the forty miles of beautiful river scenery between Hauser and Holter Dams. It varied from sheer cliffs rising 1200' above the river to a wide lake, from having no development to numerous cabins, from seeing no one else on the water to jet skis and house boats.

We spent the night at the boat ramp parking lot next to Holter Dam, named after an early Helena mining tycoon, since the regular camping area was full.

After going to bed, Pixie, our dog, barked at what Kevin thought was another dog. He investigated, and found that it was an older man wheezing right before going into cardiac arrest. His relatives revived him using CPR, also calling 911. He then tried to go out on his boat to get away from everyone asking how he felt, only to have the boat keys taken away. When paramedics arrived he refused to be taken in, saying he was OK, not wanting to pay ambulance and emergency room fees. The paramedics asked the group, "I thought you said this guy just had a heart attack?" The guy who had given CPR said, "I told you he was revived didn't I?" The man appeared OK the next morning, still unhappy at his family for calling 911.

FRIDAY, JULY 18TH, 1997

It was 9:30 as we drove along a heavily rutted rough dirt road leading to the opposite downstream bank ramp from Holter Dam. Deep ruts precluded backing the low clearance van closer and using the Zodiac wheels. A Dory type fishing boat rigging up for the day also blocked easy access. With the Zodiac fully loaded, it was a struggle to carry it to the river's edge, with a fisherman giving us a welcoming hand.

While legal as to the horse power limit, I felt guilty using a motor since the next thirty miles is very popular for trout fishing and not normally traveled by a power boater. We passed many fishermen in hip waders and floating Dory's, whose response varied. Some would wave, some ignore, and one motioned for us to slow down. I always maintained as much distance from them as possible.

Having arranged to meet Debbie at Prewett Creek, I stopped where I figured it to be and talked to a couple camping who confirmed that it was Prewett Creek. With it being just a short walk to the highway, I posted Kevin to watch for Debbie there while I checked out the area. He checked back shortly after, saying Debbie drove by without seeing him standing just ten feet from the road. I said to watch until 11:30, and at 11:28, she came by again, this time stopping. The Prewett Creek access point was unsigned, but while crossing the bridge at Prewett Creek going in the opposite direction she noticed Kevin.

While waiting, I talked with a camper who was a personal aircraft designer. He showed me a prototype and explained its design that used a glider type parachute instead of fixed wings.

Our next agreed upon stop was Great Falls, fifty-seven river miles away. I ran aground twice as we neared Great Falls. The river drops only sixty-six feet the last forty-five miles without much visible current to define the channel.

Meeting Debbie at a boat ramp along River Drive, she joined Nate and me for the short round trip run to Black Eagle Dam. It was not obvious that the first bridge crossed under was built on a shallow rocky bottom, acting as a miniature dam. Going downstream I hit rocks passing under, so when crossing under while returning I had Debbie and Nate sit in the very front, still hitting rocks seven, or eight times, further dinging the prop.

The elevation at Three Forks is 4200', with Great Falls being 3300'. We'd dropped 900' over 189 river miles. I'd been using maps from Montana Afloat since starting, but hadn't found any information covering the forty miles between Rainbow Falls Dam and Fort Benton. We stopped at a tourist information office and asked about the dams and possible places to launch from, leaving not knowing any more than when we went in.

In investigating and videotaping them we found out there are five dams; Black Eagle, Rainbow, Cochran, Ryan, and Morony in that order.

The only place that I saw any possible access was between the first and second, with only two to three miles of river between them. I decided to bypass the approximate ten miles that separate the five dams after seeing two whitewater kayaks doing rolls in the rapids just below the first dam.

The next decision was whether or not to start from the downstream side of Morony Dam. Seeing fast water pouring around and over rocks as far as the eye could see, I was having serious doubts about attempting it. Then after reading a sign that read, 'Dangerous River Ahead' I reluctantly decided the wise thing to do was not launch from there.

We drove to Carter Ferry, about seventeen river miles downstream from Morony. In talking to Brian, the resident ferry operator, I asked if we could overnight there. He gave permission and directed us to a grassy spot.

Brian said that a family from Wisconsin had left two days earlier attempting to reach New Orleans using a motorized raft, possibly taking a year to get there. Someone in a chase vehicle would get supplies, assist in getting around dams, and arrange for lodging along the way. I don't know if they made their goal, I doubt it.

I also talked with a fisherman getting ready to head upstream using a jet drive outboard on a Bass Tracker boat. He claimed that his wife did not always pay enough attention to where they were going since he'd recently run aground on an island. I did not point out that he was the one driving at the time.

While Debbie fixed dinner, I 'fine tuned' the dinged prop using a pair of pliers and a metal file.

SATURDAY, JULY 19TH, 1997

Nate and I headed upstream to cover as much distance as possible to the bottom side of Morony Dam. Even though heading against a rather swift current, the first ten to twelve miles were not a big deal, with the rest being an adrenaline rush. As we got closer and closer to Morony Dam, it became obvious why the sign warning about drops below the dam was appropriate.

With the throttle wide open, I ran chutes of white water running between boulders. With the river running fairly wide, I figured the maximum depth had to be less than three feet. That did not allow for much of a margin of error since the Zodiac needs at least 18 inches.

We got within sight of the power lines of Morony Dam, stopping only because of a two-foot 'ledge' spanning the entire width of the river that was impossible to jump. There was a tent city to our left where Brian said a team of archeologists was studying the area.

It took 2/3 throttle just to hold the Zodiac in place while Nate snapped a picture. I wished we had brought the video camera, which we don't normally carry in the Zodiac or canoe due to the abuse and extra care it takes. The run downstream was almost as exhilarating. Since boats do not leave a track behind, I once again had to choose an uncertain route between boulders.

Originally Debbie was to leave for Judith Landing, 100 miles downstream, while Nate and I headed upstream. Brian suggested she wait, thinking I'd need to refuel if I got close to the dam. It was a good thing she waited since it took six of the eighteen gallons I was carrying to run the round trip. While I filled the tank, Brian took the boys on a round trip ferry crossing and told the following story. Ferrying foreign tourists across the mountain melt off swollen river; Brian stopped about 500 feet from shore to change his angle of approach. While doing so, he told them they would have to get in their vehicles and drive the rest of the way to shore. He said you should have seen their eyes light up with fear, whereupon he took the ferry the rest of the way across.

Leaving with three full tanks, Nate and I set off for Judith Landing. About fifteen miles below Carter Ferry, starting at Fort Benton to James Kipp Recreation Area, is a 149 mile section of river designated as 'Wild & Scenic.' The two maps that cover this stretch are available through the Bureau of Land Management in Lewistown, Montana.

This is an extremely popular place to canoe because of its natural beauty and documented campsites of the Lewis and Clark Expedition.

The first 51.5 miles of the wild and scenic designation did not affect me, only regulating the type of development that can occur close to the river. Ten miles below Coal Banks Landing, the river becomes 'no wake' for 97 ½ miles to James Kipp, except for a fifteen mile stretch around Judith Landing. Not wanting to take days to traverse the area, I'll admit that I violated the principle of no wake rule.

When I saw a canoeist, I would slow to a pace about twice as fast as they were going. Then after either getting out sight, or rounding a bend, I would open the motor back up to full throttle.

Let me explain my philosophy on this. At the risk of raising the ire of canoeist, environmentalist, and even power boaters, let me pose the question of why the No Wake restriction is in place to begin with, and then answer it from my viewpoint.

Is it because the banks are subject to erosion from wakes? No, this area varies so much in water volume, that the banks are relatively unaffected by the relative small size wake of a boat that is able to operate in the unpredictable depth.

Is it because that even a small wake can capsize a canoe? Yes, that is why whenever I passed a canoe I left the barest of a ripple of water.

I suspect that the underlying reason is to discourage power boaters from using this area, resulting in it being a haven for canoeist. I'm not anti canoeist and actually think that having this area designated as 'No Wake' is a good idea. Unfortunately many power boaters don't know or care how they endanger other craft with their wake. Having been endangered by the large wakes thrown by much larger boats, I try to be respectful of other boaters.

The point I want to make is how I feel about the *letter of law*, and the *purpose of law*. The letter of law says no wake; but I believe that the purpose is to ensure the safety of the canoeist.

Did I break the law? Probably. Did I endanger anyone? No! Actually, I believe that my zipping through as fast as I did in the manner I did actually made a better 'wilderness' experience for the canoeist since the obtrusiveness of a motor was much briefer than it could have been.

While slowly idling past a long string of canoeist towards the end of the 'No Wake Zone,' I saw a small aluminum boat with the motor hood missing approaching from downstream.

In it were two old bearded men. I angled off to allow them more room when they flagged me down.

"Nice day, Huh?" "Yea, but nicer yesterday." I replied back. They complimented me on the Zodiac and then asked, "Did you know this is a no wake zone?" I said that I did. Then one said, "We don't care, we let them go by and then speed back up. We don't want anyone to get hurt." I didn't acknowledge that I was doing the same thing, but did say that I also didn't want anyone to get hurt.

I've often wondered if they'd been sent out to talk to me by someone using a cell phone, or were truly a couple of old farts just out for a ride.

Meeting Debbie at Judith, we had lunch and refueled. During the brief stop I checked out the area, which still had several old buildings standing. There was a house with a basement, which I thought was unusual for its era.

Nate and I headed out at 5:00 for the sixty mile run to James Kipp, our goal for the night. There were fewer canoes on the water, most already settled in campsites.

The designated Wild and Scenic area is very beautiful. There are a lot of stone outcroppings and sandstone bluffs that provide an ever-changing landscape. Having said that, I've enjoyed almost all off the river views seen over the years. What I find offensive are such things as using old cars and broken up concrete to stabilize banks. Bank stabilization is a necessary evil, but it can be accomplished using natural materials.

Upon arriving at a ramp at 7:45 where a group wearing bug hats were loading canoes, I asked if we were at James Kipp. They verified that it was, so I pulled in. The van was not visible from the ramp, so I walked to the main area, finding nobody around. The mosquitoes were terrible! We pushed back out into the river, seeking relief from the swarming and biting hoards while waiting for the van to arrive. By positioning the Zodiac such that the wind blew the exhaust from the 1 to 50 oil to gas mix across us helped out the mosquito situation considerably.

With daylight quickly closing, and thinking that Debbie was delayed for some reason, it was time to think about spending the night in the tent. I told Nate to assemble the rip corded tent in the Zodiac to avoid getting eaten up onshore. He had used the tent in Cub Scouts, while I'd never set it up. Being afraid he would drop poles in the water, Nate asked to be taken to shore. Since I didn't have the slightest idea how to set it up, and being a weenie when it comes to camping, I dropped him off at the ramp to set it up on his own. Just as I was backing away, I saw the van crossing the Highway 191 Bridge. I yelled to Nate, "Here they come!" He evidently did not hear me, and continued to put the tent up. As Debbie swung the van and trailer around to back up, she saw Nate doing a 'buggy' dance. Upon opening the driver's door to back up, since she is unable to use the side mirrors to assist in backing, she immediately was swarmed by mosquitoes and could hardly see. By this time, I was onshore and took over backing the van up.

Nate was irrational due to the hoards of attacking mosquitoes and he kept trying to put up the tent instead of just chucking it in the van. We had to throw him in and shut the door behind him.

With the Zodiac loaded, Debbie broke the news that the recreation area was closed for repairs. Not an issue for me since I was protected by a metal skin from the mosquitoes, and my only goal was to swat those that had gotten in. For whatever reason, Debbie had always refused to use the propane fueled Coleman stove inside the camper van. That night was an exception!

Normally Debbie gets to meeting places ahead of me, with the reason I got there first two fold; One being that Brian had warned her against using any non-surfaced road since they quickly turn to gumbo with any rainfall, and rain was threatening. The main roads she used went way out the way while I ran a fairly straight river. Second, she also had to backtrack to buy much needed gas for the Zodiac.

SUNDAY, JULY 20TH, 1997

It rained most of the night. We awoke at 7:30 and prepared for the 135 mile trip to Fort Peck Dam. Kevin, armored with a bug hat and several layers of clothing, poured and mixed boat gas. Debbie and Nate did house keeping while I acquainted myself with the US Army Corps chart covering Fort Peck Lake.

Off at 9:00 with both boys, eighteen gallons of gas and the usual gear made for a full load. Our start was accompanied by a light rain, clearing off by 2:00.

I asked Kevin to be navigator, while I would also make sure we were on track. This may seem unnecessary as we were traveling a river, albeit backed up by a dam. Because Fort Peck Dam backs up such a large pool of water, any of the numerous bays could be misinterpreted as the route to the dam, so keeping track of your route is very important.

About forty miles from James Kipp, the channel does a 180-degree turn, changing from almost straight south to almost straight north. At the unmarked turn, another body of water continues south ten miles called Musselshell Bay. There are twenty-one lights posted as Navigation Aids, with the closest one fifty-three miles upstream from the dam. Using a compass, estimated speed, and elapsed time, we figured out our approximate location.

The light wind translated to consistently rough water due to the wide expanse of water and the treeless bluff area that is typical of northeast Montana.

Even though we'd left with supposedly enough fuel for a 150-mile run, the lack of river current, rough water, and the slim margin for error had me second-guessing. Locating the flashing green light thirty-four miles above the dam that marks the entrance to Hell Creek Bay, we went four miles out of the way to Hells Creek State Park. I bought enough gas to ensure making it to the dam and we stretched out the kinks in our bodies. The cashier said someone else had stopped there earlier in the year, planning to cover the length of the Missouri.

It was 6:30 when we arrived at Fort Peck Dam, 21,026 feet long and 250 feet high, consensus being that we had not enjoyed the last six hours due to the constant pounding taken. After promising Nate, who had taken the worst of the pounding by sitting in front, and Kevin, who had done an excellent job of navigating, that we would stop at a 'treat' place, I couldn't find one. We found a campground just below the dam, with a shower being a treat in itself since it had been over a week since we had been able to take one.

I inadvertently woke Debbie in the middle of the night while trying to find aspirin to relieve a pounding headache.

I asked Kevin to be navigator, while I would also make sure we were on track. This may seem unnecessary as we were traveling a river, albeit backed up by a dam. Because Fort Peck Dam backs up such a large pool of water, any of the numerous bays could be misinterpreted as the route to the dam, so keeping track of your route is very important.

About forty miles from James Kipp, the channel does a 180-degree turn, changing from almost straight south to almost straight north. At the unmarked turn, another body of water continues south ten miles called Musselshell Bay. There are twenty-one lights posted as Navigation Aids, with the closest one fifty-three miles upstream from the dam. Using a compass, estimated speed, and elapsed time, we figured out our approximate location.

The light wind translated to consistently rough water due to the wide expanse of water and the treeless bluff area that is typical of northeast Montana.

Even though we'd left with supposedly enough fuel for a 150-mile run, the lack of river current, rough water, and the slim margin for error had me second-guessing. Locating the flashing green light thirty-four miles above the dam that marks the entrance to Hell Creek Bay, we went four miles out of the way to Hells Creek State Park. I bought enough gas to ensure making it to the dam and we stretched out the kinks in our bodies. The cashier said someone else had stopped there earlier in the year, planning to cover the length of the Missouri.

It was 6:30 when we arrived at Fort Peck Dam, 21,026 feet long and 250 feet high, consensus being that we had not enjoyed the last six hours due to the constant pounding taken. After promising Nate, who had taken the worst of the pounding by sitting in front, and Kevin, who had done an excellent job of navigating, that we would stop at a 'treat' place, I couldn't find one. We found a campground just below the dam, with a shower being a treat in itself since it had been over a week since we had been able to take one.

I inadvertently woke Debbie in the middle of the night while trying to find aspirin to relieve a pounding headache.

off at the ramp to set it up on his own. Just as I was backing away, I saw the van crossing the Highway 191 Bridge. I yelled to Nate, "Here they come!" He evidently did not hear me, and continued to put the tent up. As Debbie swung the van and trailer around to back up, she saw Nate doing a 'buggy' dance. Upon opening the driver's door to back up, since she is unable to use the side mirrors to assist in backing, she immediately was swarmed by mosquitoes and could hardly see. By this time, I was onshore and took over backing the van up.

Nate was irrational due to the hoards of attacking mosquitoes and he kept trying to put up the tent instead of just chucking it in the van. We had to throw him in and shut the door behind him.

With the Zodiac loaded, Debbie broke the news that the recreation area was closed for repairs. Not an issue for me since I was protected by a metal skin from the mosquitoes, and my only goal was to swat those that had gotten in. For whatever reason, Debbie had always refused to use the propane fueled Coleman stove inside the camper van. That night was an exception!

Normally Debbie gets to meeting places ahead of me, with the reason I got there first two fold; One being that Brian had warned her against using any non-surfaced road since they quickly turn to gumbo with any rainfall, and rain was threatening. The main roads she used went way out the way while I ran a fairly straight river. Second, she also had to backtrack to buy much needed gas for the Zodiac.

SUNDAY, JULY 20TH, 1997

It rained most of the night. We awoke at 7:30 and prepared for the 135 mile trip to Fort Peck Dam. Kevin, armored with a bug hat and several layers of clothing, poured and mixed boat gas. Debbie and Nate did house keeping while I acquainted myself with the US Army Corps chart covering Fort Peck Lake.

Off at 9:00 with both boys, eighteen gallons of gas and the usual gear made for a full load. Our start was accompanied by a light rain, clearing off by 2:00.

MONDAY, JULY 21ST, 1997

It was 9:45 when Nate and I set out on the cold water coming out of the reservoir, a big breakfast under our belts. We'd agreed to meet Debbie and Kevin about fifty highway miles later, underneath the Highway 13 Bridge. In running upstream from the boat ramp to the downside of Fort Peck Dam, water depth was not an issue. Turning back downstream and just past the ramp we'd left from, the bottom quickly became shallow and rocky. I couldn't get off the throttle quick enough, suffering major prop damage. I had never done such damage to a small outboard prop before. I had not felt the need for a spare prop so did not have one. I got out vise grips and bent it back the best I could.

Less than a mile later I hit bottom again, throwing the motor up. Somehow this dislocated a shifting component under the hood. I resolved the shift problem and continued on with the motor vibrating due to the damaged and unbalanced prop. I hit the rock and mud bottom off and on for the next two hours.

Arriving at the Hwy 13 Bridge, we saw the van parked on a side road next to the high bank. Debbie and Kevin were playing charades in the shade of a shed. We ate lunch, fueled, and with Kevin and Nate aboard, headed for the Highway 16 Bridge fifty highway miles away.

Fortunately my troubles didn't worsen, making it to the bridge at 6:30. With forty miles still to go before reaching Fort Buford, last years starting point, I was in a hurry to keep going with remaining daylight now at a premium.

We quickly fueled, and with Nate leery about being stranded in darkness, left with me anyway. There were numerous irrigation pumps on floats below Fort Peck.

While passing Fort Union, a historic rebuilt fort on the Montana/North Dakota border, Nate 'cranked' his arm in jubilation. "Yes, Yes, We're almost there! I made my goal!" Without having said anything, he had set a goal of boating the entire distance with me.

It took us only fifteen minutes longer than Debbie and Kevin to get to Fort Buford, arriving at 8:15. Not prepared for such an early arrival, Debbie didn't have the video camera ready so a 'reenactment arrival,' was done. I took Debbie up the Yellowstone River for a short distance, initiating yet another river trip possibility. While setting up camp next to a couple from Canada at the boat ramp, Debbie related her day.

The mornings drive had through grassy plains shifting to green grassy topped buttes with white rock exposed on the steep side as the day wore on.

She'd found the Hwy 13 & 16 bridges without a problem. Seeing other vehicles parked on the sand under the Hwy 16 bridge, she drove down after making sure that she would be able to pull out.

After a short nap, she walked to the river's edge with Pixie and talked with two mothers who routinely brought their children there to play. She met Darla and a Mr. Boysen with their kids. Mr. Boysen said it was fun to ride dirt bikes on the buttes and pointed to a bush high on the river bank, with a steep drop right after it. He'd ridden up the hill from the opposite side and skidded to a stop right by the bush unaware of the drop. Now he is more careful about going over the butte tops.

1997 BOIS DE SIOUX, & RED RIVER TO LAKE WINNIPEG, ONTARIO CANADA

TUESDAY, JULY 22ND, 1997

O ver dinner last night I revealed my plan to finish going North to South by water. They weren't excited; but agreed to it. Besides me not having to return to work until the following Monday, we were already geared up for boating. We headed east for the North Dakota/Minnesota border to check out the Red and Bois De Sioux river conditions.

The van needed an oil change so we stopped at Williston, ND and watched TV in a dirty waiting room while waiting. The owner, who also sold military style guns, was dealing with a shady looking character looking to buy.

After the oil change, I fulfilled my earlier promise of 'treats' and stopped at a Snow White ice cream parlor. It was a hot, sunny day as we crossed the width of North Dakota, stopping at Westgate Marina in Grand Forks to replace the damaged prop. I bought one with a slightly higher pitch, which theoretically means a little more speed. They didn't have one with the same pitch as the original in stock. In using it, I couldn't tell a bit of difference in speed or economy.

Over the winter, several heavy snowfalls delayed us getting to Grand Forks, North Dakota to do an upgrade to a hospital monitoring system. Once there, every uncontrolled intersection had such high snow banks that it was only after you were half way through you were able to see cross traffic. Record snowfall followed by fast spring snowmelt caused major flooding of the mostly flat Red River Valley, resulting in unprecedented damage. This would be the area I would be trying to boat through.

Trying to come up with a viable plan to head north from Big Stone Lake was not easy. The Minnesota Department of Natural Resources had yet to make a canoe map for the route we'd be taking. We had used them to travel from the upper end of Big Stone Lake three years ago to head southeast. I was unable find any river maps that follow water drainage as it heads north. The route being: Lake Traverse, to Mud Lake, to the Bois De Sioux River, to the Red River, and ending up at Lake Winnipeg in Manitoba, Canada.

The best resource I came up with was a spiral bound publication called Minnesota, Travel and Recreation Guide, put out by Rockford Map Publishers, Inc. It listed activities occurring within Minnesota, with its primary goal being to promote places to stay and eat. The main reason for buying it was the county maps showed in 8 ½ by 11 inch format some detail of local roads and river flow. It did not show river or lake access points.

From Grand Forks we followed Highways 220 & 75 south, since they closely parallel the Red River, and checked out places to meet as we'd head back north. While time consuming, it proved to be very valuable that we checked out most of the roads that spurred to the river. Debbie made notes in the margins of the guide detailing what we found. Her notes varied from no access, to poor access, to mud ramp, to paved ramp, and camping and gas facilities seen along the way.

We camped at Lindenwood Park, which is next to the Red River in Fargo North Dakota just north of the I-94 Bridge.

WEDNESDAY, JULY 23RD, 1997

Debbie fixed an egg/muffin breakfast while I primed myself with caffeine and planned the day. We crossed back over to Minnesota and continued south, still checking out potential access points along the way. As we followed occasional gravel roads, dust poured in through open windows. With the A/C not working, airflow was needed in the already hot day.

The furthest south we went was County Road 16 in Traverse County, which crosses the border into South Dakota.

The next one north, Highway 55, crosses into North Dakota.

It was obvious in seeing the paltry flow of water, less than a foot deep and not much more than that wide, that a start from here was impossible. Unless a larger volume of water could be instigated? We three males lined up facing downstream, discretely positioning ourselves as if we were going to add water, when a less than amused Debbie refused to continue videotaping.

We returned to the Highway 55 Bridge access. While also having minimal water flow, it appeared doable with the canoe and four-horse. This would have us starting midway up the Bois De Sioux River, with the term river being used loosely. It was basically just a deep wide trench with farm fields on either side. Nate was forced to stay behind.

I told him it would not be a fun trip, which turned out to be very true. I didn't give sixteen-year old Kevin a choice.

It was 12:30 as we left with the water going from shallow to very shallow. The motor was unusable for the most part, even in shallow water drive. There wasn't even enough water to paddle, so we poled ourselves along. There were numerous places where we got out and pulled the canoe a fair distance. The thick, heavy river bottom mud stuck to our shoes. Then when we would jump back in the canoe, it would be slippery and cause us to almost fall back out.

While in a ribbon of water just wide enough for the canoe, a fish jumped and landed in an adjacent pool. It was almost as if the fish was giving us room to pass.

Three hours and about nine miles later we arrived at the County Road 6 Bridge. There was a bright orange bag hanging from it, our prearranged signal that Debbie was parked nearby. We'd crossed under three old bridges with flood debris packed underneath along the way. While eating sandwiches we related our experiences and then put back on the water, such as it was.

Kevin and I had nine more miles to go before arriving in Wahpeton, ND, our planned camping spot. Most of the wildlife we saw flew or ran off ahead, except for a large pelican that ruffled its feathers and filled its sack as we approached. I told Kevin to have his paddle ready in case it attacked as we passed within fifteen feet of it.

With Breckenridge, Minnesota, on the right and Wahpeton, North Dakota, to the left and with the addition of the Otter Tail River, we were now at the official beginning of the Red River. So there is no confusion, there are at least two Red Rivers. The one I had explored the possibility of boating in the South two years ago, and the Red River that we would be heading north on now.

Just after rounding a bend, we unexpectedly encountered a small dam with water dropping about three feet over a one hundred foot width with Debbie waiting just below it. There was a flat area on the right bank that made an easy portage. Worn out physically from pulling, poling, paddling, and very little motor use, yet still feeling playful, I gave Debbie a 'full moon' from across the river. She and Nate were socializing with two boys and a girl while their father fished at Kidder Park.

We loaded up and found a Jaycee Campground in Wahpeton, which at first sight appeared full. It turned out to be a potluck appreciation picnic held in honor of the city employees for their outstanding effort during the spring flood. Not having a dish to share, we found a spot away from the crowd to set up camp and ate what we had on hand.

THURSDAY, JULY 24TH, 1997

I switched over to the Zodiac, and with Nate on board, left from Kidder Park and headed north on the Red River with Fargo being the next meeting spot.

The Red River twists and turns and twists and turns along most of its length. This is because the Red River Valley is so flat that any downhill gradient change causes a change of course. There was sufficient water depth as long as I read the channel correctly, which usually meant staying to the outside on turns. There was an enormous amount of partially submerged tree debris to avoid. In many places the banks were piled high with trees, showing how severe the flood had been.

I had the time of my life! It was a real adrenaline rush to run with the throttle wide open while navigating the twists and turns coming up so rapidly while still watching for fallen trees. I'd compare it to driving an open wheel Indy type car on the closed street course of Monaco.

Using the race course analogy, while entering one of the few 'straight-aways,' I noticed a change in the horizon. It is just one of those deals where you say to yourself, "What is wrong with this picture?" I slowed up to analyze. The tree line was different. Then it hit me. There was a dam ahead! There hadn't been signs, or even if there had been at one time they would have been washed away by the floodwaters.

While my research hadn't been thorough, the thought of dams on the Red River had never entered my mind. I'd considered the one portaged around with the canoe an anomaly since it was in a town. This one was in the middle of nowhere. Looking back, I still don't know how I could have researched any differently.

Nate and I pulled over to the left bank and tied up to a tree to check out the situation. There were cement abutments sticking out about five feet from either shore, with water flowing over its entire width. The vertical drop was about ten feet, with a fast flow. There wasn't an easy way to portage the Zodiac around even if we'd had the wheels with us, which we didn't. There wasn't enough consistent width to pull it between the trees sideways with the motor mounted. Also with just Nate and me, it would have been physically impossible to pull it up and over the steep and slippery mud bank.

A possible solution would be to take motor off and carry the Zodiac on its side instead of its width. I discarded that idea due to the deep mud I'd have to wade through to carry the heavy motor.

What helped hasten the final decision was Mother Nature. Mosquitoes! And lots of them! Not as bad as when Nate tried to set up the tent on the Missouri, but bad by any standard.

I decided to portage everything except the Zodiac and motor, then use ropes to guide it over the dam in a controlled fashion. Nate didn't think much of my idea but having faith in the stability of the Zodiac I decided to do it anyway.

While Nate videotaped, hopping around due to being bitten by mosquitoes, I let the Zodiac float over the crest of the dam. The stern went over first and promptly hung up. The Zodiac now vertically bounced in the backwash of the dam with the motor held just inches out of the water because of the tubes that extend past it. Now what? From my precarious position atop the cement abutment, I reached out and was able to turn the Zodiac 90 degrees and land it right side up. I then passed the rope around brush and pulled it within ten-foot of the river's edge. We had to wade through knee high mud to reload the Zodiac.

Having overcome the unexpected dam, I was now apprehensive about how many other dams might lie ahead. Nate and I encountered two more before Fargo, both vertically shorter than the first. Since I had had success in

letting the Zodiac float over, we followed the same procedure. When the Zodiac went over the second one, I directed it so as to go over the crest sideways. It landed much better, except for being drawn into the backwash and requiring all my strength to pull it back out. It was full of water, quickly draining and never close to sinking due to its inherent buoyancy.

Debbie videotaped our arrival back to Lindenwood Park at 4:30 doing my now infamous high speed victory turn.

From trip notes comes the following; "Two 'mud bunnies' came smoking from under the I-94 Bridge".

When Debbie registered, the girl asked if she had had relatives camp there two days ago. She'd recognized the last name while not tying it to Debbie's face.

4:30 was the earliest I'd ever stopped for the day, if my increasingly poor memory is correct. I was worn out after portaging in the deep mud and travelling less than fifty statute miles, well over that in river miles.

FRIDAY, JULY 25TH, 1997

After yesterday's experiences, I drafted Kevin and let Nate rest. The next dam had a rock apron with only a four-foot drop that made carrying things around it easy. I smugly floated the Zodiac over, barely getting any water in it. Kevin probably thought that I had exaggerated yesterday.

Then came the dam from Hell! It was about a ten foot drop, the same as the one where the Zodiac had hung up vertically before. Following precedent, we carried around everything except the motor. There were differences. The concrete abutments extended further into the river and more small trees lined the approach. This meant that as the Zodiac floated downstream I had to pass the rope around more trees. Just as it was ready to go over the dam sideways, as planned, the rope hung up on the final tree. This caused the Zodiac to turn and go over stern first, where it hung up vertically again.

Unlike before, I couldn't reach it from atop the abutment. While trying to pull it closer with the guide rope, it went over backwards. Now upside side down and held by the backwash I was unable pull it out by myself. Kevin missed videotaping the actual part where it went over backwards since I had yelled for his help.

The fun had just begun! It took our full combined strength to pull the Zodiac out of the undertow. The upside down motor dragging on the bottom prevented us from pulling the Zodiac to shore. While trying to flip the boat back over, it kept sliding away. The solution was to carry the upside down Zodiac to shallow water where we were able to roll it over. I had the banged up fiberglass motor hood repaired and Johnson decals replaced upon our return home.

Now would the motor start? Optimistically we loaded back up. The first pull on the manual start motor resulted in my falling into the boat when the starter cord didn't budge. It was locked up! Figuring the cylinders were full of water, I decided to pull both spark plugs. That's when I found out the Zodiac repair kit kept in a bungee corded net spanning the transom containing the spark plug wrench gone. It evidently fell out while the boat was upside because we inadvertently overlooked removing it during the portage. I went back trying to pull start. After tugging a while to no avail, Kevin gave it a shot. Kevin, after a bit, was able to partially pull out the starter rope. We switched places and a few pulls later the recoil finally allowed full pulls. I continued to pull for all I was worth as the motor started to sputter and cough, finally staying running.

"Hang out the sign Boys, We're back in business!" The second time in as many weeks I'd had a motor underwater.

At 1:00 we met Debbie next to County Road 25 just west of Hendrum, MN, having gone about twenty statute miles in four hours. We ate lunch, fueled, and agreed to meet about twenty-two miles north at County Road 7 bridge. We'd be winging all meeting points from now on, as we had not checked out the immediate Grand Forks area, the point from where we had headed south in North Dakota.

Arriving at County Road 7 Bridge at 4:45, identifiable by the orange bag, we looked for Debbie. Yelling from an unseen location, she said to not come ashore because there wasn't an easy way up to the bridge. I had enough gas to reach Grand Forks, about twenty statute mile distance, so we agreed to meet there.

She said later that the view from atop the bridge showed nettles and logs piled on top of broken off trees. While swallowing mosquitoes and startling a white tail deer trying to find a way down to the river, she'd heard us. While walking to the middle of the bridge, placing and picking up the bag, vehicles stopped both times to offer assistance thinking she'd broken down.

Seeing the van parked close to a railroad bridge on the Minnesota side at East Grand Forks we pulled to shore. With the wheels mounted on the Zodiac, we slipped and slid in mud pulling it up a ramp to a campground whose only facility was a flush toilet. The few campground occupants were not there for recreation; they were construction workers there to rebuild after the massive flood. The thick stinky mud drew an inescapable number of common houseflies, making just being in the area miserable.

Floodwaters had crept up to mid first floor range in the downtown business area across the river when a fire broke out. Since traditional fire fighting methods were useless, a good number of buildings were destroyed.

Just as a heavy rain started to fall, we found a restaurant featuring an all you can eat Friday night fish fry.

SATURDAY, JULY 26TH, 1997

Was I glad we hadn't camped closer to the river. Last night's rains had turned it into a quagmire! We talked to a kid who said that a Toyota and another 4x4 next to the river's edge had been stuck there for a long time.

The road to the ramp wasn't too bad. I tied the Zodiac to the back of the snowmobile trailer, intending to pull close to the ramp and handwheel it down. I told Nate to videotape the train. He looked towards the train trestle bridge and said, "Train, Is there a train coming?" It was a funny misunderstanding with me equating our van, trailer, and Zodiac to a train.

While pulling on the lower unit to get the Zodiac through the mud into the river, I noticed the attaching nuts were loose. I hadn't noticed the progressively louder exhaust noise. A simple tightening of the bolts restored the sound level to normal.

Within a mile Kevin and I encountered another dam, quickly returning to the ramp hoping to find Debbie still there. She wasn't. With the dam right next to a golf course the wheels would have worked great. After the last fiasco I was determined to not float the Zodiac over if there was an alternative.

With the bank close to the dam steep and brushy, we drug the Zodiac and motor about a ¼ mile alongside the 17th Hole fairway. Where is a golf cart when you want one? We had hoped to talk a golf cart driver into pulling it, without one passing by. I talked to a golfer carrying his bag who said there were at least two more dams ahead. A golf ball stamped with a leaf and Grand Forks Country Club logo is now a souvenir. It would have been easier to carry the motor and then drag the Zodiac. I'd bolted the motor to the transom and the tools to unbolt it were part of the kit previously lost.

When I was little, a good friend of my father died due to a small boat accident. While checking fish bank lines on a log-strewn river with his son and another young boy they hit something that caused the motor to fly off, hit him, and capsize the boat. Fortunately both boys made it safely to shore. With search efforts failing to find the body, they asked Dad to run our speedboat up and down the river in an attempt to dislodge the body from wherever it was hung up. Knowing first hand what can happen, I had bolted the motor on and always wore a life jacket while in the canoe and Zodiac.

The river snaked much less radically, and we met at the Highway 317 Bridge on the North Dakota side to refuel and have lunch. Our next meeting spot would be at #175 bridge heading west out of Hallock, Minnesota.

Finding the bridge out at #175, and via shouting we agreed to meet around the town of Pembina, North Dakota, not knowing if the bridge crossing over to St. Vincent, Minnesota was intact.

The first actual posted sign warning of a dam was just after passing a power plant called Drayton Dam. Having no idea of the potential drop, and understandably nervous about approaching it we pulled off into brush. Walking the Zodiac downstream, anticipating a headwall of rushing water, we found a drop of 6", yes ***that is inches***. Any posted information is helpful since, without the sign, I might not have noticed such a small drop and taken out the motor upon hitting the cement ledge.

Our arrival to Pembina North Dakota at 7:00 coincided with a nice red 4x4 pickup truck backing a Bayliner down the ramp. It appeared they were the first ones to use the ramp since the flood because there were no other tracks in the mud. The two young kids were novices; with the one in the boat unable to start it. The pickup truck driver got in and started it up, then didn't know enough to lower the out drive. He would hit the throttle and throw water in the air. After hearing my yelling to lower the out drive and doing so, they took off leaving the pickup and trailer blocking the access. Dumbstruck by their rudeness, we had a hard time getting the Zodiac around them. I felt like using river mud to write on their windshield 'Ramp Hog' or 'Move Me,' but didn't.

We spent the night in a campground that was just over the levee from the boat ramp.

SUNDAY, JULY 27TH, 1997

It rained from 6:30 to 7:30 with the sun coming out at 8:00. Not wanting to get in trouble with US and Canadian custom authorities while crossing the border two miles north of Pembina via the Red River, we drove there and talked to them. They didn't have any objections after explaining the plan of Nate and me entering by water, with Debbie and Kevin coming across by highway.

We returned to Pembina, getting underway at 10:00. Meeting places would now become even more uncertain since our only resource was now a large-scale highway map. The next hopeful meeting spot was two miles to the border, plus another forty-two kilometers highway distance away in Morris, Manitoba at the Highway 23 bridge crossing. A mile times .6 equals a kilometer.

Seeing Debbie waving her arms at a ramp just before the #23 bridge, I did my high speed victory turn and hit something hard in the process.

It was 1:00 so we ate lunch and discussed the morning's activity. Just before crossing the border Debbie had filled the four six gallon gas containers carried on the front of the trailer. The idea was to buy cheaper gas on the US side since Canadian prices were higher. We were thwarted in our attempt to save money since she was assessed $7.39 US to bring it in. The exchange rate at the time was 1.35 US to 1.00 Canadian.

Upon arriving at Highway #23 Bridge she found a park and an associated boat ramp. While checking out the area she talked to a park ranger who said there was a partial underwater dam just above the ramp. She'd been waving her arms trying to warn me, and not understanding her hand signals, I hit it anyway. I assume its purpose is to prevent the rivers flow from washing out the ramp. The ranger said that the only other change to the river before Winnipeg is a diversion canal designed to channel flood water around the city.

Back on the river at 1:30, and with Nate and me covering less than ten miles since leaving the Highway #23 Bridge, the motor suddenly over revved. Something had broken! While the motor itself ran fine, the prop wasn't turning. Evidently running with the lower unit bolts loose and/or hitting the underwater dam had taken its toll. Now what?

About 1/8 mile downstream we saw a floating swim platform, so we got out the paddles and aimed for it. Debbie's waiting spot was at Ste. Agathe, about twenty miles north of the Highway 23 Bridge. There was a small unoccupied cabin on wheels close to shore with a narrow lane leading away from the river. I decided to see where the lane went, figuring it would hit a main road, and then try to hitch a ride. I told Nate to stay put on the swim platform since it was the least muddy place to be, and I felt confident he'd be safe in the isolated area.

Just a short walk through the trees I saw a large log home and knocked on the door. This surprised the man and woman inside since their three large dogs hadn't barked. Bill Skelton said the dogs normally barked when company arrived, not realizing I'd come from the river side and not the road. I explained the situation and Bill immediately volunteered to drive Nate and me to find Debbie at Ste. Agathe. Bill lived south of a small town called Aubigny. We had a very enjoyable conversation while he drove his small sports car north. Knowing the area, Bill figured she'd mostly likely be at a small park overlooking the river, a popular tourist spot because of an old hotel, and there she was!

Debbie happened to glance at a car pulling in and was surprised to see me sitting in the passenger seat.

Bill's brother-in-law, Travis, sister, nieces, and nephews were at the house when we got back. They helped me swap motors and I helped them drag two jet-skis through the thick sticky mud to the river. Nate learned how to fly a kite with the nieces and nephews while Debbie schmoozed with the women. It was like we were blood relatives. The cabin built on wheels was a good idea, especially considering the flood conditions just experienced. When the river is high Bill pulls it next to the log house that sits a good deal higher and back from the river.

Because Bill and Travis had jobs in Winnipeg, they knew of a boat ramp close to where they worked. It was in Crescent Drive Park at the end of Crane Street, marking the location on a city map so Debbie could find it. Bill would not take any money for the map or the ride so we sent him our unused Canadian money and a thank-you note upon returning home.

We stayed a while longer to see them use something called an Air Chair pulled behind one of the jet skis. It is a ski with a fin fastened two feet below and a seat above. I had seen videos of people using them. You are supposed to be able to do flips, but they weren't successful.

It was 5:00 before I once again was headed north to Ste. Agathe, this time with Kevin as the designated rider and using the four-horse. Getting there took one hour twenty minutes with my estimated speed less than ten mph, a far cry from the previous twenty-five mph. We threw in another tank of gas and headed off to meet at the boat ramp in Winnipeg.

Off and on I saw a huge Canadian flag; as I rounded bends it would appear and disappear. Finally I realized it was a hot air balloon shaped and colored to look like the Canadian flag. Around nine we saw the diversion canal that had saved the City of Winnipeg from flood damage by diverting floodwater around the city, with us staying in the river channel.

The measure of progress to find Debbie was to count **X#** of bridges passed under, and then look left for the ramp. Two hours after entering Winnipeg in the moonless night with city lights providing little illumination on the river, I started to doubt our whereabouts. Had we miscounted bridges? We stopped in a well-lit area with a lot of people milling about and asked if they knew where Crescent Drive Park was. Being told it was still downriver an unknown distance we continued on.

Suddenly Kevin grabbed the flashlight and shined it towards shore, the first time he'd done so. From behind the trees came an answering light. Then we heard a voice calling; "Ron? Kevin?".

Kevin yelled back. You'd think I'd be ecstatic at making contact, but for some reason that I still can't explain said, "Let's get out of here. They know who we are!" Kevin kept me from leaving. It had been a long day, having spent over eleven hours on unfamiliar water with the last two in the dark.

It was almost midnight as Kevin and I slogged through mud to reach the van, leaving the Zodiac tied to a tree.

MONDAY, JULY 28TH, 1997

Over breakfast Debbie related her story, while joggers and pet walkers passed by. She'd found the park without difficulty, only to find the boat ramp gate closed and padlocked to prevent usage with its fifty foot distance to the water covered by very thick mud. Seeing a sign that said parking was reserved for vehicles pulling trailers until 9:00; she drove through the rest of the park to make sure there was not another ramp. Upon returning, she parked on the grass of the dead end secluded street outside another set of gates. Nate and Debbie then carried chairs to the riverbank and sang songs from 9:30 to 10:15, with mosquitoes driving them back to the van.

Park security came by, looked at the van, and locked the entrance gate without ever talking to them. Now parked outside the unlit park, she listened and watched from the van, twice going to the river upon hearing motors. Debbie fell asleep at 10:45, waking up at 11:00 on hearing a motor. She ran to the river again. Seeing navigation lights, she knew it wasn't us. Depending upon boat size, navigation lights are legally required. This was the first time I had the Zodiac out so late in an area where there might actually be other boats. Kevin's beam of light came just as she just happened to take one more peek out the window by the bed and she saw the light from the river scanning the trees. Debbie said it must have been divine intervention that made the connection possible.

I was surprised that park security or the police did not knock on the van during the night, especially considering our Minnesota license plates. Park security not only opened the park gate, but the previously locked ramp gate as well.

It was hard to get motivated to start the day's trip. I was worn down, physically and mentally, but get started we did. As we squished back through the mud to the Zodiac in the light of day, I was amazed that Kevin had recognized it as a ramp from the water. It was just an open area between thick trees, and obviously hadn't been used since the flood. Using the city map key symbols, we found another ramp to meet at next at called North Perimeter Park.

It was nice to be in the light of the day while winding our way through Winnipeg. Kevin amused us with his new found Canadian dialect while we ate Dinty Moore stew at North Perimeter Park.

Yesterday Travis had told a humorous story of finding bats in his A frame. Some parts of Canada seem to use 'Eh' in any conversation over about fifteen seconds. Anyway Kevin retold Travis's story using exaggerated facial and arm movements. Bats in the A frame, 'Eh'! We were in stitches!

The next stop would be at Lockport, and actually is a lock that allows passage around the dam spanning the river. We had a hard time finding the lock master; who was then crabby about locking us through. I had to sign an insurance waiver, which is probably standard procedure.

The day seemed to just drag on from there. This is not a reflection on the lack of beautiful scenery, which there was plenty of. I had been vacationing for almost four weeks now and was active every day. I was beat and needed to get back to work to rest up. I am not looking for sympathy. Anyone who has ever overdone his or her favorite activity knows that it is possible to reach a point where it is no longer fun. I'd reached that point!

Our final bridge crossing meeting point had a nice park with a swimming pool, campground, and boat ramp. Nate played with the other kids while waiting.

The road by the park dead-ended just short of the wide-open expanse of Lake Winnipeg, our last meeting point. Debbie easily got there ahead of me. While walking around the resort, she talked with an eighty year old man who said that he used to come there with his now deceased wife. He now came there just to remember her. Pretty Sweet!

I climbed the watch tower at the resort. Seeing water in three directions, I debated whether to continue on into the open water of Lake Winnipeg. I decided to end the trip right there, figuring the last thing I needed would be for the four-horse to quit working and end up stranded on the huge lake.

We loaded up and headed home.

The following is what I've learned about the 1997 flood and the Red River since taking the trip.

The average slope of the Red River is just one half foot per mile. A combination of record-breaking snowfall, a late spring blizzard, already saturated soil conditions, and flowing north into the still frozen water caused the flood to be so massive.

Grand Fork's normal snowfall is 38 inches, actually getting 97.9 inches in 1997, breaking the 1896-97 record of 91 inches.

One reason which caused the Grand Forks area prediction of a maximum 49' flood stage to reach 54' was overland flooding, which basically bypassed the rivers and streams that normally feed to it.

From a website provided by US Army Corps of Engineers, St Paul District Water Control Center I have since learned the Red Rivers length and where the dams were at.

Mile # Description
548.7 Ottertail and Bois De Sioux Rivers-headwaters
546.4 Kidder dam, Wahpeton-Breckenridge
496.56 Christine Dam
482.7 Dam number 3, Fargo-Moorhead
458.1 Dam number 2, Fargo-Moorhead
452.15 Dam number 1, Fargo-Moorhead
448.9 Dam "A" at Fargo-Moorhead
296.1 Riverside dam, Grand Forks
????? 206? – I know there is one next to the power plant close to Drayton ND which they don't note 155.0 International boundary

15

1998 BOIS DE SIOUX, MUD LAKE, LAKE TRAVERSE, MINNESOTA

Shortly after returning from last summer's trip, I found a job back in computer operations. I'd mostly enjoyed installing medical monitoring equipment and was making good money, but as a temporary contract employee, I didn't have job security. My new employer, besides having a 4 ½-day workweek, also allowed an additional two-week vacation by reducing every paycheck giving me four weeks.

Since last July's very low water level had precluded finishing my goal of traveling North to South by water, I was determined to catch this spring's highest water level without fighting ice.

WEDNESDAY, APRIL 22ND, 1998

I left Lakeville about 6:00 PM in the camper van using the snowmobile trailer to carry the canoe. I had so much stuff loaded, and with just me going, I knew that I couldn't have over looked anything. Only to find out I forgot my two pillows, causing a restless night sleep at an Interstate 94 rest stop. Everybody's sleep comfort level is different, mine requires two pillows.

THURSDAY, APRIL 23RD, 1998

It was a beautiful spring morning, with many farmers out working their fields. While daydreaming about my younger days spent on the farm, I missed two turns before arriving at the Bois De Sioux River. I'd be starting from the Wilken County access again, heading south instead of north.

I videotaped the area, loaded the gear into the canoe, and was ready by 10:00. Just as I was about to start the four horse, a local retired farmer drove up and asked how the fishing was. I told him of my plan and some of the places I'd been river tripping. Embarrassingly I only went 100 feet before sputtering to a stop. The gas tank connection at the motor wouldn't stay attached.

The farmer volunteered his help, with me saying I had things under control. One of the things my father instilled in me was to always have a backup plan.

I pushed back to the bank and grabbed the other gas tank I'd brought. By placing both full tanks towards the front, it also helped offset the weight of me and the motor clear at the back.

The current was surprisingly strong considering how flat the surrounding terrain was. At one especially shallow spot, I had to push with a paddle to assist the motor. The 'river' is basically a deep ditch between farm fields designed to drain water as quickly as possible. The banks were at least six feet above my head, although slightly more than a year ago I'd have been boating through fields.

I arrived at White Rock dam, which backs up Mud Lake Reservoir, Elevation 972 feet, about 1:40. From atop the dam I memorized the southerly view so that I would recognize the approach to the dam from that side. There were many carp swimming and jumping in the fast water of the spillway.

Not able to see over the close high banks, most would consider this to be less than a scenic trip. During the round trip I saw a brown fox, geese, ducks, a mink, and a muskrat. It was enjoyable just being out in the sunny 80-degree day. The approximate thirty mile round trip was faster on the way back because of 'going with the flow'.

The view heading south and west on gravel road #9 into Traverse County was of flat farmland and raised river banks. I went to a service station in Wheaton, Minnesota to buy gas and asked if there was a public access to Mud Lake. Yes there is, follow #27 southwest about one mile, take a right at # 76 over Mustinka Creek bridge to a junction, go right to the junction with #9, then left on #76 to the Public Access sign at Mud Lake Wetland.

The public access area was pretty flat and marshy. It was 6:00 by the time I unloaded the canoe and got started. After clearing the channel that had been dug through reeds and marsh to reach the more open part of the lake, I headed north to the dam outlet. For the most part, it was very shallow with scattered rocks and mounds of earth rising above the surface.

Finding White Rock Dan dam at 6:50, I headed toward the south part of Mud Lake. Speed was at half throttle in shallow water drive because of the rocky shallow bottom.

Arriving at the south shore, I couldn't find the lake inlet. With the sun quickly setting, I decided to return to the van without wasting time trying to find it.

Darkness was settling in at 8:30 when I saw the white camper van top. I had trouble finding the meandering channel back to the ramp. While videotaping and remarking about how Nate would have felt right at home due to arriving in darkness, the camcorder battery gave out.

I loaded up and found my way to #117, where Reservation Dam helps form Lake Traverse, and parked in front of a sign that said No Camping. Dinner was meatball stew and I settled in for the night. In trying to charge the camcorder battery using my small Honda generator, I found that I'd forgotten to bring the camcorder battery charger. I slept restlessly, where are my pillows? There was very little traffic on the gravel road leading to and over the small dam and spillway that separates Mud Lake from Lake Traverse.

FRIDAY, APRIL 24TH, 1998

Over frosted flakes and morning coffee, I formed the day's plan. It amazed me how thick the carp were in the fast water flow of the four foot spillway.

It was 8:30 when I backed the trailer down the ramp that gives access to Mud Lake and was underway. I knew I wouldn't have to go very far to finish the upper portion of Mud Lake I'd been unable to do yesterday. Following the dug channel through marsh to where it opened into the lake, I then hit bottom many times. Rounding a point, I recognized where I'd been previously and returned to the ramp.

From Reservation Dam on #117 there wasn't an access to Lake Traverse unless I'd wanted to drag the canoe across the road and through muck, which I didn't. So I loaded up and headed south on Hwy 27 hoping to find a Public Access sign. I saw one, but was going to fast to brake for the turn. My attention being drawn to a 'For Sale' sign on a 59-60 Chevy Impala like a high school chum, Larry Miller, used to have parked alongside the road. It took two or three miles before I could find a place to turn the camper van and trailer around.

The Public Access was nice, actually having a dock. As I headed north to Reservation Dam, there was mild chop and a harsh wind blowing. Spray broke over the canoe, getting me wet. Having left the rain gear in the van, I slowed to stay dry. I stayed a ways away from shore to avoid several spots where rocks were sticking above the waters surface, not wanting to tip the canoe over upon hitting one. I'd had hypothermia once before after putting a snowmobile through the ice in mid January 1988, and didn't wish to experience it again. You need to be especially careful when no one is expecting your return and you are the only one in the area.

After making it to the dam, I returned to the van to put on rain gear and then headed for the southern most part of Lake Traverse. There was a major point jutting out from shore with partially submerged rocks extending out about 1000 feet from shore. I stayed well away upon seeing the waves expose rocks on the down swell. Two fishing boats passed going south - first boats I'd seen. There were a few cabins & mobile homes dotting the shore.

My arrival to the south shore completed my goal of going North to South by water! There is less than five miles of land separating southern Lake Traverse from the north side of Big Stone Lake, where I'd been in 1994. I was at the closest point it gets to where water flows either to Lake Winnipeg or to the Gulf!

The wind turned around in my favor with two miles left to go on the return trip, resulting in less spray and decreasing waves. Arriving back at 4:00, I loaded up for the return trip to Lakeville. Just as I was pulling out bread to make a sandwich, a resident living next to the Public Access walked over carrying two Miller Lights and offered good food. Reminiscent of a TV beer commercial line, "It doesn't get any better than this!" Having just completed a major goal, I was in the mood for a celebration.

It was his fourth spring living there and he always put on a party just prior to the opening of fishing season, which was the next day. The fishing season opens two or three weeks sooner on border waters with South Dakota than the rest of the state. I think he was anxious to get the party going when he saw me.

We'd just started to chat and enjoy the feast he'd laid out when a friend of his dropped by. The friend asked how long it had been since he'd hit a cow on the road, being three years. The visitor's dad had hit a cow recently and was trying to get the cow's owner to pay damages. The Insurance Company was fighting it. They were both characters! The visiting farmer said the insurance company's policy was that if a cow gets out once - Act of God - they are not responsible- if they get out more than once they cancel your insurance. It was a Catch 22 situation. The cow, which his father had hit, was not even fenced in, just turned loose in a field. He was getting signatures from neighbors saying that this particular farmer allowed his cows to roam across the highway.

His father hit it at night while heading down a hill close to town. A Sheriff checking speeds saw headlights coming down the hill towards town, and in seeing them disappear, investigated, finding out that the pickup had hit a black cow.

They also talked about the local game warden and his night spotter scope capable of seeing 2-3 miles.

As more people arrived I increasingly felt out of place so I went to a Travis County Park where camping was free.

There were approximately 15 - 20 units there, all with boats getting ready for the fishing opener.

SATURDAY, APRIL 25TH, 1998

I headed home, taking highways I had never been on before, enjoying the spring scenery. Arriving home at 3:00 and feeling lazy I had the boys do most of the unpacking.

SUNDAY, APRIL 26TH, 1998

Midwest Mountaineering had a demonstration day where you could test paddle various kayaks on Lake Nokomis. I tried out a couple and later bought a sea kayak from them.

Bois De Sioux River	30 mile round trip
Mud Lake	12 mile round trip
Lake Traverse	34 mile round trip
Two days on water	76 miles total

1998 BIG HOLE RIVER

In finishing the North - South back in April, I used last year's carry over vacation days. It took special permission from the president of the company to take four weeks in a row for the next long trip.

I spent an enormous amount of time getting and organizing information on the Big Hole, Clark Fork, Pend Oreille, Columbia, Snake, and Yellowstone Rivers. My goal was to take the Big Hole to the Jefferson; thereby boating as much as is possible of the westerly water drainage flowing east and south to the Gulf. Then I would cross over the Continental Divide, pick up the Clark Fork at the shortest distance between it and the Big Hole, and try to boat it as much as possible, figuring to bypass parts of it due to Class IV rapids to the Pend Oreille, which crosses Idaho and flows north in Washington State into Canada where it joins the Columbia, and follow the Columbia to the Pacific. Using any time left; I also had plans to travel significant portions of the Snake and Yellowstone on the way back.

It was an aggressive plan requiring long days on the water and good coordination with Debbie supporting me along the way. On the snowmobile trailer was the sea kayak, canoe, 25 hp Johnson mounted on the Zodiac, 4 hp Johnson bolted to a support board, and four six gallon gas cans. The four of us were packed like sardines in the camper van due to also carrying a fifteen horsepower long shaft four-stroke Honda outboard along with everything else. I had bought the Honda as a backup after breaking the drive shaft on the 25 hp last year, and made a mount for the Zodiac to raise it. The difference between a short shaft and a long shaft motor is about five inches. Most newer boats have a higher transom height to help prevent water coming over the stern. Both the four and twenty-five horse Johnson's are short shaft.

FRIDAY, JUNE 17TH, 1998

We left after I got off work at 11:30 AM, finding a camping spot close to the Big Hole River in western Montana just before dark a day and a half later.

SUNDAY, JUNE 19TH, 1998

Debbie fixed breakfast within the screened enclosure of an old cabin, very helpful since there were a lot of nuisance bugs swarming around. From our about 6000-foot altitude, the morning view of snow capped mountains was absolutely beautiful.

The entire length of the Big Hole River and most of the Clark Fork River does not allow motors. Not wanting to put the Boys at risk paddling the canoe in fast water, I'd purchased the sea kayak. It is more maneuverable and less susceptible to sinking due to the waterproof skirt worn around the body. Paddling around our lake at home, I spent a fair amount of time getting acquainted with the internal foot pedals connected via cables to an external retractable steering rudder at the back. The one thing I hadn't practiced was how to right myself in the event of a rollover. There are ways to use the dual blade paddle to do a complete rollover without capsizing. Being up front and honest, I knew there was no way in Hell once tipped that I wouldn't immediately bail out.

Squaw Creek Access, Mile 82 descending, is a rough and tumble area meant for higher clearance vehicles than ours. We carried the kayak to the Big Hole's river edge where I readied myself for the day. What does ready mean? Well, it means putting on neoprene boots to keep your feet warm and protected from rocks upon entry and exit. It means putting on neoprene gloves to avoid cold hands and aid in gripping the paddle. It means slipping into a waterproof skirt that attaches to the cowling around the opening where you sit. It means dressing for conditions and putting a life jacket on.

Since it seems like I always make a mistake getting started, I got it over quickly by falling in the river while trying to slide into the kayak. Actually I didn't get that wet since I got up very quickly.

The only paddling required in the fast current was to help steer. Debbie videotaped as I wound my way around the wide sweeps of river visible from the highway.

I stopped at Fishtrap Creek, Mile 75, and Sportsman Park, Mile 71.6, and East Bank at Mile 65.2 to touch base with Debbie and the boys.

There are two things I don't like about the kayak; First, once in there is little room to readjust, Second, it is not motorized. Duh! Of course I knew it wasn't motorized when I bought it. That doesn't change the fact I don't like to paddle.

The next stop on the Big Hole River was at Jerry Creek, mile 55.6, elevation 5680', and just below where the Wise River enters. Debbie had prepared sandwiches for the quick stop. Knowing that every day's distance was important to my end goal, I was anxious to press on. As I left the access, something didn't feel right.

I'd forgotten to put my life jacket back on! The swift current prevented me from paddling back upstream to Jerry Creek, so I continued on, reasoning that the river thus far had not been difficult. The next scheduled stop was six miles away at a mandatory portage around the Big Hole Pumping Station. I could have stopped three miles downstream at Dewey, blowing by it before recognizing it as an access.

Almost immediately after passing Dewey, the river narrowed, dropped, and I was in rapids. They were about three feet high separated by about ten feet. While this does not sound like a big deal, the spacing and height were a bad combination. The sea kayak is seventeen foot-long and tapered at both ends with a concave bottom. It is relatively stable when the center is sitting in the water. Picture the kayak supported at the front and back on two different waves, leaving the center unstable. This is exactly what happened and over I went. What a shock being in the cold snowmelt without a life jacket! I quickly exited and made a dumb decision to let the kayak go. The front and rear watertight compartments would have enabled it to float while I held on. With the river only twenty feet wide, I decided to swim for shore. I stroked and stroked not gaining an inch. Panic, swallowing cold water, and swimming all contributed to shortness of breath.

I heard myself yelling I didn't want to die. The thought occurred to me to just stop swimming, tuck my feet up, face downstream, and move only my arms enough to keep my head above water. About a mile from where I'd dumped, the river widened and slowed enough to enable me to grab some brush, halting my downstream float.

While trying to catch my breath, I saw Kevin scrambling down the steep bank on the opposite side yelling, "Dad I've got your life jacket!" Still out of breath, I couldn't respond. I was afraid he was going to jump in and try to swim to me. Finally able to pull myself out, I told Kevin to stay where he was.

Just below me, some men fishing in a raft had caught the kayak as it came through and ferried it and me over to Kevin.

Just after I'd left Jerry Creek, Debbie realized that I'd left my life jacket behind. She and the boys saw the kayak floating upside down through the rapids from the road that closely follows the river. We pulled the kayak up the steep bank and overnighted in the overflow area of a campground.

MONDAY, JUNE 20TH, 1998

During the night I did some serious soul searching. Faced with your own mortality tends to do that. I realized that I didn't know what I was getting myself in for. Being from the Midwest and with most of my prior water experience being somewhat controlled by dams I hadn't come to realize the raw power of water as it descends elevation. Debbie had tried to warn me, with me pooh poohing her as not being adventurous.

While eating breakfast a Montana Fish & Wildlife official intrigued by the variety of watercraft on the snowmobile trailer dropped by. Not knowing about yesterday's experience, he commented that not many sea kayaks came to the area during early summer melt off. This only added to my concern about continuing.

There are two distinctly different types of kayaks. The type I'd bought is designed for open water and the other for white water, being much shorter and wider in the center. I was aware of their differences, not intending to be in white water sections. Having said that, I do not think the standards of classifying rapids are applied the same between the Midwest and the West. It is relative to what you consider the norm. For example a climb for a Midwesterner might start at 1000', whereas in the West you might start at 5000'.

I jokingly told the family that they had tried to do away with me by hiding my life jacket, and on Father's Day! On a more serious tone, I proposed a radical idea. Instead of the proposed river trip plan, change it to be a family non-boating vacation. Other than Debbie questioning me if that was what I really wanted to do, there was zero resistance. I said, "Yes."

Not having been to the Pacific as a family, we wound our way through Montana, stopping at Lewiston, Idaho for the night.

While getting an oil change at a full service drive through, they added fluid to the rear differential. Midway between the Idaho border and an area referred to as the Tri-Cities in Washington State, I stopped so Debbie could videotape. She yelled the van was on fire! I saw smoke rolling from the rear of the van without an actual flame. Returning to the very small town just left, we found a gas station with a limited service bay. A very helpful gentleman using a creeper rolled under the van and using the age-old smell test said we were losing rear end fluid.

Not equipped for that type of repair, he refilled the differential and we continued at a slower speed.

We made it to a Tri-Cities Midas shop, arriving just before closing. The manager allowed us to push the snowmobile trailer into one of the open bays and took us to a nearby motel that accepted pets. As background, the right rear axle was replaced at a Midas just prior to starting the trip. Evidently the shops are locally owned, as it took several phone calls back to the Minnesota Midas to get the OK to replace what turned out to be a defective axle. I must acknowledge that not only did the Minnesota shop cover the cost of repair, but also paid our motel and extra food expense as well.

Two days later, we continued west, somewhat following the Columbia River. The rest of our trip consisted of a whirlwind of different activities and sights.

Some of the highlights along the way were; Hiking the trail to Multnomah Falls in Oregon to the point where it had collapsed preventing our further ascent.

Seeing Mount Saint Helen's volcanic crater in Washington.

Kevin snowboarding Mount Hood, getting a major facial sunburn while doing so.

Traveling the Pacific coastline of Oregon.

Being awestruck by the giant redwoods of northern California.

Debbie and I boating around Lake Tahoe in the Zodiac.

Touring the Mormon Tabernacle and huge open copper pit mine at Salt Lake, Utah.

Attending a rodeo and fireworks display at Steamboat Springs, Colorado on July 4th.

Viewing the beautiful scenery of Rocky Mountain National Park, and almost losing our brakes on the descent.

And seeing the Corn Palace in Mitchell, South Dakota.

1999 COLORADO RIVER (POWELL, MEAD, MOHAVE, HAVASU)

After last years near death experience on the Big Hole River, I was less aggressive in my thinking about future boating adventures. Debbie and I discussed boating in the Southwest. She preferred to stay home: her main objection being the notorious summer heat.

Honoring her thoughts and preserving two weeks vacation time, I left after Debbie returned to school. My broad plan was to travel the Colorado River as much as possible: starting from the upper end of Lake Powell in Utah to where Parker Dam borders California and Arizona. I'd be using The Boat as much as possible, and had the Zodiac and 25 HP Johnson inside the camper van.

FRIDAY, OCTOBER 1ST, 1999

When I left Lakeville at 9:30 AM, the van odometer showed 136,940. Besides pulling The Boat, I also had the Zodiac, two outboard motors, and a lot of miscellaneous paraphernalia, making a full load.

I drove I-35 South, to I-80 West and pulled in around midnight behind a gas station somewhere in western Nebraska to sleep.

SATURDAY, OCTOBER 2ND, 1999

I continued on I-80 through Nebraska, to I-76 in Colorado, picking up I-70, taking it to Hwy 24 south in Utah, connecting to Hwy 95, and then to 276, camping, next to a big gravel pile with two other RV's. It was about 1:00 AM and I was about two miles north of Lake Powell. The reason for detailing the road route taken to reach the upper portion of Lake Powell is to give scope to the 1372-mile distance just to get there.

SUNDAY, OCTOBER 3RD, 1999

Picture falling asleep at home and awakening in an alternate world the next morning. That is how I felt. Instead of seeing the turning leaves of autumn, there were not any trees, except for the few palms next to the marina. Instead of seeing the small lake we live on, there was now a huge expanse of water. Instead of seeing the fall corn harvest in progress, there was now only bare desert or rock bluffs. Arriving under the cover of darkness, the morning's view was just as described.

The National Park Service employee at the visitor center where I bought a lake map was from Wisconsin. He had enjoyed being stationed there and was returning home in two weeks.

Trying to avoid the hurry up and get started mistakes typified by prior trips, I took longer to get organized.

From Bull Frog Marina I went south five miles on Bullfrog Bay to Mile 94, and then headed towards what would have been upstream before the Colorado River was dammed.

My view varied from wide-open expanses to places where canyon walls were quite close and high. Utah 95 crosses over a steel arch bridge at a place called Narrow Canyon. This is the only bridge crossing the Colorado River between Moab, Utah, 75 miles as the crow flies NE, and US 89 at Page, Arizona, 142 river miles SW. The scenery changed drastically as I passed under the bridge. The fact the area is called Narrow Canyon speaks for itself.

Shortly after rounding Mille Crag Bend, ten miles upstream from the bridge, I stopped to help a lady on a disabled PWC. She declined my offer of a tow, deciding instead to use my VHF radio to call her husband for assistance.

Passing a floating sign stating the upper limit of navigation, I continued on an undetermined distance. I went through an area I thought was appropriately named Cataract Canyon, since I could not visually confirm my location.

As the silt laden river became increasingly murkier and narrower, with more and more scrub brush growing along the banks, I decided against proceeding further upstream. It was too early into my planned goal of traveling the major Colorado River Reservoirs to break down due to striking bottom in shallow water.

I bought gas at Hite Marina (Mile 140), and headed back to Bullfrog Bay. It was 4:30 as I videotaped and added gas from a six-gallon container while floating in the wide expanse of the bay. Looking up after refueling, I found myself disorientated. Instead of using my handheld compass to determine position, I headed for the closer of the two visible marinas, which turned out to be southerly Halls Crossing, my expectation being northerly Bullfrog Marina.

In retrospect this was a plus since I had been debating about heading to the dam. Having wasted valuable daylight, and needing to use the van and trailer anyway to continue west, I decided to return to Bullfrog Marina, load up, and drive to Glen Canyon Dam.

I do not claim to be a good navigator, tending to go with a 'gut feeling' rather than looking at maps or instruments. This has not always stood by me in good stead.

There is a ferry crossing between Bullfrog and Hall's Crossing, but I did not check out the cost or their hours of operation. Driving #276 & 95 to Hanksville, then 24 west, to ½ mile past the junction of 62 south, I spent the night parked next to a historical marker sign.

It had been a long day and I had driven somewhat slowly, (40 to 50 mph) due to the unfenced open range livestock grazing area. I saw cattle and deer off on to the side of road six different times, with the altitude varying from Lake Powell's approximate 3700' to a summit of 8406'.

MONDAY, OCTOBER 4TH, 1999

The historical marker memorialized the settlers and Indians of the era who had reached an agreement to co-exist, with the peace never broken.

It got quite chilly during the night, with icicles hanging from irrigation equipment as I drove southwest on Hwy 62 I took a brief tour of Glen Canyon Dam, which included a slide show showing the dam's construction.

Lake Powell & Glen Canyon Dam general info taken from a brochure put out by the U.S. Dept of the Interior Bureau of Reclamation;

Started filling March 13, 1963 and completed initial fill June 22, 1980.

Length of lake is 186 miles.
Miles of shoreline is 1,960 miles.
Depth of water at dam when full is 560 feet.
Height above original river channel is 583 feet.
There are 8 generating units producing 1,296,000 KW.

Driving across U.S. 89 Bridge to Page Arizona, I fueled the boat and van. It was 315 highway miles between Bullfrog and Glen Canyon Dam, with a ninety-four water mile trip one-way trip back to the midpoint between Bullfrog and Halls Crossing Marinas.

I went to Wahweap Marina and Campground, checked out the boat ramps, and got a full RV hookup site for $24 a night, which included hot shower facilities. The non-RV campground was $15, no electricity, and you had to pay $2 for shower. I got site #56 and pored over the Lake Powell chart in preparation for tomorrow's run up the lake.

There is a $5 fee to enter the Glen Canyon National Recreation Area and a $10 fee to use the boat ramps. Both fees cover a seven-day visit. Not aware of the fee at Bullfrog, I paid $15 here.

TUESDAY, OCTOBER 5TH, 1999

There is a major parking area where vehicles and trailers can be left for up to fourteen days. It was 9:30 Central Daylight Saving Time when I left Wahweap boat ramp.

I found Rainbow Bridge National Monument quite by accident. Knowing I was off course, and while looking for navigation markers, saw a floating sign directing the way to Rainbow Bridge. Wanting to go there anyway, I let myself be directed. It is almost a spiritual experience passing through canyon walls while on approach to the Arch itself.

Heading back upriver, I watched the mile marker buoys more closely. Seeing a boat that seemed to know where they were going, I followed. I slowed because they were going faster than the 30 mph pace that I wanted to run at. It was very enjoyable, calm, no boat traffic, no buoys – WAIT – NO BUOYS?

In looking at the map I found out that I was heading up the San Juan River Arm of Lake Powell. Having gone about fifteen miles, with the Arm being about fifty miles long and no fuel facilities, I turned around. While following the boat, I had blown by the buoy announcing entry into the San Juan River. Oh Well, It was certainly pretty and the boat traffic was less.

Back on track meant being back in constantly choppy water. Besides the increased number of boats, another contributing factor to chop was due to waves bouncing off high surrounding rock walls.

I then shot about three miles up the Escalante River Arm!

The Boat had traveled several thousand miles just doing river trips. If you believe an inanimate object can have a personality, then The Boat does. It seems that it just naturally heads up rivers, **Rivers!** Not side channels or canyons, just rivers.

Since there are just the two rivers joining the Colorado River within Lake Powell, The Boat stayed the course the rest of the way to Halls Crossing Marina. The only gas option beside the 50:1 mixture used for two cycle outboards was detergent gasoline priced at $2.12 a gallon compared to the then auto station price of $1.309. Buying just twelve gallons since I still had eighteen gallons in the six-gallon containers aboard, I asked the cashier what time it got dark. She said 7:45. It was 4:30 Minnesota time, so subtracting the one-hour time zone difference, I figured I had four hours to travel the ninety-five miles to the dam and return to the marina before dark. At 30 mph, it would take just over three hours to make the return trip, assuming I would not shoot off into a side canyon, with about an hour to spare.

I stopped numerous times to video and verify course. Around Mile 12 there is a large island called Antelope where one of two routes to reach the southernmost part of Lake Powell can be taken. Having taken the northerly route up, I took the southerly route past Glen Canyon Dam on the way back.

With gas getting low, I was concerned about making it back Wahweap. The return gas mileage was 2/3 of what I had experienced on the way up. I found out later it was due to using detergent gas. Because houseboats consume the vast majority of gas on Lake Powell, detergent gas is sold because that is the best way to protect their heavily loaded engines.

Having mentioned houseboats, I would like to comment what a wonderful area this is to vacation at. Sometime I would like to return and rent a houseboat, accompanied by what I hope will be an extended family. I am looking forward to the boys getting married and being able to spoil grandchildren. Many of the houseboats also pull other boats behind them. I'd seen one towing an I/O, two PWC's, and an aluminum fishing boat.

Upon entering the southerly route, waves changed from a slight chop into actual white caps. The sun increasingly got lower and lower, finally shining directly into my eyes, making navigation difficult. I missed actually seeing the dam even though I passed within 1/8 of a mile of it.

It was to gathering darkness when I arrived back at Wahweap Marina boat ramp. Fortunately, I had not wasted too much time making the return trip; Lake Powell is no place to be on at night unless you are familiar with it.

After loading The Boat, I talked to the owner of a whitewater raft with a 25 hp motor setup who said he ran the Colorado River professionally. He had made a couple of setup changes and was testing it.

I had traveled the reservoir length twice; and look forward to exploring the numerous side canyons on future trips. Returning to Wahweap campground, I asked for and got site #56 again. I called home and finished off two cans of stew, having not eaten all day.

WEDNESDAY, OCTOBER 6TH, 1999

I changed the van battery with one taken from the tractor used to maintain our gravel driveway. The van battery had failed twice and I had had to use the 12-volt portable jumper battery to start it.

While checking out of the campground, I picked up a copy of the daily Lake Powell posting, which is just a single page. The weather forecast was for it to become partly cloudy, with a high of 78 and a low of 55. Sunrise was at 6:23 with sunset at 6:05. Lake level was 3691.21, with surface water temperature being 72 degrees.

I wanted to go to Lee's Ferry, which is a river access with about a fifteen-mile upstream run to Glenn Canyon Dam. Raft trips also start from there to run the Grand Canyon. After climbing to an altitude of about 6,500 feet coming out of Page, Arizona and not knowing how steep Alternate 89 was going back to the river I decided not to. The camper van was already overworked as it was. My next boat put in would be on Lake Mead.

Following Highway 89 South to I 40 West to Kingman, Arizona, I stopped at a Goodyear tire store and bought two boat trailer tires just before they closed. The thirteen-year-old original tires showed signs of weather checking and had an uneven wear pattern. The uneven wear pattern was due to striking a post with the right fender at a boat ramp years earlier when taking a corner too sharp. I didn't think much about it at the time. When I'd taken the boat in for a tune-up before leaving, the mechanic pointed out a problem on the trailer. The U-bolts holding the axle to the frame were pushed back about two inches on the right side, causing the tires to run slightly crooked.

The purpose for sometimes going into more detail than seems necessary is to hopefully educate readers who can learn from my mistakes.

After fueling the van and boat, I headed north on Highway 93 to the Temple Bar exit and drove twenty-eight miles on an asphalt road that meanders and dips through scrub brush to allow for the infrequent rain to flow over it. It was late when I arrived at Temple Bar Campground, midway up Lake Mead's southern side. I self registered and quickly fell asleep.

THURSDAY, OCTOBER 7TH, 1999

Anxious to get started, I awoke early and drove to the marina. While waiting for the marina store to open and buy a good Lake Mead map, I turned on the VHF radio and listened to the weather and boating condition forecasts. Winds were gusting up to 50 mph, with small craft advisory warnings out. I also talked to a National Park Service ranger, who successfully convinced a family from California with a small jet boat having very little freeboard from going out on the water. He told them that he did salvage work on the side, making good money recovering sunken boats like theirs.

Since I'd already prepared the boat, I decided to launch and motor out just past the point of land protecting the cove. It was rough! It didn't make sense to go out in such conditions so I decided to wait at least a day for the weather to change. Just as I loaded the boat, a second red flag was being raised on the pole at the dock indicating a change from small craft advisory to a gale warning.

Las Vegas was just one hundred miles away and with nothing better to do, I headed there. I videotaped Lake Mead and followed Lakeshore Scenic Drive and Lake Mead Boulevard into North Las Vegas. I got an RV site at Circus Circus with the cost being very reasonable considering having pool and shower privileges and easy walking distance to The Strip.

I gambled from 7:00 PM until about 1:00 AM, giving my fair share to keep Las Vegas green.

FRIDAY, OCTOBER 8TH, 1999

After five long days on the road and two on the water, my lack of decent sleep caught up with me. Upon initially awakening, I turned the van's roof A/C up a notch and drifted off for another four or five hours of sleep.

I spent the afternoon looking at the Lake Mead map, swimming in the pool, and generally relaxing. I took in an evening show at the Rivera and walked the strip without gambling until about 2:00 AM. The free Pirate Ship Battle at Treasure Island, and water show to music at the Bellagio were both well worth watching.

SATURDAY, OCTOBER 9TH, 1999

Now fully rested, I launched at 10:00 AM using a very shallow rate drop off ramp at Lake Mead Marina. It was a problem getting the trailer into deep enough water to push The Boat off.

The water temperature was comfortable with the air temperature being about 80 degrees. Before leaving the marina, I talked to a United States Park Service Ranger in a Boston Whaler about the depth of the Colorado River above Temple Bar and the Lower Grand Canyon National Park. In hearing that I would be using a Zodiac inflatable and a 25 HP outboard, he said I shouldn't have problems as the water level was high. He confirmed the distance from Temple Bar to the upper legal limit of navigation of Grand Canyon National Park is about seventy miles.

Arriving by water above Hoover Dam was awesome. As a regular viewer of the History Channel, The Learning Channel, Etc I knew what an effort it had taken to build it.

I turned northwest and followed what would have been the original channel thirty-six miles to Temple Bar, the scene of my wisely aborted trip two days earlier.

About three miles above the dam there must have been at least forty Miami Vice type boats running back and forth across a portion of Lake Mead. There was also a helicopter buzzing overhead following their general course. I waited for a gap in traffic and zipped across.

The run to Temple Bar was uneventful. Not trying to take anything away from Lake Mead's scenic view, it is less dramatic than Lake Powell's. Whereas Lake Powell has a myriad number of places to explore off the main channel, there are just a few on Lake Mead. Instead of seeing the almost intimidating view of Lake Powell's sometimes-sheer cliffs, Lake Mead's mostly distant bluff seemed almost friendly.

While meandering my way back to Lake Mead Marina from Temple Bar, the place where I had been three days earlier, I inadvertently took the long way back. With fuel and daylight not an issue, I paid little attention to navigation markers. I took short stops at Callville Bay Boat Harbor, and Las Vegas Bay Marina to get navigation bearings.

The Boat seemed to enjoy hitting and jumping the other small boat wakes encountered, while I enjoyed the unique scenery.

Upon returning to Lake Mead Marina, I decided to load up at a different ramp from where I'd put in. I tied The Boat about twenty-five feet back from the water's edge to a dock and went to get the trailer. When I got back, there was a guy loading up a thirty-foot Miami Vice type boat right next to where I had to go. Seemingly nonchalant I backed up with relative ease and at a fast pace, keeping about four-foot distance between his trailer and mine. Stopping with the rear van wheels barely touching water I jumped out to winch it up. The boat owner next to me said, "You must have done this before". I didn't initially know what he meant saying, "I've been boating in at least twenty different states". I then saw where the trailer was in relation to the dock and boat. It was **perfect!** I was about three inches from the dock with the right rear fender and the trailer rollers perfectly centered under and touching the keel! It was actually a calculated backup, with me trying to stay 'X' distance away from him.

I drove back to Temple Bar, got a campsite, and prepared for the seventy mile run into the lower end of the Grand Canyon National Park using the Zodiac.

Preparations included charging the camcorder battery, inflating the Zodiac, putting the wheels under it, mounting the 25 HP, and mixing oil with the gas. I was taking twenty-one gallons, spread between three tanks, and one 6-gallon auxiliary container.

SUNDAY, OCTOBER 10TH, 1999

I left the campground for the one-mile drive to the ramp pulling The Boat on its trailer, towing the Zodiac behind. With the water calm, I made good time until missing a right hand bend at Paiute Point, heading into Grand Wash Bay three miles. I backtracked three miles past the initial mistake before figuring out where I was. This resulted in an additional twelve miles to the days run.

Paiute Point is twenty-four miles upstream from Temple Bar, with the area beyond it having shifting sand and mud and houseboats not allowed. Six miles later, I had to put the motor in shallow water drive to get past the delta formed by the silt that drops out as the river hits the reservoir. Just after passing the signage buoy 'Entering Grand Canyon National Park", I encountered current.

My goal was to go upstream until encountering rapids where I would turn around. The view was beautiful with massive colored rock walls veering up both sides. I continued about 30 minutes **past** the point where I had used up half the gas, turning around without seeing rapids.

I met a group on a non-motorized inflatable finishing the typical two-week trip that it takes to float from Lee's Ferry to Pearce Ferry, Mile 66 at Lake Mead. They were having a good time, singing loudly. Tour helicopters were flying about and landing next to the river. There was about three gallons of gas left when I made it back to Temple Bar.

Using previous gas mileage figures the 18 gallons used should have taken me about 150 miles. With the navigation mistake of 12 miles subtracted, I figured I'd gone about 69 miles upstream, 32 of them in Grand Canyon National Park. It was a great trip, in great weather, and in calm water. I deflated the Zodiac, loaded the gear, and drove to Kingman, Arizona where I filled the van, boat, and the 6 six gallon containers.

The Colorado Rivers sixty-six mile distance between Hoover and Davis Dam, known as Lake Mohave, is within the Lake Mead Recreational Area of the National Park Service. Using their brochure as a guide, I drove west on Hwy 68, and arrived at Katherine Landing camping area after dark.

MONDAY, OCTOBER 11TH, 1999

After spending yesterdays long trip in the cramped Zodiac and too lazy to inflate it, I decided to take The Boat, launching from Katherine Landing.

Lake Mojave's length is more like that of a wide river than a reservoir. The six or seven miles just below Hoover Dam had a good current. I ran three or four sets of rapids before getting within sight of the dock where rafters depart from without actually seeing the dam.

I'd seen the same dock earlier from Hoover Dam itself. Still without a depth finder and seeing bottom through the clear clean fast water exiting the turbines I played it safe and turned downstream. I videotaped part of the rapids, and a raft powered by a jet- drive outboard heading upstream. While adding gas, I talked with a guy in a nearby boat whose wife was a teacher. She worked at a year round school, had one month off every three or four, and enjoyed that schedule. The last twenty miles above Davis Dam got increasingly busy with boaters and jet skiers, with many boats pulled up on beaches.

I loaded up and drove to Laughlin, Nevada, where I registered at Riverside RV Park. It was HOT! While gambling at Riverside Casino and throwing around more money than usual, the pit boss asked what he could do for me. I said a free room, which he set up. All I had to do was go to the front desk and register. By the time I decided to call it a night I wouldn't have gotten much use of the room so I slept in the van. I wanted to start Lake Havasu at daylight.

TUESDAY, OCTOBER 12TH, 1999

Daylight found me sleeping in. It was10:00 by the time I launched The Boat from a public ramp, next to Riverside Casino. The bottom was clearly visible but there was sufficient constant depth to run in. In talking to a blackjack dealer last night, he said there were many areas where you had to know the river or you would run aground.

The terrain was flat with many nice houses along the rivers edge the first 15 - 20 miles, especially on the Arizona side.

About five miles north of Lake Havasu City there was a lot of sand along shore and a noticeable increase in river width and a decrease in current. Seeing a boat coming from the right side of an island at high speed, I assumed it was deep. WRONG! Just a quarter-mile past first seeing the oncoming boat, I saw the water was REALLY shallow! The prop started to hit bottom off and on. I reluctantly pulled back the throttle knowing that when I did the boat would settle very quickly as it came off plane. It Stopped Fast And Hard! I went from 30 MPH to a complete stop within thirty feet. This might not seem like a big deal to someone used to driving a car. What caused the quick stop on The Boat was due to dragging the out drive through sand.

With the water only 18 inches deep, it sat at an angle with the lower unit partially holding the stern out of the water. I wish I had videotaped it. At the time, it was not humorous or something I thought I would particularly want to remember. When I initially hit the power trim switch to lift the lower unit, it made kind of a sickening whine with no resulting lift action. It took hitting the switch five or six more times before the sickening whine sound changed and the lower unit actually came up. I pulled The Boat about one-hundred feet, got in, started the motor, and idled to deeper water.

The river became a lake. Not knowing the distance between Davis and Parker Dams, I purposely ran the fuel tank empty to calculate distance, running dry about three miles above Parker Dam. Using prior gas consumption experience, I figured I had gone about seventy-five miles. It was probably further than that considering I had been running with the current for 2/3 of the way.

The upstream view of Parker Dam was typical; I wondered what happened to the outflow. While trying to find gas at Lake Havasu City, I noticed unusually heavy PWC (Personal Water Craft) activity. While asking a Jet Skier where to buy gas, I found out the World Finals for Personal Watercraft Competition was this coming weekend. Fueling at a marina in Lake Havasu City, I went by an on the water treat stand which sold everything from ice to hot dogs to ice cream.

Taking the other side of the island from where I had previously run aground, I still hit bottom, but at a much slower speed and it was only shallow for about fifty feet. Why no warning buoys? Typically, heavily used areas have warnings posted.

Shore camping areas exist below Lake Havasu City, with the eighteen miles above day use area only. Darkness was closing in as I neared Laughlin so the flashing casino neon lights made it a pretty sight.

As I loaded up in semi-darkness, a thought occurred to me. Maybe I could still get the free room passed on last night. The desk clerk made two phone calls. A half hour later I was in a room with an excellent view of the river and soaking in a whirlpool bathtub. I went out on the town until 7:00 AM, having a very good time while not winning any money.

WEDNESDAY, OCTOBER 13TH, 1999

After only three hours of sleep and being kicked out by the cleaning staff, I headed home. The drive on I-40 has a more varied landscape than you might expect. My day ended at 8:30 when I camped behind an abandoned gas station close to the New Mexico border.

THURSDAY, OCTOBER 14TH, 1999

The crossing into New Mexico completed my being in all of the lower 48 states within six years. I'd received a puzzle of the US while having rheumatic fever and it gave me a sense of satisfaction having visited all of them in the same vehicle. I stopped at Albuquerque to visit Debbie's sister, Chris, between her appointments as a speech therapist. Continuing on I-40 East to I-25 North I arrived at Colorado Springs to visit my sister Jean. While having my first decent meal in almost two weeks, we caught up on happenings since last talking.

FRIDAY, OCTOBER 15TH, 1999

Hwy 24 to I-70 into Kansas was very windy. One gust pushed me to the side of road where rumble strips or road debris caused the right rear tire to blow. The outer portion of the tire separated and wrapped itself around the axle and brake drum. I had a hard time prying it off and I was concerned that the wind from passing semis would cause the van to fall off the jack. The spare seemed low so I inflated it more with a 12-volt compressor. Taking the next exit north I went two miles to a service station where I had a front tire switched to the rear since it was more suitable to the load carried.

At Hays, Kansas I stopped at a Pennzoil Quick Lube for a needed oil change. Just as it got dark with a light rain falling, I encountered a major road construction project diverting traffic into a single lane just outside of Kansas City, Kansas. My long hours of boating, highway driving and night life caught up to me as the flashing lights became a bewildering obstacle course. Fortunately, I found a rest stop to sleep at.

SATURDAY, OCTOBER 16TH, 1999

After leaving the rest area and connecting with I-35 North, I considered myself on the home stretch. I once again stopped at Jim Hansen's place in Indianola, Iowa.

Jim was with me on my first ever river trip. I don't know who suggested or planned the weekend, but it was not well done. Five of us in two canoes left Ledges State Park on the Des Moines River on a September Friday evening intending to camp along the bank and make Des Moines sometime Sunday. Since there were an odd number of people, it made sense that one canoe would carry more cargo than the other. Jim and I were in the canoe carrying the unprotected sleeping bags and most of the five cases of beer. To this day we still argue about who stood up to relieve themselves, tipping the canoe over in the process. In any case, we agreed the group stood in the middle of the river and searched for loose beer cans as they rolled downstream, recovering most of them. Then after establishing camp and trying to dry out the soaked sleeping bags over a roaring fire, we came to the consensus that we'd already had enough of camping and canoeing.

With darkness approaching, we threw everything back in the canoes and paddled to the first bridge we came to. We then hitched a ride in the back of a pickup to a nearby bar where Jim called Genie, his girlfriend and future wife, to come pick us up. We must have been a sight while waiting outside in our muddy and disheveled condition. The five of us squeezed into her Mustang along with the girlfriend accompanying her making it a tight fit. We returned the next day, picked up the rented sleeping bags, tent, and canoes, and were not refunded the deposit since everything was returned wet and dirty. This was a rather inauspicious beginning to my water trips.

Now with 141,359 miles on the van, I returned home at 6:00 PM, putting 4,417 miles on the van and 848 boat miles.

2000 YELLOWSTONE RIVER

Dissatisfied with my job for a number of reasons, I planned to give appropriate termination notice and take the summer off to further river tripping goals.

I wanted to go east to complete the gap from the last lock on the Allegheny to the Atlantic, then start back west. I'd spent many Friday afternoons calling numerous helpful people, receiving a lot of correspondence enabling me

to put together a viable plan.

The eastern route, though not the order to be taken in, consisted of the Allegheny, Conewango, Cassadaga, Chadakoin Rivers, Lake Chautauqua, ten miles of land, seventy miles of Lake Erie, Erie Canal, and the Hudson River to New York City.

The western route plan was fluid, based on water level and flow rates upon completing the eastern portion. Knowing some areas were unsafe to attempt on my own, I'd gathered information about local guides. Using what we'd learned while transiting the highway route along the Columbia two years ago, I updated plans.

With a picture of the World Trade Center Towers hanging in my cubicle to get me through to the day when I would quit, my boss called me into her office knowing I was unhappy. We had a frank discussion, and were on track to resolving our differences when a major unexpected event occurred.

On May 3rd, after sharpening the blades on my older riding lawn mower, I set out to mow the yard. In reversing to position for an incline, then putting it in forward while still rolling backward, the front end came off the ground throwing me off backwards. The mower balanced on its back tires, did a 180-degree turn, and dropped where I was still lying. Instinctively putting up my right hand with fingers extended, they were then cut off several times at various lengths. Fortunately, the impact of my hand being hit also rolled me out of the way as the mower finished coming down. **Man did that hurt!**

Debbie was at a center serving meals for the disadvantaged. Nate and Joey, a young neighbor, were just out of sight jumping on the trampoline. I managed to walk up the hill while trying to stem the flow of blood with my right hand. I yelled at Nate to call 911 and for Joey to see if Jan, our next-door neighbor and retired nurse, was home. Jan immediately got a towel to wrap my hand in. Surprisingly the bleeding had already stopped with minimal loss.

Since this book is about boating and not the medical profession I won't go into details, but suffice to say it dramatically altered summer plans. Because my occupation requires fast and accurate keyboarding, and due to having paid extra to upgrade the standard company short and long term disability policies, I never returned to work.

Between surgical operations and therapy, we took Kevin back to Montana State for his sophomore year with Debbie and me stopping at Gardiner, Montana, the northern gateway entrance to Yellowstone National Park. We made reservations with Yellowstone Raft Company for a rafting trip the following day and camped on a bluff overlooking the Yellowstone River.

It was chilly when we checked in for the 17 ½-mile raft trip, during which the altitude would drop about 1000 feet. Besides the oarsman, two charter pilots on a layover accompanied us. The flow rate was about as low as it ever gets due to a less than average snowfall and the time of year. Our starting point was just outside of Yellowstone National Park with the first 1 ½ miles classified as whitewater but tame due to the low flow rate.

Our guide did a good balance of pointing out areas of interest and just letting us enjoy the view. Midway through the day we enjoyed a shore lunch. The last four and one half miles took us through Yankee Jim Canyon. A rafter needs to be knowledgeable how to approach it during different water stages or it can flip a raft.

Taking out at Carbella, we'd thoroughly enjoyed the day. Even though the Yellowstone River was not part of the east-west planned route, I now felt compelled to follow it to the junction of the Missouri.

One day 17 ½ miles.

Our guide did a good balance of pointing out areas of interest and just letting us enjoy the view. Midway through the day we enjoyed a shore lunch. The last four and one half miles took us through Yankee Jim Canyon. A rafter needs to be knowledgeable how to approach it during different water stages or it can flip a raft.

Taking out at Carbella, we'd thoroughly enjoyed the day. Even though the Yellowstone River was not part of the east-west planned route, I now felt compelled to follow it to the junction of the Missouri.

One day 17 ½ miles.

On May 3rd, after sharpening the blades on my older riding lawn mower, I set out to mow the yard. In reversing to position for an incline, then putting it in forward while still rolling backward, the front end came off the ground throwing me off backwards. The mower balanced on its back tires, did a 180-degree turn, and dropped where I was still lying. Instinctively putting up my right hand with fingers extended, they were then cut off several times at various lengths. Fortunately, the impact of my hand being hit also rolled me out of the way as the mower finished coming down. **Man did that hurt!**

Debbie was at a center serving meals for the disadvantaged. Nate and Joey, a young neighbor, were just out of sight jumping on the trampoline. I managed to walk up the hill while trying to stem the flow of blood with my right hand. I yelled at Nate to call 911 and for Joey to see if Jan, our next-door neighbor and retired nurse, was home. Jan immediately got a towel to wrap my hand in. Surprisingly the bleeding had already stopped with minimal loss.

Since this book is about boating and not the medical profession I won't go into details, but suffice to say it dramatically altered summer plans. Because my occupation requires fast and accurate keyboarding, and due to having paid extra to upgrade the standard company short and long term disability policies, I never returned to work.

Between surgical operations and therapy, we took Kevin back to Montana State for his sophomore year with Debbie and me stopping at Gardiner, Montana, the northern gateway entrance to Yellowstone National Park. We made reservations with Yellowstone Raft Company for a rafting trip the following day and camped on a bluff overlooking the Yellowstone River.

It was chilly when we checked in for the 17 ½-mile raft trip, during which the altitude would drop about 1000 feet. Besides the oarsman, two charter pilots on a layover accompanied us. The flow rate was about as low as it ever gets due to a less than average snowfall and the time of year. Our starting point was just outside of Yellowstone National Park with the first 1 ½ miles classified as whitewater but tame due to the low flow rate.

19

2001 CHADAKAKOIN, CASSADAGA, CONEWANGO, ALLEGHENY

Since last fall, I'd had three operations done to my hand, one a procedure to lengthen what remained of the thumb. I'll describe it only because I think it's interesting. First, the skin is opened, exposing the bone. Then the bone was separated by drilling through it. Two pins were screwed into both sides of the separated bone and attached to a device that holds everything together, but slightly apart. My job was to use a wrench and turn the device a quarter turn twice daily to further separate the bone. The bone grew back from both sides. Talk about painful! I would take a pain pill one-half hour before turning and crank the stereo up just before turning so I could not hear myself moan with pain. Over a period of six weeks my thumb palm bone was 1 ¼ inch longer, enabling me to have a pinching ability, not possible before. Within a week of removing the lengthening device, I broke my 'new' thumb and wore a split until the break healed.

After a less than an enjoyable winter and basically unable to use my right hand due to the splint, I wanted an adventure. Considering the laughable distance covered last year, this years goal was equivalent to the Wright Brothers saying after their first flight they wanted to land on the moon twenty years later.

MONDAY, JUNE 25TH, 2001

Debbie, Nate, and I left Lakeville at 6:45 AM. I drove the camper van pulling The Boat carrying all of our clothes, food, and camping gear. Debbie drove the Ford Aeorstar pulling the snowmobile trailer carrying the canoe on the overhead rack, inflated Zodiac with the 25 HP Johnson, and inside the Aerostar van was the 4 HP Johnson for the canoe, 15 HP Honda, and whatever we could not find a place for. I'd put in a back lit compass and paid to have a through hull depth finder installed in The Boat. Kevin was working a summer job and stayed home, taking care of the lawn and dog.

Our arrival to Chicago on I-90 was in the midst of rush hour traffic. We were trying to stay together, with me in the camper van taking the lead. Debbie fell behind, passing by where I was waiting outside a tollbooth because she was unable to pull over. It was half an hour before we caught sight of each other. And when we did, I was in the express lane with Debbie using local traffic lanes, separated by concrete dividers. I breezed by with her waving in acknowledgment of seeing me. She caught up ten miles before we took the South Bend Indiana exit. Debbie's parents had a meal of salad, turkey, and sweet corn ready for us. Who knew how long it would be before we ate such a feast again? Better eat up!

We left the Aeorstar and The Boat there, taking the snowmobile trailer and camper for the first part of this trip. Of course this required totally rearranging and switching trailers.

The first phase is to boat Chadakakoin Creek from where it leaves Lake Chautauqua in western New York about three miles to where it joins Cassadaga Creek, follow it for eight miles to where it joins the Conewango River, be on it for twenty-five miles to where it joins the Allegheny River and follow it to Lock 9, about 118 miles later. The approximate total one-way distance is 143 miles.

I had spent many hours researching and gathering the material needed to accomplish this trip during the winter of 1999/2000.

TUESDAY, JUNE 26TH, 2001

Leaving South Bend at 6:15, we picked up I-90 toll road to Pennsylvania, then I-80, and meandered byways that headed south to check out Brady's Bend on the Allegheny River. Our goal was to check out the most logical water access points to meet along the way, doing so in reverse order, south to north, so we'd end up at our starting point.

The roads to Brady's Bend were a lot like the ones traveled in West Virginia during our family vacation in 1995. It was slow driving on narrow winding roads. The brakes would heat up going downhill, and I used low gear to go uphill. I pulled over and let traffic by whenever the opportunity arose.

Shortly after stopping for an ice cream cone break at a wayside country store, a small deer darted across the road. I swerved to avoid, with the trailer still hitting it. I'd been peering at the Allegheny flowing by through trees that almost met overhead. I saw from my rear view mirror that its back legs were broke as it tried to crawl off the road. It seems strange that the back and not the front legs were broke as it had been running towards me and was hit on the driver's side, but that is the way it was. I pulled into a roadside rest a short distance away and looked for a knife to cut the deer's throat since there was no way it could survive with two broken legs. A car heading south also stopped. Hearing what I first thought to be firecrackers turned out to be the guy in the stopped car shooting at it with a handgun! Missing the first three times, he ran down the ditch and put a bullet in its head. Meanwhile his car was on the narrow two-lane highway, driver door open, with vehicles swerving around it.

After encountering unknown dams on the Red River in 1997 and not wanting to be surprised again, I investigated the three small rivers we would be boating. I contacted a Pennsylvania Department Conservation officer based out of North Warren Pennsylvania, who in turn called The U.S. Corp of Engineers, about potential dams. The Corp said there were two, one at the southern outlet of Lake Chautauqua, and one in Warren 'just past the Middle School and just upstream from Burger King'. We checked out the one in Warren so I would recognize it heading downstream.

We camped at Hidden Valley in Jamestown, New York.

WEDNESDAY JUNE 27TH, 2001

Happy 15th Birthday Nate! We checked out McCrea Point Park as a possible launching spot for The Boat to travel the length of Lake Chautauqua for phase II.

The thirty foot across dam at the southern outlet of the lake is just downstream from a power plant with water dropping about five feet or so.

Two hundred feet downstream is a street bridge that crosses Chadakoin Creek with a Chinese Buffet restaurant right next to the creek. It was too early for it to be open, so we hurriedly carried the canoe across their lawn, mounted the four horse, and loaded gear. A guy walking by stopped to talk, telling us that at Buffalo Street was a dangerous dam, and that the creek then went underneath a building. I was totally unaware of their existence. So much for all my prep work!

Nate and I were off. Debbie met us at Buffalo Street and helped do an easy portage around the dam. There was plenty of clearance to go underneath the building spanning the creek, but not much depth. Debbie videotaped as we bounced off exposed rocks and kept hitting bottom.

It continued to be shallow so we were constantly getting in and out, pushing, and pulling the canoe. One time as I jumped in, the canoe bottomed out and I fell in. Nate thought it was just hilarious! Shortly after, he jumped in one side, slipped, and fell out the other! It was my turn to laugh.

Our arrival at the junction of Chadakoin and Cassadaga was to log jams and downed trees! We encountered at least ten distinct logjams. Sometimes it was an easy portage up and over, or easily bypassed by scaling the slippery bank and pulling the canoe behind us.

One logjam in particular needs the details told. It was an especially big one with steep vertical heavily brushed banks on both sides. The current ran too fast to get in the waters unpredictable depth sweeping underneath. Not wanting to be pulled down and trapped under logs, I decided the best way was up and over the ten-foot high jam.

With my back to the jam, since I could only use my left hand, Nate and I were pulling the canoe up at about a 45-degree angle when it hung up. The back started filling with water and was being pulled down by current. Trying to hold the canoe in place, and thinking the problem was a couple of small branches, I told Nate to break them off.

"Dad they're not going to break!" With my patience and strength both on the short side, I told him again to break them off! "Just look and you'll see what I mean." Managing a look behind me, Nate was absolutely correct. What I had thought to be branches were in fact six to eight inch limbs lying horizontal. By sliding the back of the canoe around we managed to tie it out of the water and formulate a plan.

By putting the bow under the offending 'branches,' we slid the canoe through. This sounds much easier that it was, and in the process we broke off the four-horse shift lever while in forward gear. Fortunately the motor does not have a safety feature and starts in gear.

At some unrecognizable point, we joined the Conewango where logjams turned into an occasional downed tree blocking our path. I would take a run at it, and tip the motor up as we went over. They don't build canoes that take that kind of abuse anymore.

Near the end of the day, we met Debbie at a bridge close to Frewsburg, New York, covering about fifteen water miles, but only five as the crow flies. We were only two miles away from Hidden Valley campground, so we checked back in. I was pooped, while Nate still had enough energy left to swim in the pool.

THURSDAY, JUNE 28TH, 2001

A vise grip clamped to the broken shifter made a good temporary fix. Starting off from Frewsburg, Nate and I made it to Tidioute Borough. This is a Pennsylvania Fish & Boat Commission boat ramp on the Allegheny River about twenty miles downstream from where the Conewango joins. There had been six dam/water spillways before reaching the Allegheny when I'd expected two. It had been shallow with the going slow, but no logjams. We spent the night at Eagles Campground in Tionesta.

FRIDAY, JUNE 29TH, 2001

Putting back in at Tidioute Borough, Nate and I traveled fifteen miles in three hours to Tionesta where we met Debbie. Other than depth being unpredictable, it was uneventful.

Our next meeting spot would be at Oil City. Debbie had been reading a book I'd purchased as a resource and noticed there were Class II rapids as you entered Oil City. She videotaped us from a bridge as I picked a course through the boulder field and fast water using the 4hp to steer. It was eight blocks back to the boat ramp where she'd parked the van and trailer, so Debbie rode in the canoe with us to the ramp.

It was 3:00 as we ate lunch and decided the final stop for the day would be at the town of Kennerdell, twenty-five more miles. Debbie expressed concern about roads as we were getting back into the steep and winding part of Pennsylvania where the brakes had heated up before. I said just don't push it and it will be OK.

Nate and I started to see lots of fishing boats, most equipped with jet drive outboards instead of props. Just after passing through faster water, not rapids, and around the tip of an island we met a boat powered by a 90 HP jet drive. The operator asked if it was safe to go upstream. In hearing I'd made it without touching bottom and that I only needed a foot of water, he roared upstream.

We met Debbie at Charlie Meyer's boat ramp on the east side of the Allegheny at the bottom of a steep drive just above a high bridge crossing the river. I asked at the house at the top of the drive where Debbie had paid a $3 ramp fee if we would owe an additional $3 tomorrow morning. No, it was an unload/load combination.

Using the AAA campground guide, we found a campsite at Kennerdell.

SATURDAY, JUNE 30TH, 2001

While backing down the long ramp at Charlie's at 8:30, a jeep followed me down. It turned out to be Charlie.

Thinking I was in trouble for not paying the launch fee, No, he just wanted to know long we would use the ramp.

Charlie ran a marine repair shop across the street and wanted to test drive a boat just fixed.

I told him where we had started from Tuesday and about some of the boat trips taken. Charlie observed my missing fingers, which somehow led to the story of how he had almost drowned the year before.

Charlie acquired a WW II amphibious landing vehicle (DUCK) and spent about 1,000 hours rehabbing it. Taking it on its maiden voyage, he put in on the high fast Allegheny River at his ramp, with his son-in-law and another friend aboard. They were quickly swept downstream about a quarter mile to a bridge support work site. The DUCK got catawampus when the front hit one side of the narrowed channel protection barriers and the back swung around hitting the opposite side, effectively blocking the current. The overhead construction crew lifted his son-in-law and friend, but was unable to get to Charlie before the current rolled the DUCK over. A construction worker threw a life jacket and jumped in to save Charlie. It was about eight foot deep at the time and The DUCK sank upside down just below the bridge. Two days later the construction crew raised it with their crane. It was at Charlie's shop with a few holes awaiting repair.

The ten-mile stretch above Brady's Bend was visually hard to see if it was shallow due to black rocks. I wondered if the black came from being one of the first petroleum areas of the nation and settled residue. I don't know the answer.

Arriving at Brady's Bend we loaded the canoe, and unloaded the Zodiac to travel the fourteen mile round trip to Lock and Dam 9. A major thunderstorm interrupted the boat exchange for an hour.

The three of us made the run to the lock where Debbie and I had been on the other side of in 1994.

We stayed overnight at Gaslight Campground in Emlenton, Pennsylvania, right next to I-80. They very specifically told us to stay on the gravel path as the recent heavy rainfall had left the ground very soft. Another big thunderstorm rolled through right after dinner.

SUNDAY, JULY 1ST, 2001

A six-hour drive put us back in South Bend. Besides returning for The Boat Debbie's brother from Texas and sister and brother-in-law from New Mexico were due to arrive since we'd left.

MONDAY, JULY 2ND, 2001

It was Socializing, Reorganization and Regrouping Day. I switched The Boat trailer back to the camper van, and left unneeded items either in the Aeorstar or on the snowmobile trailer. Debbie did laundry and organized her part of Phase II. Both of us had a good time getting caught up with the relatives.

Due to timing issues, I tried to sleep while the rest of the group enjoyed a home fireworks show. We left at 10:30 PM and I drove all night to Buffalo, New York.

2001 BUFFALO TO TROY TO NYC TO ALBANY NEW YORK

TUESDAY, JULY 3RD, 2001

D riving all night from South Bend, Indiana following I-80 & I-90, I stopped to check out a boat launch at Barcelona, New York on Lake Erie around 6:30 AM.

It is time to outline Phase II goals. From Barcelona heading south, I would have ten miles of land and about twenty-five miles of Lake Chautauqua to travel before reaching where Nate and I started down the Chadakoin six days ago. From Barcelona going east, I would have seventy miles of Lake Erie to Buffalo New York, picking up the Niagara River, to the Erie Canal, to the Hudson River and New York City.

Back to Barcelona; the person collecting the boat ramp fee said to stay off Lake Erie if winds were northeast as the lake can change character within ten minutes. He also said to stay away from shore and come into the harbor through the north opening, not the sides.

With wind and waves high, and not knowing where to meet in Buffalo if I left by boat, we drove to Buffalo. Tourist information signs led us downtown. We pulled into a church parking lot and saw a young man in a security uniform. Thinking he must be the guard for the church, I approached and asked if we could park there while visiting the tourist information center two blocks away. It turns out he was a night security guard for the building where the tourist information center is housed, and was just waiting for a city bus. The information center would not open for an hour so we drove around, and in seeing signs giving directions to Naval Park and Marina, followed them.

The Naval Park had a couple big ships at the dock and the marina's name was Erie Basin Marina – they have a security guard house and charge $5.00 for the public to launch. This is a city owned facility with at least two hundred slips rented out on a seasonal basis. Briefly explaining about wanting to leave the camper van and trailer for two to three weeks, the guard said to ask Chris, the harbormaster. Chris was not in his office at the end of the breakwater so a maintenance worker radioed to find him. Driving to where he was supposed to be, and finding a group of city workers, I asked the most senior looking if he was Chris, "No", who then pointed him out. Chris was quite young, and in telling of our trip plans and asking if we could leave the camper van and trailer there for an extended period, he said it was okay as long as we obtained a parking permit from the marina store. I asked directions to get to the Erie Canal, with Chris suggesting buying a chart they normally carry, but were temporality out of.

Chris penciled directions to West Marine where we bought NOAA Chart #14833 and a fifty-dollar season pass for the New York Canal system. The West Marine cashier said security is good at Erie Basin, where he occasionally pilots a catamaran. On the way back we fueled The Boat with 'cheap' gas.

We then stopped at the Erie Basin Marina store and asked Ed, the store clerk, about getting the required parking permit. There was confusion about the cost of and how long a parking pass is good for, then by special permission our 'Temporary Parking Pass' was free. Initially written for July 3rd, through July 19th, and afraid it might take longer, I asked Ed to change it to be through July 26th. Ed changed it to July 30th to be on safe side. While buying ice, I asked Ed what VHF channel Black Rock Lock monitored. He was unsure but said a Coast Guard cutter moored just outside giving a tour of their boat would know.

Nate and I really enjoyed taking the excellent tour of the Coast Guard boat, learning about the specialized equipment carried and their purpose. With watertight hatches in place, the boat can do a complete roll and come back up OK. They said to call Black Rock Lock on channel 16 and after making contact switch to 12.

It took a while to pack the following in some organized manner; three sleeping bags, pillows, Coleman cooking stove with extra propane canisters, life jackets, throwable boat cushions, rain gear, tools, safety kit (containing first aid supplies, three kinds of flares, whistles, extra fuses, etc), two anchors, VHF radio, backlit compass, searchlight, box of music cassettes, two extra props, spare starter & alternator, jumper battery, extra rope, boat fenders, two coolers, camcorder, 35 mm camera, enough clothes & towels for at least two weeks stuffed into a Duluth pack, & numerous misc. items.

I mounted the 15 hp Honda on the auxiliary motor bracket and attached its starter cables to the boat battery. Part of the preparations before leaving home included buying two 11-gallon portable gas containers on small plastic wheels called 'Gas Pals' to replace the smelly, leaky, six gallon containers.

With the van and trailer left parked within 150 feet of the twenty-four hour security guard post, parking pass hanging from the rearview mirror, I never gave them a thought the rest of the trip.

We were on our way! It was choppy as we approached Black Rock Lock, even though somewhat protected from Lake Erie by the Outer Harbor seawall. The lockage went quickly and we were soon on the Niagara River. It is about seven miles from the lock to the entrance of the Erie Canal, which we missed due to the exuberance of starting another adventure. I should have been on the right side of the river as we approached Tonawanda Island, but was in the center channel just taking in the sights. Oh Well, I hung a turn around the north side of the island and found the entrance to the Erie Canal by heading south. At least we did not continue on and make headlines by going over Niagara Falls.

The first speed limit sign read six mph, with ten mph being the normal speed limit on most of the canal system. The depth finder read a constant twelve feet while passing through the very early part of the canal. Planning for the Erie Canals 338 mile length, thirty-three locks, fifteen lift bridges, and numerous Guard Gates came from several sources. A Guard Gate is like an enormous guillotine, except the 'blade' is not angled or sharp and its purpose is to plug the flow of water in the event of a lock failure.

Having bought "The Cruising Guide to the New York State Canal System", I made two subsets of the information gathered. The first subset detailed the distance between locks, their normal rise or fall, and the typical time it takes to travel between each based on having to wait for bridge lifts and speed limits. The second subset noted the availability of gas and overnight facilities. Not knowing the minimum clearance, I hoped to pass under most of the bridges due to our low height. I will not detail passing through all the locks and under the lift bridges in the system, while mentioning some.

The first lock, appropriately called Lockport, is actually two, E34/E35. They share a common gate and lower fifty feet as you head east. Do not let the high number of E35 mislead, as there is no lock E31 or E1. Wanting to check the reliability of my marina information, I went to Nelson C. Goehle Marine Park, after exiting Locks E34/E35 and passing under two bridge lifts, and couldn't find an attendant. I asked the operator of the third Lift Bridge about gas availability. "Gasport" and a good place to spend the night would be at Middleport where dockage along the canal wall was by donation.

Nate drove while I slept in the bow, having driven most of the night with only a two-hour nap in South Bend interrupted by nieces & nephews. Nate slowed while passing though a large boat wake that rocked and rolled the boat, waking me up with a start.

Stopping at Gasport Marina, it took two phone calls made by a seasonal tenant to track down the marina operator, who then unlocked the fuel pump and sold us gas.

It was late when we arrived at Middleport and tied up to the lock wall at the far end of a city park. Looking for a bathroom, I asked a couple walking by where one might be. They pointed towards the back of a large maintenance building with a light shining over its entrance. I used it, and pointed the bathroom light out to Nate. He came back after not finding the bathroom, seeing an ambulance in a garage. I walked Nate to the correct building and door. Nate then pointed out sources. A Guard Gate is like an enormous guillotine, except the 'blade' is not angled or sharp and its purpose is to plug the flow of water in the event of a lock failure.

Having bought "The Cruising Guide to the New York State Canal System", I made two subsets of the information gathered. The first subset detailed the distance between locks, their normal rise or fall, and the typical time it takes to travel between each based on having to wait for bridge lifts and speed limits. The second subset noted the availability of gas and overnight facilities. Not knowing the minimum clearance, I hoped to pass under most of the bridges due to our low height. I will not detail passing through all the locks and under the lift bridges in the system, while mentioning some.

The first lock, appropriately called Lockport, is actually two, E34/E35. They share a common gate and lower fifty feet as you head east. Do not let the high number of E35 mislead, as there is no lock E31 or E1. Wanting to check the reliability of my marina information, I went to Nelson C. Goehle Marine Park, after exiting Locks E34/E35 and passing under two bridge lifts, and couldn't find an attendant. I asked the operator of the third Lift Bridge about gas availability. "Gasport" and a good place to spend the night would be at Middleport where dockage along the canal wall was by donation.

Nate drove while I slept in the bow, having driven most of the night with only a two-hour nap in South Bend interrupted by nieces & nephews. Nate slowed while passing though a large boat wake that rocked and rolled the boat, waking me up with a start.

Stopping at Gasport Marina, it took two phone calls made by a seasonal tenant to track down the marina operator, who then unlocked the fuel pump and sold us gas.

It was late when we arrived at Middleport and tied up to the lock wall at the far end of a city park. Looking for a bathroom, I asked a couple walking by where one might be. They pointed towards the back of a large maintenance building with a light shining over its entrance. I used it, and pointed the bathroom light out to Nate. He came back after not finding the bathroom, seeing an ambulance in a garage. I walked Nate to the correct building and door. Nate then pointed out purpose. With watertight hatches in place, the boat can do a complete roll and come back up OK. They said to call Black Rock Lock on channel 16 and after making contact switch to 12.

It took a while to pack the following in some organized manner; three sleeping bags, pillows, Coleman cooking stove with extra propane canisters, life jackets, throwable boat cushions, rain gear, tools, safety kit (containing first aid supplies, three kinds of flares, whistles, extra fuses, etc), two anchors, VHF radio, backlit compass, searchlight, box of music cassettes, two extra props, spare starter & alternator, jumper battery, extra rope, boat fenders, two coolers, camcorder, 35 mm camera, enough clothes & towels for at least two weeks stuffed into a Duluth pack, & numerous misc. items.

I mounted the 15 hp Honda on the auxiliary motor bracket and attached its starter cables to the boat battery. Part of the preparations before leaving home included buying two 11-gallon portable gas containers on small plastic wheels called 'Gas Pals' to replace the smelly, leaky, six gallon containers.

With the van and trailer left parked within 150 feet of the twenty-four hour security guard post, parking pass hanging from the rearview mirror, I never gave them a thought the rest of the trip.

We were on our way! It was choppy as we approached Black Rock Lock, even though somewhat protected from Lake Erie by the Outer Harbor seawall. The lockage went quickly and we were soon on the Niagara River. It is about seven miles from the lock to the entrance of the Erie Canal, which we missed due to the exuberance of starting another adventure. I should have been on the right side of the river as we approached Tonawanda Island, but was in the center channel just taking in the sights. Oh Well, I hung a turn around the north side of the island and found the entrance to the Erie Canal by heading south. At least we did not continue on and make headlines by going over Niagara Falls.

The first speed limit sign read six mph, with ten mph being the normal speed limit on most of the canal system. The depth finder read a constant twelve feet while passing through the very early part of the canal. Planning for the Erie Canals 338 mile length, thirty-three locks, fifteen lift bridges, and numerous Guard Gates came from several the bathroom door light to Debbie, who misunderstood and ended up under a light pole in an alley next to a bar. She finally found it. I warned her to not to shut off the light switch on the inside as it controlled the light on the outside. It is an overlong description of such a simple thing as finding a bathroom, but it goes to show that every stop requires an orientation process, especially in the dark.

WEDNESDAY, JULY 4TH, 2001

I filled one of the 'Gas Pals' with ten gallons at $1.63 a gallon and returned with milk and ice.

The Boat was able to go under the Middleport and Medina lift bridges, with the canal then crossed **over** Oak Creek seventy feet below.

Culvert Road, about 2 ¾ mile east of Medina, we passed over the only road passing **under** the Erie Canal, being built in 1923. Tying the boat to a tree, we went down the hill, under the canal, and up the opposite side. The bridge/tunnel seeped water, but seemed well built.

Continuing on we then passed under the Knowlsville Rd Lift Bridge with just three inches to spare, but could not get under the bridges at Albion. The bridge lift operator could not figure where we had come from since we had cruised under the last three lift bridges. By way of explanation, sometimes one person operates multiple lift bridges, driving between them as boats proceed. Others send a message ahead to the next lift operator.

Between Holly and Spencerport, I met a large boat going too fast, causing a huge wake to crest over the bow where Debbie was napping. Initially not a happy camper, she quickly found humor in the situation and laughed. I turned on the bilge pump and it ran for quite a while. The experiences for the bow occupant have gradually gotten worse. Me being bounced around but not wet, then Debbie getting half soaked. Nate was now afraid a bad wake would throw him out, although he did finally fall asleep in the bow. We videotaped as he awoke with a start upon hitting the first major wake. While The Boat has seating for six behind the windshield, only two places were open due to the load carried. If a third person sits behind the windshield, it has to be on a cooler between the driver and the passenger seat immediately across the aisle.

Rochester, New York has many bridges passing over the canal, while the canal has a bridge crossing over the Genesee River. River traffic was almost non-existent considering it was the Fourth of July.

After locking through E33 & E32 and hearing Fairport has an excellent ice cream parlor, we pushed on arriving at 8:30.

The riverfront of Fairport was that of an idyllic picturesque – almost like Twilight Zone- atmosphere. The canal reflected the street, lift bridge, and seawall lights. In viewing the townhouses across the canal, we never saw anyone go in or out, nor do any lights go on or off.

Choosing not to dock between nice large cruisers, we continued east to the dead end of the public walkway tying up just ten feet away from picnic tables. It was not as private as it sounds since people still intently watched from a nearby bridge while we ate and set up for the night. The cost was only $4.00, with bathrooms and a shower close by.

After buying large ice cream cones, we watched fireworks from the Parker Street Bridge right above The Boat.

Unfortunately we were next to the only boat running its A/C, making sleeping a little more difficult.

THURSDAY, JULY 5TH, 2001

In reading a dockside bulletin board, I learned ice was available at the gift shop but no directions were given how to get there. Nate and I asked a very polite woman with a distinct New England accent on a rental Erie Canal boat for directions. Her husband had bought ice last night so she called to him below deck, "There are some gentlemen out here looking for ice". He had an even thicker New England accent and very politely said he had bought it at Vix, a grocery store, and gave directions how to get there.

A security alarm went off as we entered Vix and a cashier looked up. "We couldn't have stolen anything, we just walked in!" "It's been going off all morning," she replied. It was no problem finding milk, but ice was another story. Where do you keep the ice? "Aisle 10." After walking aisle 10's length and not seeing ice, I asked again. "Aisle 10" was the same reply. We finally found the 'Happy Ice' sign, with no ice there. I asked a worker if there was any in back. He went to check looking 'unhappy.' A different worker emerged, limping, and slowly pushing a cart with fifteen bags. I told Debbie 'Happy Ice' came from unhappy employees.

Between Debbie and me, Nate is busy when we stop – helping unload, load, rearrange, and refuel the boat. He also cooks, but when traveling he does the 'teenagers favorite pastime' – SLEEP! When not asleep, he reads, plays Snakes & Ladders with Debbie or one of his travel games.

The Lockmaster at E30 said there were nice places around Cross Lake to overnight, taking us four to five hours to get there without much in between.

Trying unsuccessfully to talk with the lockmaster at E-26, we saw the top of one of the three cruisers locking up. A woman heading west outside the closed ascending lock called 3- 4 times, with him talking to no one. We drank melted 'Happy Ice' while waiting.

Shortly after passing through E-25, we entered Montezuma National Wildlife Refuge. While I'm not particularly interested in birds, Debbie views their variety as part of an overall balanced ecological sign of life. I did stop so she could videotape a Bald Eagle in its nest atop a power pole. Also saw: Heron in a tree, Hawk, and a Golden Eagle flying low over the water in front of us.

Looking to buy gas and use a bathroom, we stopped at Eagle Bay Marina. It was a kind of rinky-dink outfit with gas priced at $2.20 a gallon. I walked around trying to find a gas attendant; finding out 'Steve' had left for a doctor appointment. We were advised not to wait as Steve was kind of a 'free spirit,' and it was impossible to predict when he'd return.

We **need** gas. I had not thought gas would be an issue on the canal. The Boat has a planing, not displacement hull, and gets its worst gas mileage while running at the ten mph speed limit. Gas mileage issue aside, handling is terrible at that speed. The bow runs at an elevated angle making forward vision difficult and to maintain even the semblance of a straight wake, steering requires *constant* adjustment.

I understand bank wash has to be kept to a minimum, but even running at just ten mph the big cruisers threw out a wake that The Boat could only aspire to. The ideal situation would be to have speed rules based on boat size and draft, except they would be impossible to administer.

Eight miles later, we stopped at family run Midway Marina. A young teenager came down to the fuel dock. I bought only 9 gallons because I thought the price was too high at $2.00 a gallon. The kid was curious, "Are you traveling?" "Yea – from Buffalo to New York City." He asked how much the two portable gas containers held and the purpose of the big plastic zip bag we use to keep our sleeping gear dry. I said we usually got at least four mpg but now only two because of the slow speed limit. The kid said, "No one follows the speed limit here. I've never seen a sheriff out." I said, "I don't want to be the first to get a ticket! Do they water-ski through here?" "No, No water-skiing. Do you want to fill up the red tanks?" "No, not at $2 a gallon." "Its $2.20 at the next marina." He reminded me of myself at that age.

At the seemingly breakneck speed of 25 mph we crossed the four miles of Cross Lake and into the Seneca River. I slowed upon entering the narrow State Ditch Canal Cut where the Seneca River meanders south, and then resumed speed when the Seneca rejoined the canal. Seeing a fishing and pontoon boat approach, I once again slowed. As they passed Debbie heard them shout and she saw someone point in the direction we were headed. As we rounded a bend, there sat the first water patrol boat we'd seen. Fortunately, I was already going slow because of the warning. Not too much further someone was water skiing. "What is the speed limit? This irks me."

It would be nice if I could give some sense of when, how, why, and what modifications have been done to the Erie Canal, but that would be a book in and of itself. It is interesting to see rivers and streams flow *in, out, and under* and how the lakes and lowlands fit into the system.

At 7:30, we stopped at South Shore West Trail to see about staying the night above Lock 24. It was in a windy, wide spot in the canal with the boat bouncing unprotected. Not finding restrooms in the cold exposed area we decided to lock through and check out Lions Community Park – Transients Allowed.

Lions Community Park didn't have docks to hold us off the rocks piled on shore, so we continued on a short distance to check out three marinas at Cold Springs. Not finding anyone around at the first two, we stopped at the last one, Cold Springs Harbour. Still not finding anyone around, we pulled into an empty slip and set up for the night. Dinner was just about ready when a man in a blue pickup truck drove up. "What do you think you are doing?" I said the Cruising Guide lists you as accepting transients, and since no one was here we tied up. "It'll cost at least $20." He had just been returning to an apartment above the office. In asking about buying gas, I found out they only sell to members of the marina. We were able to use bathrooms and take a shower. The day's weather had been generally cool, with occasional big fluffy cumulus clouds.

FRIDAY, JULY 6TH, 2001

While Debbie fixed breakfast, I checked the engine oil level. This involved moving everything in the stern and untying ropes used to stabilize and support the auxiliary motor. I kept a knife at the ready to cut the ropes to drop the motor quickly if the need arose.

The oil level was fine, but there was an excessive amount of water in the bilge. I started the motor and found water leaking around the exhaust bellow. A simple tightening of the four band connectors took care of the problem.

Wanting to become a part of the larger boating community Debbie and I joined the United States Power Squadron, a national group promoting boating safety, education, and social interaction. Each chapter has a small flag called a burgee unique to them. I'll describe our local chapters, Hiawatha Valley Sail & Power Squadron, burgee; There is a field of blue representing our sky blue waters. The letters H & V, representing our chapter name, are one above the other on a red triangle depicting the Civic, Fraternal and Self-Education sides of the

USPS. Then a blue line runs most of the white feathers length. The feather represents all the different kinds of people on earth and joins us together in good spirit to share our knowledge and interests. The blue line through the feather represents our journey and the courses we travel.

I fastened Hiawatha's burgee to the upper part of the VHF antenna with cable ties before leaving the marina.

Not able to buy gas at Cold Springs Harbour, we went upstream to J & S. Marine. It took a while to find someone to run the pump, filling everything at $1.84 per gallon, costing $52.50. While relating river trip goals and experiences to the age 65+ attendant, he asked if we were on an Odyssey. He said boaters who transited to Cross Lake in a boat our size thought that they were on an Odyssey. Noticing my missing fingers, he proceeded to tell about a neighbor who cut off his hand with an airplane propeller, a nephew who lost an eye in a firearm accident and then cut off the tips of his fingers in a planer at the high school shop.

He pointed out a large three-deck cruiser with a green cover that took 450 gallons to fill ($828.00 at that day's price). He warned that today's winds out of the West would make Lake Oneida choppy. "Got a bow cover?" We do not. He said to write our story so he could read it and that we were living the Odyssey.

The morning was cool, so we bundled up, putting on jackets and long pants. Nate left his usual spot in the bow to sit on cushions between Debbie and me. We shut the front window and used the Duluth pack to block wind from coming in.

I saw a nice fender floating amongst reeds, making up for one lost earlier. For non-boaters a fender generically is a round plastic device to absorb impact from a dock or prevent a boat from being scratched while locking through. Nate used our extendable docking pole to grab it.

Lock 23 was very busy. While waiting for five boats to lock up, we talked with two 20-year-old guys who had been boat camping on one the Finger Lakes and headed home to Utica. The Finger Lakes region is as its name implies. If you place the palm of your hand centered above Lake Ontario with fingers and thumb pointed south, the thumb and four fingers surprisingly emulate the placement of your hand. Three of the fingers are accessible via the Erie Canal; the Seneca, Cayuga, and Onondaga Lakes.

I followed the 19-20' boat from Utica through the first navigation buoys as we entered Lake Oneida at 12:12. What can I say about Lake Oneida?!?!

Debbie, ever the cautious one, expressed concern about crossing the lake. The two to three foot waves were close together as we entered the west end of the lake with the wind from the West. Remember what the gas attendant said?

Nate went up front for a thrill ride. Every tenth wave was a splasher. He rode there with a life jacket on for 20 - 30 minutes, coming behind the windshield when he started to feel seasick. I ran about 20 mph – "I thought we'd be able to open her up out here!" The two larger boats we had started across with were out of sight. We found ourselves south of a navigation buoy – dangerous shoal area. The waves got higher and harder to gauge how to hit them- right on or quarter? The Boat did not respond quickly to higher throttle nor turn very precisely. We had overloaded the boat more than I had thought. Due to rough water causing increased gas consumption and not filling the main tank before starting across the lake, it was now dangerously low. The Gas Pals were still full.

The fuel tank fill spout is at the stern and outside of The Boat. Trying to fill the tank in the choppy following sea while on the go would have splashed water into the tank, so I headed north to find calmer water. Lake Oneida is approximately five miles wide with navigation buoys positioned slightly north of center as it runs west to east. I picked through whitecaps to the north shore where Debbie and Nate added gas while I circled. Nate then laid down in the bottom of the boat and actually fell asleep! I followed the shoreline heading east, thankful for the depth gauge. Reaching the east shore, I then headed south to find the Erie Canal entrance. The swells were now seven to eight feet high with crests further apart. By definition, a swell is a long wave that moves continuously without breaking. A crest is the top of the wave. I watched the stern and adjusted steering as wave crests caught up. Using just enough speed to maintain control, the boat wallowed in troughs. Sometimes it was like surfing – with waves picking up the stern. Sometimes the waves hit us sideways, tipping the boat hard to port, then back to starboard. While we got wet, it was not from actual waves, rather water blown off the top of wave crests. And Nate still slept!

Our joy in seeing the rock breakwater protecting the canal entrance quickly subsided upon finding we were on the wrong side of the entrance and closer to shore than the breakwater extended. I now had to head into the waves to get out around the breakwater. Debbie kept track of our progress while I timed turns to avoid the worst of the waves and tacked into the smaller ones.

Finally rounding the breakwater and able to go with the waves again we woke Nate so he could see what he had missed. The burgee just fastened to the VHF antenna was gone. Too much rocking and rolling from side to side must have flung it up and off.

It took us two hours to cross Lake Oneida's eighteen-mile length. We could have gone faster than that on the canal. I had been looking forward to going 30 mph.

I had Nate drive and cracked a beer to relax after the harrowing crossing.

Arriving to Lock 20 at 6:00, and with ten miles to Lock 19, we decided Ilion would be our overnight stop.

Lock 19 was ready, and at 8:15 we pulled in at Ilion. Overhearing comments from a group lounging around the dock why we had so much gear, I said in an over loud voice we'd started from Buffalo and were headed to NYC.

Over dinner, I voiced thoughts about not taking the Erie Canal back to Buffalo once reaching NYC. It took about five days to travel the 338 miles from Buffalo to Troy. Time aside, I really was not enjoying the Erie Canal because of speed restrictions. I am not trying to deter anyone from taking the trip, there are increasingly numerous places to stop, shop, and tour and the scenery is nice. Due to the aforementioned low speedboat handling problems, I did not want to do a return trip.

My thought was to hop a bus at Troy, New York, return to Buffalo to pick up the van and trailer, then drive back to Troy.

SATURDAY, JULY 7TH, 2001

Wanting to get under way before the marina pumps ($1.95) opened at 9:00, Nate and I took the two 11 gallon Gas Pals three blocks and bought 20 gallons ($1.57).

Our morning's view is the top of land off in the distance as all the locks going east from E-20 descend.

The countryside scenery changed from marsh to rock cliffs at Little Falls, with the canal using the Mohawk River. At Fultonville, Nate and I pulled the Gas Pals up a steep twenty-foot bank to buy fuel from one of the several service stations while Debbie kept the boat from bouncing on rocks. Using mooring lines from a secure foothold, we lowered the Gas Pals.

The lockmaster house at E-12 is the nicest one we saw.

At 8:00, we stopped at Wilson Marine Services looking for transient dockage. Being Saturday night and finding a noisy bar very close to the boat slips we moved on to Mohawk Valley Marina.

They had quite a few slips, with very few unoccupied. Temporarily tying up in the westernmost slip, Nate and I went to see if any slips were open. The owner said he would let us overnight at the dock next to the boat ramp, a spot not usually used. We told Debbie that the few empty slips left were for boats still on the water and that the marina was full, which was true. I backed the boat out mumbling I did not know what to do. Cruising just a short distance, I pulled in next to the boat ramp. Gotcha!

A picnic table was right underneath an overhead light and within thirty foot of the boat so it made preparing the evening meal easier. Due to the opposite side of the dock being used for loading and unloading boats, there was more activity than we would have liked. It did make for a short walk to the bathroom and showers.

SUNDAY, JULY 8TH, 2001

It had rained more than the predicted tenth of an inch. The canvas kept Debbie and me mostly dry, except where a corner had come loose and gotten my feet wet. When Nate woke up from his sleeping spot in the bow and seeing the sag of the water-laden canvas, he tried to push it up and off, resulting in the rainwater coming inside instead of rolling out. It was good we'd kept many changes of clothing dry since the only thing of his that was out not getting wet were his water shoes.

We looked forward to locking through the "Waterford Flight" - Locks 5 through 2. The 150-foot change of altitude to the Hudson River was done in the shortest distance of any canal in the world at the time. The sky was overcast – with a 40 % chance of rain. We zipped through the first four locks; with the doors of one open and ready for the next. Westbound traffic waited for us. At Lock E-2, there being no E-1, some very large vessels caused me to back off into a side channel, as they did not share the channel when the lock doors opened.

Docking at Troy Town Dock & Marina on the Hudson River, Debbie and I walked several blocks to a AAA visitor center, finding it closed due to being Sunday. The only reason for going there to begin was that we were

BA members and trying to find a way for me to get from the Hudson River/Erie Canal junction back to Buffalo, New York. While passing back through the guard gate, The Dockmaster suggested taking Amtrak. Being from the Midwest where mass transit options are very limited, the idea of Amtrak never entered our minds. The Dockmaster looked up Amtrak's number, dialed it, answering questions about where the different stations were and how far from the closest marina they would be.

The train depot that worked out best was in the town of Rensselaer. Debbie jotted down departure and corresponding arrival times to Buffalo. We then stopped at Albany Yacht Club, across the river from its namesake and about six blocks from the Amtrak Station. I asked if it would be possible to dock the boat there, leaving Debbie and Nate aboard on the return trip, while I retrieved the van and trailer, finding it not a problem. At 1:30 we headed south on the Hudson for the run to NYC.

At 4:30, after just missing a storm to the West and with the sky looking stormy to the South, we went up Rondout Creek just south of Kingston looking for transient dockage. We checked out a city dock next to a historic section of town, and not seeing a good place to cook and eat off the boat, we continued on to check out other facilities.

It was early and the storm we thought was going to hit had moved on. We ended up at Rondout Yacht Harbor. Richardsons' Chartbook did not indicate they accepted transients, with their sign stating they did. Jeff, the Dockmaster, was quite busy. I topped off the main gas tank and put six gallons in one of the Gas Pals. The skipper of a large boat just completing a ninety-four mile round trip to the Catskills refilled it with 85 gallons costing $178, laughed at the expense, saying it was his boss's boat and charged it to his account.

Jeff walked Debbie to an open slip close to a picnic and play area. When I pulled into the slip the guy fishing there seemed a little ticked at having to reel in. He was loud and yelling at his wife and daughter.

After dinner, I talked to the loud angler and another man, telling of our goals for this trip and about past trips. Chris, the angler, and Jerry, his friend, both were season slip holders at Rondout. Chris was of Greek ancestry and was there with his wife Dee, and daughter Mandy. Jerry, married with two grown children, was off work due to health reasons.

Chris told about an old man who had sold hot dogs to vendors for many years, describing them as the best ever. They could be in the freezer and he could still smell 'the hickory flavor.' Owning the business for many years, he raised a family, put the kids through school, and upon retiring gave it to the kids who were bankrupt within a year.

Chris and Jerry are quite the pair, like Abbot & Costello, or Rowan & Martin. Our original impression of Chris changed dramatically as we talked with him. First, he is hard of hearing, which at least partly accounts for the loud voice. We found out loud and seemingly antagonistic behavior between friends and family around NYC is part of who they are.

Chris and Jerry would argue about anything, just to argue. They would insult and tell stories on each other, and then when the other was not listening, would say, "He is a good guy", all the while puffing big cigars.

When Chris cast out into a lagoon next to the picnic area, the reel hung up causing the dough ball bait to go one way and the hook another. Mandy brought out some string cheese since Chis had lost the last of the 'special recipe' dough ball bait. Jerry said he would not catch anything and wagered five dollars. Chris guaranteed he would catch a carp and cast out leaving the pole resting against a log. While Chris was getting another round of beer, Jerry saw the line move. He picked up the pole, set the hook, and called out for Chris to reel it in. Jerry claimed he caught the fish as Chris reeled it in. As Chris tried to land it from the high bank, he called out to his wife and daughter. He had Mandy hold the pole while he went down the bank to release the ugly carp.

Chris and Jerry then good-naturedly argued over who actually caught the carp and was entitled to claim the bet. Was it Jerry who hooked it, Chris who partially reeled it in, or Mandy who had the final turn at the pole? I do not remember if they ever settled it.

Chris had been saying he had eaten every kind of fish and loved them all. After catching the carp Chris said, "Carp don't have to worry about me keeping them anymore." In trying to eat one his wife cooked, he kept thinking it tasted like shit, and then halfway through eating it, told his wife so.

MONDAY, JULY 9TH, 2001

In awakening at 6:45 and upon hearing the days forecast of 85 degrees, partly sunny, with fog in the morning we were not in a particular hurry. After showering and starting to heat water for coffee, Jerry invited us aboard his boat, Quiet Time. We talked and drank at least four cups of coffee apiece while the fog burned off. Jerry had bought the boat six years earlier as a 'fixer upper' with it now being very nice inside and out.

It was 9:00 when we arrived back to the calm as glass Hudson River. I cruised with the stereo cranking out favorite tunes; does it get any better than this?

West Point Military Academy sits on a western bluff in a bend of the Hudson about forty miles above NYC. The Hudson narrowed and upon hitting more open water it became choppy and stayed so.

At Penny Bridge Marina we bought 11 ½ gallon for $23. Just as we approached NYC, and for no apparent reason, the motor started to cut out.

Since Debbie has this thing about bridges, I have to mention we passed under the Tappan Zee and George Washington Bridge before arriving at Newport Harbor on the Jersey side. A seasonal slip boater at Rondout Yacht Club recommended staying on the New Jersey side. Reason being is the most impressive sight of NYC is the Manhattan skyline, which is only viewable if you are across from it. I had not thought about it that way, but he was right.

The Hudson was calm between Manhattan and Jersey except for ferry wakes. Locating Newport Harbor and per the posted NO WAKE signs I was idling in when I noticed a 120-foot yacht rapidly overtaking us. Damn the No Wake area; I forged ahead and ducked into a restaurant mooring area with the yacht sliding by right behind us.

The Dockmaster office adjacent to the restaurant dock was unoccupied while they assisted the yacht. I watched as they used a walking tape measure to ensure the yacht would fit between boats already docked. The yacht must have bow and stern thrusters as it effortlessly turned 180 degrees within its own length.

Feeling very self-conscious about our small size boat after they had just docked the yacht, I asked about transient moorage. The female Dockmaster said there was a 30-foot minimum charge and it would be $72 a night. She suggested Liberty Harbor Marina might be a better fit. For one of a few times ever, I felt very outclassed and out of place. Giving Newport Harbor credit, we were not rejected as unacceptable by any standards they may have, formal or informal.

While idling south we discussed what to do in NYC and how long it would take, agreeing to stay two nights. We would circumnavigate Manhattan Island yet this afternoon, try to get to the Crown of the Statue of Liberty and Ellis Island tomorrow, and leave Wednesday morning.

After buying gas at Liberty Harbor Marina, we left the boat tied to the gas dock and found the office to arrange transient dockage. Linda, the Dockmaster, was busy. Securing two night's dockage for $70 total, we walked to the assigned spot and found a boat already docked there. Linda, ticked at the inaccuracy of the help who had just updated dockage availability, found us another slip that worked out better by being in a quiet, backwater on the north side.

I asked about leaving a few things at the office to lighten our load for the afternoon run around Manhattan, but with them locking up at 5:00 did not work out. The trip around Manhattan was awesome! Just south of Ward Island where the Harlem and East River meet, known as Hell Gate, the water churned as if going through rapids. The depth went from 50 to a 100 foot in a very short distance. Other than being apprehensive of why water acted that way, it did not cause any problem. Just as we completed the northern sweep around Manhattan on the Harlem River, a railroad swing bridge closed. We slipped underneath by lowering the VHF antenna.

The Hudson was *very* choppy while returning to Liberty Harbor Marina with the motor cutting out again. I do not understand how it can run perfectly for two hours then not be able to run over 1500 RPM after that. I made sure to stay out of the way of the ferryboats as they made beeline routes across the Hudson.

We videotaped and watched the NYC skyline from the Sand Bar, an outside bar that was part of Liberty Harbor Marina, while socializing with other patrons.

TUESDAY, JULY 10TH, 2001

I got Debbie and Nate up early to take the 7:30 NY Waterway Ferry, Yogi Berra, across the Hudson to the financial district of Manhattan. I chatted with the pilot as he steered the ferry with a joystick. In my telling about going through Hell Gate yesterday, I asked if the name came from being a bad area of NYC. "No", it came from the era of sailboats trying to navigate the turbulent water.

As we walked alongside the Hudson River heading south, there were a lot of people jogging, biking, and walking in the green way area of Battery Park. The long line waiting to buy tickets started to move just as we arrived at 8:00.

Having visited NYC in the summer of 1995 and leaving by ferry from the New Jersey side, we knew it first stopped at Ellis Island, then at Liberty Island where the Statue of Liberty is. After spending a lot of time at Ellis and while standing in line at Liberty Island to ascend the Statue, they stopped admitting people due to the time of day. If you leave from Battery Park at the southern tip of Manhattan, you stop at Liberty Island first, then Ellis, and back to Battery Park. Therefore, the reason for leaving from Battery Park was to reach Liberty Island with plenty of time to climb the Statue of Liberty.

While in line to board the first ferry, vendors were hawking various things, watches, bagels, crowd tickets, etc. Crowd tickets? What is a crowd ticket and why would you want one? I listened more closely to the 'hawker', "Now listen up people, if you don't take one of these 'crown' tickets you won't be allowed up". We got three and they were free.

The ferry was crowded, but we found seats and drank a morning coffee. We heard an announcement informing us that the ferry running to Ellis Island was not going there for an indefinite time due to President Bush performing a citizen naturalization ceremony there.

While waiting in line under a canopy shielding us from the sun, we read signs saying that from June 30th - Sept 3rd only people with crown tickets could climb all the way up. I took credit for being psychic and getting us up and around early. There are 354 steps to the crown, with the slow line making it an easy climb. Nate said he was "embarrassed". "Why?" "He had never been in a lady's dress before!"

The crown was only large enough for two or three people at a time to look out the glass pane windows and see the impressive view.

After descending from the crown, we toured the museum with Nate, who did not remember seeing it on our prior visit. At 1:00, right after eating lunch and just stretching out for a nap in the shade, we heard Ellis Island was open and caught the first ferry going there.

We listened to most of a Park Rangers roving tour of the Ellis Island facilities that were open to the public. Much of it is a state of decay, awaiting funds for restoration.

At 3:00, we arrived back in Manhattan without a game plan. Debbie and Nate shared a "Famous Pizza" while I had a sausage sandwich.

Trying to find milk, we came across an ice cream truck parked just east of the World Trade Center complex.

Enjoying the ice cream, we sat and people watched. I said we should videotape the area for about thirty seconds. Almost immediately a well-dressed woman walking across a steel grate caught her high heel spike shoe, continuing her stride without it. A fellow New Yorker retrieved it and they were both on their way. I like to people watch.

At the World Trade Center Plaza, we rested on benches facing the reflecting pool. It seemed one security officer's job was just to keep people from using it to cool off.

I still wanted milk. In trying to buy one at a sandwich shop, they directed us to a restaurant on the west side of the plaza. A manager there asked if we wanted seated. "No" We want to buy milk. Saying they did not sell milk, a passing waitress corrected him by saying, "Yes we do". While this seems much ado about nothing, it amazed me that it was so hard to find such a basic commodity as milk in a city of millions.

Returning to the World Trade Center Plaza, an Irish American band started to perform. It was hard to understand their words above the strong wind whipping through. The music was a combination of traditional Irish ballad and American bluegrass rolled into the same song. Moving on an hour later, we walked through one of the buildings that comprise the WTC complex to reach a ferry that returned us to Liberty Harbor Marina. Two months and a day later the twin towers no longer stood.

Getting back to Liberty Harbor Marina about 7:30, we found a round about way to a point of land called 'Morris Canal Park.' The 'Colgate Clock' is across from the park, separated from it by a now defunct canal. Our night shots of Manhattan did not turn out due to bad time exposure and shaking lenses.

WEDNESDAY, JULY 11TH, 2001

With today's goal being to catch the 4:20 PM train out of Rensselaer, we got up at 5:35 AM. I changed the condenser in the distributor hoping to fix the cutting out motor problem. A Weather Service report valid until 10:00 broadcast thunderstorm warnings. Ferry traffic was heavy, making it a rough ride as we headed north.

Less than ten miles and short of reaching the George Washington Bridge, threatening rain forced us to duck into Von Dohln Brothers, a private marina on the Jersey side. Seeing a lot of lightning and with heavy sprinkles starting to fall we put the top up causing the rain to promptly stop. Still seeing dark clouds off to the North, we waited a while longer before leaving.

Trying to keep the load down, I had not filled up at Liberty Harbor Marina and now needed gas. Finding Engelwood Boat Basin gas dock closed, we went to Alpine Boat Basin, which did not open until 9:00. It was 8:40 so we waited. The attendant explained how ocean tides affected river current and why they occurred at predictable and varying times.

More boat and barge traffic was heading north than we'd experienced going south. The motor originally started cutting out when the gas tank got low, then started to even with a full tank. The gas mileage also went to half of normal. I changed spark plug wires which made it run smoother for a while, but it soon it went back to cutting out.

Twelve miles short of reaching Albany Yacht Club, from where I would catch Amtrak, and desperately needing gas, we stopped at the town of Hudson upon seeing a 'Power Boat Club' sign. It evidently is private as no one was around. Nate and I grabbed a Gas Pal and went in search of a gas station. Seeing a man sitting in a car a block away, I asked where the closest gas station was. Hearing it was quite a ways and with him volunteering to drive, I accepted.

Along the way, I learned he was a retired bartender who had worked at the Copacabana in New York City sometime in the 40's. His favorite baseball team was the Cincinnati Reds, taking a lot of flak for supporting them. Years ago, he had written the team, and upon receiving an autographed photo of his then favorite player, Jack Martin, became a staunch fan. We also learned there were over 100 antique dealers; helping save the town from decline after some major industries had left.

It was 3:55 when I left on foot from Albany Yacht Club, with the scheduled departure time for the Buffalo train being 4:20. Coming to a three-way junction just a block from the marina, the directions given at the marina did not make sense. I went left towards the river, which turned into an entrance ramp for a bridge crossing the Hudson River. I then headed east, figuring I would encounter railroad tracks leading to the depot at some point, alternately running and walking as endurance permitted. I stopped at a gas station and asked the last person in line to pay if he knew how to get to the Amtrak depot. I could tell you how to get there but it would not make sense so I will show you. Stepping outside he said, "Do you see the new construction off to the northeast with the spire above it? The old depot is next to the spire and they are building a new one next to it. OK, do not go that way. You have to continue on this street, cross the bridge, take a right down the stairs, and another right from there."

I ran up the street, across an uphill bridge, down the stairs, and north to the new construction. Needing to save time, I ducked through a hole in a construction fence, crossed over planking spanning a parking ramp, and down a two-story stairway, only to be blocked from reaching the old Amtrak station by a padlocked chain link gate.

Finding a small gap in the gate, I squeezed through and ran into the station, immediately hearing the "Final Call" for the 4:15. Saying I wanted a ticket for the 4:20 train to Buffalo, the ticket seller's question was which station in Buffalo. Hearing Erie Canal Boat Basin was my destination; she determined the Exchange Street stop was the closest. While close enough to walk to the marina, she did not recommend it. "Take a taxi; it won't cost you an arm and a leg." Telling her I had been in hurry up mode since leaving NYC by boat, she said to relax since the train would not arrive until 4:35.

The train sat in the station fifteen minutes after arriving. My seat assignment put me close to a very polite mother who had a very obnoxious child. Fortunately, they got off an hour and a half later. The Amtrak rail line closely followed the Erie Canal and I recognized a few of the spots. A high school graduate going to Buffalo for college orientation was concerned about getting off at the right stop.

Arriving at the Buffalo depot about 10 PM, I asked the lead driver of four taxis if he knew the way to Boat Basin and what it would cost.

He talked to the other drivers in trying to figure out where Boat Basin was and said it would be about $10. With $7.80 on the meter and upon seeing the Navel slip area adjacent to the Erie Basin Marina I said, "That's it down there." It was a ways before he could turn around and head back. With $13.50 showing on meter upon arriving at the guard gate, I gave him $15.

The taxi driver said Erie Basin Marina was one of the safest places to have left the van and trailer in downtown Buffalo, being so close to the guardhouse and well lit. He told of a couple who took the train to Pittsburgh, leaving their car in a ramp with no overnight security. They came back and found their car on blocks; with the tires and radio gone, he had felt so sorry for them.

I checked in with the guardhouse, receiving permission to sleep in the van overnight. With the Coleman stove in the boat, I ate a cold can of chili and found a pudding for dessert.

It was a chilly night; I found two pillows and a sheet. I used the inflatable mattress Nate sleeps on as a blanket.

THURSDAY, JULY 12TH, 2001

As I headed west, I-90 turned into a toll road. I stopped at an oasis service area to figure out the toll fee, arriving at $13.40. In my rush to catch the train yesterday, I had overlooked taking more cash with me. With only $7 in my billfold, I counted out $6.40 in change from the ashtray to cover the toll road expense. Still having $1.95 in change I went to 'Dunkin Donuts' at the oasis. Explaining that $1.95 was all the money I had; we analyzed the options, buying a coffee and pastry with 7 cents left over. I suppose I could have used a credit card, but charging such a small amount would have been a nuisance. I handed the $7 in cash and a coffee cup with $6.40 in change to the tollbooth attendant in Buffalo, getting change back. It was better to get back than to owe and not have it.

With the family back together, we loaded The Boat at a public boat ramp on the west side of the Hudson as Albany Yacht Club does not have a ramp. For the second time in less than 24 hours, I was headed west. Our destination being Barcelona boat harbor where we'd checked out Lake Erie almost ten days ago, arriving at 11:30 PM.

Planning to spend the night there and while just getting settled in, a police cruiser displaying a Westfield door emblem passed through without telling us to leave.

FRIDAY, JULY 13TH, 2001

During the night I dreamt I was in school and was asked the question; "Where are you?" The correct answer being Lake Chautauqua, but in order to get credit I had to spell it correctly, which I could not.

At 6:30, Debbie went to make coffee in the public women's restroom and found the electrical outlets dead. A man filling water jugs outside the door asked the Dockmaster why they did not work. The Dockmaster, Mitch, invited Debbie to make coffee in his office and they talked while coffee brewed.

Today's prediction for Lake Eire was 10 - 15 mph NW winds and three to four foot waves. Mitch said not to trust tomorrows forecast of one to two foot waves. Last week nobody went out for a scheduled fishing tournament because of bad weather and rough water.

We decided to head straight south to Lake Chautauqua and come back to Barcelona the following day hoping the wind would drop. The ten-mile stretch of land between Barcelona and Lake Chautauqua is the only land that separates New York Harbor from the upper reaches of the Big Hole River in western Montana using the following route.

From East to West: Hudson River, Erie Canal, Lake Erie from Buffalo to Barcelona, 10 miles of land, Lake Chautauqua, Chadakoin River, Cassadaga River, Conewango River, Allegheny River, Ohio River, Mississippi River, Missouri River, Jefferson River, and then the Big Hole River.

While drinking coffee, I talked with an angler waiting for a fishing buddy to show up. He said his grandchildren were coming from Canada for a visit, and he wanted to make sure the boat was in good working order. Giving up on his buddy, he invited us to follow him to a good boat ramp on Lake Chautauqua where it would be much calmer. The angler warned of rocks and shallow water in the southern part of the lake.

Before leaving from Prendergast Point Park boat dock, I removed the spark arrestor cover and sprayed the dirty carburetor throat with Gumout.

Not having a lake map, I carefully watched the depth gauge as we headed to the northern most part. At a depth of three foot and fifty feet from the northern shore, I turned south. The motor ran perfectly, making it fun sharing the relatively calm lake with the sail and powerboats that were out.

The southwestern end got shallow and very weedy. While pulling weeds from the prop, we could see boat traffic reaching the southeasterly section without problem. A nearby weed harvester was cutting them off about four foot below the surface, using a conveyer belt to dump them into a storage area.

Trying to find the outlet of Lake Chautauqua, I followed an unmarked channel running about eight feet deep on the southeast side. A sheriff in a patrol boat overtaking us said, "Its beautiful back here isn't it?" Trees and water lily pads on both sides obscured most signs of civilization.

As we passed under bridges and got closer to Jamestown, birthplace of Lucille Ball, the depth became increasingly shallower. Going quite slowly under one of the last bridges and on the opposite side of the center pier from where I wanted to be in deference to some young fisherman, I hit something solid. In the process of trying to put the boat in neutral with my injured right hand, I threw it in reverse and backed over whatever I'd hit the first time! Aside from the occasional ding filed off, this was the first real prop damage sustained in the several thousand miles taken with The Boat.

A short distance later, we passed the power plant that utilized the pool of water backed up by the small dam from where Chadakoin River flows. Another connection made, we headed back to the boat ramp. The wind had come up and the lake choppy with the boat running great except for a vibrating prop.

Humoring Nate, we found a campground with a pool that the proprietor uncovered just for us, saying it would be cold. Now Nate had to use it. The water felt warmer once you were actually in it, as we all found out.

While I reorganized the boat and replaced the prop, Debbie cooked a great meal. It had been ten days since we had left South Bend, with this our first real campground.

Over dinner I announced that I was ready to take on Lake Erie. The boat was now 400 pound's lighter without camping equipment, extra clothes, food, etc, and one less person, as Debbie would be driving the van back to Buffalo to meet us.

SATURDAY, JULY 14TH, 2001

I was up at 7:00 listening to the VHF marine forecast for Lake Erie. One to two foot waves, with the wind supposed to lie down as the day progressed. "Let's go! We're doing it!"

We arrived back at Barcelona Harbor Ramp in time for the Saturday morning coffee klatch of the locals gathered in the Harbormasters office area. They thought we were going fishing, even after trying numerous times to it make clear that Nate and I were headed to Buffalo. How far off shore should I stay? Would a half-mile be OK? "Oh that would be OK, There's bass there." Or go further west and depth wouldn't be a problem."

When they finally understood I was not fishing and our destination was Buffalo the reply changed to; "Oh, you really are going to Buffalo?" "Then stay pretty far out, especially from the first point going east."

The Harbormaster let me use a very high power set of binoculars to see past the breakwater. It was rougher that it appeared from shore. He agreed the waves were supposed to settle down more as the day wore on.

Nate and I left at 8:55, with Debbie to meet us at Erie Basin Marina boat ramp after our '*three hour tour.*'

Seeing white water bouncing off the bow once past the protection off Barcelona Harbor, she stopped at the next major harbor heading east called Dunkirk City Harbor & Ramp in case I'd pulled in because it was too rough.

We had 'good sailing' all the way to Buffalo with the motor functioning perfectly. It was hard to discern our position without having GPS, charts or knowing the landmarks, but gauging from the mph and elapsed time I counted down the distance to Buffalo.

Two years ago, Debbie and I participated in a regional Predicted Log event sponsored by our chapter of the United States Power Squadron. The goal is to predict how long it will take to run a course using just the tachometer to determine speed. The speedometer is either disconnected or covered, and the skipper is not allowed to use a watch. The round trip Mississippi River course we ran was about twenty-five miles and went through two no wake zones. It was supposed to be run in legs, with each leg timed individually. If you run one minute long on one leg and one minute short on the next, they do not cancel each other out. Over the course of the twenty-five mile run, I was off five seconds from my total time prediction. I don't remember how the individual legs worked out as they ended up judging based on the total elapsed time margin of error. We won, with the award being a plaque and hosting the event next year. We ran it as it was meant to be done, with each leg timed individually.

Debbie stayed at Dunkirk until 10:30; moving onto Erie Basin Marina where she arrived at 11:47, figuring it would be at least an hour wait Nate and I plugged along at around 25 mph, stopping once to add fuel. I kept my feelings in check about making it to Buffalo until about ten miles away.

Identifying the approach to Erie Basin Marina, I felt relieved upon completing the most apprehensive part of the journey between NYC and the upper end of the Allegheny River.

We tied to the dock at the launch ramp at 11:50 and went to find Debbie. While climbing the steps to the parking lot we saw the high top camper van where Debbie was poring over a crossword puzzle. We snuck up and surprised her. She could not believe we made it so quick considering the chop we went through. I reminded her that it would be 'a three hour tour' and was within five minutes of the prediction.

During her wait at Dunkirk, she had not seen us go by since I had stayed far off shore.

After a major boat cleaning and reorganization, we went to Niagara Falls since we were so close. We had been there in 1995, but it is a sight worth seeing many times. The sheer volume and accompanying thunder of water cascading over is awesome.

Not trying to burst anybody's bubble about the purism of the falls, it is a little known fact its waterpower makes electricity. In somewhat of a compromise agreement between tourism and using the falls productively, during the night gates are raised from the bottom of the Niagara to divert water. According to a TV special only 50% during the day and 25% at night of the Niagara Rivers flow actually goes over the falls, with the rest used to generate electricity. By law, a certain minimum cubic feet per second must be allowed to flow over.

5:30 on our way back to South Bend we stopped at Barcelona for the fourth time finding the wind indicator bouncing between six and ten mph and the waves back to three to four feet. So much for the VHF marine radio prediction of the wind lying down later in the day!

Two days were spent visiting in South Bend before we left to drive both vans pulling trailers back to Lakeville. Anxious to get home, I pushed the camper van harder in the summer heat than it could take. About two hundred miles from Lakeville Debbie passed and motioned to pull off the interstate upon seeing smoke rolling out from under the van. The problem turned out to be transmission fluid coming out of somewhere and hitting the exhaust pipe. Even with a transmission cooler, the fluid had overheated, losing almost two quarts. I refilled the transmission after letting it cool. Driving slower, we arrived home with no apparent damage done to the transmission.

2001 PEND OREILLE RIVER

Having completed the Eastern part of going East to West by water, the plan for the Western component of 2001 is to start from the Idaho/Washington border on the Pend Oreille River, boat it about 90 miles into British Columbia, Canada, where it joins the Columbia, taking it to the Pacific.

Upon returning from 'Out East,' I asked Debbie when she would be able to leave for 'Out West', with her picking August 8th.

TUESDAY, AUGUST 7TH, 2001

Hot! Hot! Hot! 97 degrees – 79% dew point – 105-heat index. There had been 18 days above 90 degrees in the Twin Cities area so far this year, most of them since we had returned from out East. With the factory A/C in the camper van not working and because of the discontinuance in the production of Freon and cost of repair I didn't have it fixed. Because of the heat, I suggested we leave half a day sooner and drive in the cooler evening temperature. Debbie put the laundry into fast forward, enabling us to reach Interstate 94 rest stop in North Dakota about midnight where we spent the night.

WEDNESDAY, AUGUST 8TH, 2001

The air was dry and very windy. We ate dinner at the I-90 Bozeman Montana rest stop, home of Montana State where Kevin would soon be starting his junior year, and stopped for the night about 60 miles past Butte Montana.

THURSDAY, AUGUST 9TH, 2001

In trying to find information about nearby Clark Fork River, we stopped at the St Regis, Montana visitor information center. The nice middle-aged lady assisting us reminded Debbie of her Aunt Jean. Born in Montana, she'd moved to Oregon and had recently returned. Debbie poured two cups of complimentary coffee, placing them on the information desk. While picking through brochures, I noticed a 3-D relief map of Montana hanging on the wall that dramatized the changes in altitude. After almost drowning on the Big Hole, the visual of how fast the Clark Fork dropped altitude was scary.

In telling the information clerk why we were traveling through, I got expressive and knocked both cups of coffee on her desk. The only thing ruined was a daily weather forecast report.

We then went to the Trout & Tackle store two blocks away to browse. In seeing a rubber inflatable pontoon boat for an angler to sit on while floating downstream, I asked Debbie if she could imagine me floating the Clark Fork on it. At close to $1,000 it was a bit pricey for a single use.

A circuitous route found us at a visitor center in Spokane, Washington. I told the staff I had been to the World Fair, hosted there in 1974; my remembrance of the theme being reuse/recycle. They looked it up and confirmed my memory.

The World's Fair visit was part of a 6,000-mile, two and ½ week road trip vacation with a friend, Art, and my sister, Jean, in my 1971 VW Beatle. Besides the Worlds Fair, our stops included; Grand Teton's, Yellowstone National Park, ferry ride on the Puget Sound, San Francisco, Disney Land, Tijuana Mexico, Las Vegas, and the Grand Canyon.

Art's grandfather had taught him an amazingly authentic hog call. A booth at the World Fair had a decibel gauge used to measure noise pollution. Art nearly pegged the meter doing his 'hog call!' He also did it while he and I were in a small cave just below the lip of a tourist overlook of the Grand Canyon. Jean, who'd stayed at the overlook, said you should have seen the crowd's reaction. They grabbed binoculars and searched for the 'wild boar.'

At 2:30, we crossed over the Pend Oreille River from Newport, Washington into Old City, Idaho and went to Albeni (pronounced Albany) Dam visitor's center in search of a boat ramp. In asking young Rangers sorting recyclable materials about a boat ramp, they said their supervisor was en route and could better answer questions. The supervisor directed us to a nearby Forestry Management Office. The only thing they told us was the distance between the Albeni and Box Canyon Dam was about thirty-five miles, which turned out to be almost twice that.

A brochure entitled Albeni Falls? Some Questions Answered; stated the falls had been spelled three ways over the years, the intent being to name them after the first settler, a French Canadian named Albeni Poirer. Nobody could pronounce his last name so he was known by his first. The Great Northern Railroad spelled it Albany and the U.S. Geological Survey crew spelled it Albane. In 1952, the editor of the Newport Miner spearheaded the effort to officially correct the spelling.

The Pend Oreille River is pronounced "Pond O' Ray." Over the years, its spelling has also changed. The three spellings often used are Pend Oreille, Pend d'Oreille, and Pen d'Oreille.

Pend Oreille is derived from the French name given to the local Kalispel tribe because of the pendant ornaments worn in their ear lobes. The Kalispel's lived around the river and lake. A fall fishing site and winter hunting base was at Albeni Falls. In their native language of Salish, it was called sxwe uwi (shwe u wee), which means, a portage around the falls.

Generically speaking, I knew from talking to various people that a boat ramp close to the dam existed. We went north off Hwy 2 about three miles in a state park and found a concrete ramp stopping short of the water, with a further gradual decline over uneven rocks. In talking with two young men and a girlfriend wading, I found it got deeper the further out you went. Having traveled for almost two days I was anxious to get started. Not wanting to inflate the Zodiac, I decided to use The Boat. Even with the van backed the full length of the ramp; the boat was still high and dry on the roller trailer. It took our full combined effort to push it off.

Nate and I idled out to a depth of twenty feet and slowly headed south, which is upstream. While passing between an island and the bank to our right we encountered a grass field with a depth of only two feet. Is it going to be like this the whole way; going from twenty foot to two foot with no warning? Right after passing under the Hwy 2 Bridge we saw huge rocks in the clear water, some just six inches below the surface. Numerous sunken logs were also visible. With a marina being on the same side, water this shallow is unexpected. A very steep boat ramp was now visible on the southeast side of the bridge. With Nate in the bow watching for big rocks, we continued to inch our way to the bottom side of Albeni Dam. The depth finder transducer is only one foot ahead of the lower unit; by the time a big rock registers, it is too late to avoid hitting it.

In videotaping Albeni dam and mistakenly calling it Noxon, I realized I had left the maps and prepared trip notes with Debbie due to my usual haste to 'get started.' Our next meeting was to be on the west bank at whatever place she could find that had a ramp close to Box Canyon Dam.

Reaching Albeni Dam, we turned around and headed north for quite a while in the uncertain and varying depth. I asked Nate "Don't you wish that we were back on the Erie Canal?" Although their speed limit was 10 mph, depth was never an issue. He agreed.

Seeing five teenagers in a 14-foot aluminum runabout with probably a 50 horse Mercury suddenly take off ahead, I told Nate, "We'll follow their wake!" My hope was they knew the shallow areas, and I continued to watch the depth finder. They suddenly veered left, and a quick glance at the depth gauge showed only three foot, I wondered if they really knew where the channel was after all.

They continued for a while, slowed, and then stopped. Following their example, I did the same. Then off they went again! I took up the chase and followed in their wake three more miles where they stopped again. This time it appeared they might stay put for a while so I idled up and asked, "How do you know where the channel is?"

There were no channel markers and we had just passed a sandbar with people standing a good way out from it in knee-deep water. "You have to be out here and learn from experience." Saying we were from Minnesota and headed to Canada to where the river joined the Columbia, which we'd take to the ocean on a one-time trip their response was; "Well, Oh? Well, Follow us." Off we went.

We barreled through a narrow area with a depth of only two and a half foot; at least the bottom was now mostly sandy. Right after passing through a twenty foot depth and seeing four feet on the depth gauge they really slowed down. Everybody's head was moving and looking out the bow and sides as they moved forward. It was interesting why they were so intent while passing through a depth of four feet and had sped through the two and a half foot spot so casually. Just a short distance later, an adult waved them over to a dock on the left bank. I figured they were trying to look cautious for parents, but that is just a guess.

In talking with the adults; "Stay in the middle! It should be deep the rest of the way." However, it was not! It made me wonder when they had last been to Box Canyon Dam since a drought was occurring in the Northwest causing water levels to be abnormally low.

We went through some grassy areas where milk jugs on strings marked either a shallow area or a lucky fishing spot. In any case, I gave them a wide berth.

Right after crossing under a bridge, we saw twenty foot poles spaced about fifty feet apart running at about a 30 degree angle bank to bank with the upper most one 1/2 mile above the lowest. I assume their purpose was to corral logs back in the days when they floated rather than hauled them to mills. While passing through the widest space, I noticed two pilings cut off right at or just below the present water level. From there to the dam, it was fairly deep.

At 7:30, we spotted Debbie at a public boat ramp. I idled in so she could complete the run to Box Canyon Dam with Nate and me. She said the boat trailer suspension had broken and was at Newport, Washington awaiting repair. I told her of a major problem also; "The cassette player does not work!" Music is an important part of the trip.

Adding five gallons of gas to bring the gauge to empty, we headed for Box Canyon Dam. The dam is not visible from the point where a fence stops downstream progress. During the planning phase, I'd found out a canoe party from Europe hadn't heeded the warning sign before entering the steep canyon walls and were swept over the spillway, hence the reason for the fence.

Directly adjacent to the public boat ramp is Ione Motel & RV Park, with dockage on the river. We lucked out; getting an overnight spot for the van and moorage at the dock. With the trailer being repaired, the boat had to stay in the water.

While having dinner Debbie related what had happened to her. Right after crossing the Highway 20 river bridge and entering Newport, she heard a terrible racket coming from the trailer. A suspension part on the trailer had broken causing the right tire to lock up against the fender. As luck would have it, she was right across the street from a tire store and a young man came running out to help. The trailer was incapable of being pulled forward but could be backed. Al, the auto parts store owner on the same side of the street where the trailer broke, agreed to let her park it at the back of his lot. Al put Debbie on the phone with E & L Automotive. E & L called a welder who said he did not like to bring his equipment out without knowing what needed done. E & L's owner then went with Debbie to look at the trailer, saying it would not be a quick fix. He would do it, but not before noon tomorrow. With that understanding, she headed north to find us.

When Debbie arrived at the public boat ramp, she thought we should have already been there and started to worry, asking departing boaters to keep an eye out for us. Had it been too shallow? Did we have motor trouble? Were we trying to find her? Our arrival to the ramp was a full two hours after hers.

FRIDAY, AUGUST 10TH, 2001

With our bodies still tuned to Central Time, it caused us to wake up early so we took much-needed showers. Over breakfast, we discussed what to do until the trailer was ready. Intending to pull the radio/tape player out and buy a replacement, Nate suggested we use the portable CD player and cassette adapter instead. His idea worked fine since the only problem with the cassette player was that the tape transport motor was running slow.

Having time to kill before the trailer would be ready, we headed north to identify boat access points and check out river conditions.

I talked to a man fishing with his son at the boat ramp on the downstream (north) side of Box Canyon Dam. We learned that the Boundary Dam generating facilities were inside of the hollowed out mountain instead of part of the concrete dam structure.

Continuing north on #31 and while crossing over the Pend Oreille, I commented how narrow the river becomes just north of the bridge. We drove to Boundary Dam Vista Point and took a short hike down to a platform from where there is an awesome view of the dam and river.

We stopped a guard to ask questions about the river and if we would get in trouble approaching Boundary Dam from the Canadian side. He said that he had not seen any boats or Jet Ski's approach the dam from the North this season. Even though being in the area for ten years, he had yet to learn the river between Box Canyon and Boundary Dams. His contradictory statement is as follows; For the most part it was deep, *except*, for all the sandbars and shallow spots. He warned that the area just north of Metaline Bridge had been very rough yesterday and many canoeists had capsized there this summer. A lot depended on how much water Box Canyon Dam released at any one time.

We continued to the border and asked questions while going through the border ritual. The young female Canadian border-crossing official was of no help, professing she didn't even know the Pend Oreille went into Canada, let alone knowing about access points and dams that are on it. She gave us a cutsie tourist map that, while giving no real detail or scale, did show a gravel road running along the Pend Oreille. Driving ten miles north and not seeing a gravel road going west, we turned back south and found it. Right at the Border Crossing building! It was even called Pend 'Oreille Road.

The gravel road followed the river valley for the most part, winding up and around the mountainous terrain. The area is heavily pine treed and slopes steeply down to the river on both sides of the bank. The only access point is just before a bridge that crosses the Salmo River. Trying to find out if the road continued onto Seven Mile Dam, we continued a short distance past the Salmo River Bridge, encountering a Road Closed sign on a gravel road that follows the river. Seeing a one-lane trail going off to the right, Debbie encouraged me to take it saying she was sure it would loop around and end up at Seven Mile Dam. Against my better judgment, I followed the trail as it got steeper and rougher. Due to the vans low clearance and the trail seemingly going nowhere, I found a spot to turn around and headed back down the trail.

Back at the access point, we talked with two young moms swimming with their four children, ages one through ten. They remembered how the river looked before damming, saying it used to be just a stream running deep in parts. The water level was temporarily high due to Boundary Dam releasing a lot of water. They said the gravel road blocked by the 'Road Closed' sign continued to Seven Mile Dam but after washing out was not repaired. The trail we'd been on was nothing more than an old logging road.

On returning through US Customs, we told of our plan. They said to check back when we would actually be crossing the border by water.

While zipping back to Newport for the trailer, Debbie thought I was driving about 60 mph when I was only doing 45. It always seems faster when you are in the passenger seat on winding, hilly roads.

At 2:30, we arrived at E & L Automotive who had managed to pull the trailer from Al's auto parts store, using a 'C' clamp to hold the broken suspension together. Since the right front bracket had failed, they took the other connection points apart for inspection. The other three had cracks, with all four sent to be welded, reassembly expected to be done by 5:00. I thanked him for investigating the other three attachment points. It could have been a disaster if one had broken at highway speed with a boat on it.

Probably the single most overlooked and under maintained item of a trailer boater is the trailer itself. My trailer is rated at 2500#s, with the empty boat weight being less than 1800#'s, giving an allowance of about 700#s for gas and gear. I do not believe I ever exceeded the maximum weight while trailering. Never in salt water, replacing both inside and outside bearings less than six months ago, inspecting the surge brake master cylinder, winch, hitch jack, tires, wiring, and lights and with 99% plus towing miles on paved roads a major break still occurred without warning. Only after being dismantled were the other three cracks discovered. The only things I hadn't replaced were the rollers, surprisingly still like new. I kidded Debbie about me pulling the trailer with the boat on it from Minnesota without a problem while she'd broke the trailer after towing it five miles empty. There are two possible reasons why the trailer failed when it did. I'd cut a turn too close within a block of where it failed on the way to the ramp running the right wheel over a curb, and I'd had to back the trailer over rocks to get it deep enough to unload.

While awaiting trailer repair we walked the isles of the Safeway Grocery store to make sure we hadn't overlooked anything. Prices were high compared to Minnesota. Needing to replace an overhead van map light we went to Al's, finding he'd closed three months ago and had just happened to be there when the trailer broke. Finding a NAPA store nearby, a young employee glanced at the bulb, identified it as a #1004, and went back to get one. It took numerous key strokes to ring up the purchase. I joked the bulb would probably cost us $100. "Yeah, each punch is 25 cents." I asked where we could buy ice cream cones; being directed to an old grocery store with a soda fountain reminiscent of one on the town square of Washington, Iowa, the closest 'big' town to the boyhood farm. That was tasty! I read real estate ads while there. Housing was inexpensive compared to Lakeville, which would partially make up for the seemingly higher cost of groceries.

Everyone in Newport was so friendly and helpful. From the young man at the tire store who helped when he heard the noise, Al at the now closed auto parts store, the man at E & L, his friend the welder, the checkout cashier at Safeway, the Napa employees, and the soda jerk.

The trailer repair expense was very reasonable at $107.50. We returned to Ione Motel & RV Park where we loaded the boat and stayed the night. The real plus to having investigated the route to British Columbia is we now knew that using the Zodiac was the best option.

Rather than pull The Boat in steep and hilly terrain, and since the Pend Oreille loops and joins the Columbia River that mostly heads south, it made sense to leave it at the RV park in Ione. Fortunately, they allowed us to park it in an out of the way spot.

SATURDAY, AUGUST 11TH, 2001

It was 6:15 when we headed up #31 for the downside of Box Canyon Dam. The hand pump used to inflate the Zodiac was very noisy and probably sounded very intrusive to the people in the nearby campground considering the early morning hour. I tried to quiet it down by greasing the slide. It took an hour to get ready for the seventeen mile run to Boundary Dam. Before we could hand wheel the Zodiac down the long ramp that stopped well short of the river, rocks had to be cleared.

Debbie bought gas on the way to Metaline City Ramp, six miles downstream, with her arriving while our wake was still swirling. With everything OK, we said "Hi" and were off again.

Between Metaline and Boundary Dam, there is awesome scenery, especially when passing through an area with sheer rock cliffs.

Meeting at Boundary Dam ramp, a popular spot for campers, boaters, and anglers alike, we quickly deflated and loaded the Zodiac.

Per US Customs request yesterday, we again told of our plan. After being asked two or three times what boat we would be using, a U.S. border-crossing official took my drivers license and told me to park by the yellow curb while he called his supervisor. We waited, and waited. I was getting antsy. Finally the Border Patrol agent returned asking additional questions; "Were we getting out at the dam?" "No." "Were we leaving anything there?" "No." He told us to not get to close to the dam, as outflow changes are unpredictable and dangerous. Hearing I had respect for dams and would keep my distance, "OK, Go On". He had tried to reach his superior without success.

We then stopped at Canadian Customs and talked to the same woman as yesterday. She still does not understand what/or maybe why we are doing this. She asks if we have permission to use the water access. I said there was no one to ask permission of. She let us proceed.

Hoping to overnight at the unofficial access point to the Pend Oreille, next to the Salmo River, we found a camper trailer blocking access. In talking with the woman sitting underneath the awning, we found out her husband worked at both the Seven Mile and Waneta Dams. She said both dams were on a paved road accessible from the west with walk-in points to the river along the way. Seven Mile Dam was in the process of being upgraded with an additional turbine so it could match the outflow of Boundary Dam without causing so much water level fluctuation. She removed hanging lanterns from the trailer awning, enabling us to slip the Zodiac underneath.

The three (four if you include the dog) of us made the eighteen mile round trip between the two dams without being shot at by border patrol. It is a toss-up between this brief run and an especially memorable part of Lake Powell as to which is my favorite view of scenery from the water. Both have soaring cliffs rising from both sides; but Lake Powell's is of solid rock and barren of trees, while this is just the opposite. Today's water level was down seven feet from yesterday. With the original plan to overnight at the 'access' now out due to the travel trailer parked there, we deflated the Zodiac and moved on.

Debbie calculated the circuitous route we would have to take to reach Waneta Dam at seventy miles due to the gravel road no longer going through. Thinking we were making excellent time, Debbie realized the map scale was in kilometers and thus the distance was more like forty-four miles.

About five miles after picking up an asphalt road going east off 22A, we found a water access point. Inflating and equipping the Zodiac for the third time today, we were now like a NASCAR pit crew with everybody knowing their job without any spoken communication. It took just ½ hour to get ready for the upriver run to Seven Mile Dam.

With Seven Mile discharging water at a good clip, I did not try to round the rocky bend in the swift current and actually see it. The hills, while not as steep, were still very scenic. The ten to twelve mile round trip run between Waneta and Seven Mile Dam from the walk-in access point was especially relaxing due to the mostly deep calm water and the rush to keep going off. After deflating and loading the Zodiac, we took a very refreshing swim in the hot afternoon, with Debbie jumping in fully clothed.

Driving to the border, we crossed over the one-lane bridge just below Wanetea Dam and saw its outflow churning upon entering the Columbia River. It was 6:15 when we arrived at the border; finding it had closed at 5:00. Having to wait until 9:00 tomorrow for the scheduled border crossing, we found an RV park next to a McDonalds.

Using the $12.75 Canadian Nate received as change after buying 'Crunchie' and 'Krispie Crunch' candy bars, I added $4.17 US to the Canadian money to cover the $19 Canadian camping fee at the City of Trail RV Park. Ever since Kevin and I had taken the fly-in fishing trip to northern Saskatchewan in 1989, a 'Crunchie' bar, unique to Canada, has become a mandatory purchase whenever crossing the border. Nate had bought the 'Krispie Crunch' in error due to the similarity of name. I don't like 'Crunchie' bar's since they look like couch stuffing, and without actually having tasted couch stuffing, can't get over that thought while trying to eat one.

Hearing an incessant and loud barking coming from a building up the hill, Nate and I went to investigate. While walking around the chain link fence of the Society for the Prevention Cruelty to Animals (SPCA) facility, the din from barking dogs was incredibly loud. We hoped the fence was secure since they were not taking kindly to us.

22

2001 COLUMBIA RIVER

SUNDAY, AUGUST 12TH, 2001

The Columbia River part of the trip begins.

The RV campground showers required quarters to operate, and without Canadian change, we did not take one. They may take US but we did not want to cause problems with the equipment by trying. We left for the border at 8:45 for the posted 9:00 opening. Wanetea Dam was not releasing as much water as last night so the juncture where the Pend Oreille joins the Columbia was not as agitated as last night.

There was just a short wait at the border for the only car ahead of us to clear customs. The official asked the usual questions. "How many in the van?", "Citizenship?", "How long were you in Canada?" and "Why have you been in Canada?" Saying we had traveled the Pend Oreille River, he then asked how we heard about the river. I replied that I had done a lot of research on rivers. "Where is the boat?" "It's an inflatable and underneath the bed in back." "Why are you doing this?" "It's my hobby." "Where is the Pend Oreille?" I pointed back to the one lane bridge less than a ½ mile back. "Why the Pend Oreille?" I explained I was working on crossing East to West by water, and the route from the Rocky Mountains going west started with the Clark Fork, connecting to the Pend Oreille, connecting to the Columbia, and flowing to the ocean. "Are you writing a book?" "Is this why you are doing the rivers?" "No, but we do keep a journal so I may in the future." "Where are you going today?" I explained that I was looking for the first access point that I could find to get on the Columbia, then go upstream to the downside of Waneta Dam, and then downstream to Kettle Falls.

"OK, Pull up to the sign." My immediate thought was; Here it comes again, another long wait while our identities were ran through a computer, or worse, required to unload the van for an inspection. But, No! While pointing he said, "There's a road that goes down to railroad tracks. Right across from the tracks is a rocky trail that people use to walk-in canoes." He checked out the van clearance and said, "There is a boat ramp further down the road, but I don't think you have enough clearance reach it." "Check out the spot by the tracks first. If that doesn't work out come back and I'll tell you how to find the ramp."

Most of the time that he talked it was in a serious and business like manner. Looking back, when he asked if I was writing a book his demeanor had changed from that of an 'official' to that of the many helpful people we have met over the years.

We drove to the railroad tracks where I took a long time checking out if we would be able to get the Zodiac down to the Columbia River. It was at least a 100-foot vertical drop between the railroad tracks and the river. There were a few ways down, some having shrubs in exactly the wrong place, and all were rocky with a steep angle of descent. My thought was that it was doable if we all worked together.

With Nate and I carrying the main weight of the 122 lb. 25 hp Johnson outboard motor between us using a rope wrapped around our shoulders, Debbie kept the lower unit from dragging as we made the descent. It worked better than I originally thought.

Using the wheel kit, the inflated Zodiac was alternately pulled and held back by Debbie and Nate. I trailed behind; helping prevent a free wheel uncontrolled descent by having ropes wrapped around me and tied to the Zodiac.

It was 11:30 when Debbie and I left from the difficult access point with the Zodiac to run the swift upstream current of the Columbia River to the bottom side of Wanetea Dam to satisfy my phobia of covering the maximum water distance possible. Stopping back at the railroad departure point, I made Nate, who had stayed behind, go with

Debbie back to Ione to pick up The Boat. We would meet at Kettle Falls, which is at the upper most end of the reservoir created by Grand Coulee Dam.

The fifty mile river run was exciting, with the current being very swift for the first twenty or thirty miles, arriving at Kettle Falls at 1:30. I *love* running at wide-open throttle while negotiating the sweeps of a river, with every turn requiring a new set of decisions.

I sat on a shaded picnic table while waiting for Debbie and Nate to show up. I had just bought a Mug Root beer and was digging out quarters to call Debbie's parents when they pulled in at 3:30. The circuitous route they took to pick up The Boat took longer than I expected.

During the entire two hours I'd spent waiting, a young girl was on a public pay phone. How can somebody talk that long and still have anything left to say? We deflated the Zodiac, leaving with The Boat for the 102-mile trip to Grand Coulee Dam shortly after 4:00.

While I'd liked being in the Zodiac, it was nice to have a more comfortable ride and listen to 'tunes' while seeing sights not seen before. The enjoyment factor decreased as the motor started crapping in and out the last thirty miles.

We found Debbie without difficulty, loaded the boat, and ended up at an RV park called Kings Court in Coulee City with an empty 'pull through' site. While registering across the street at the Motel office the manager asked, "Are you fishing?" "No, we're headed down river to the Pacific." "They are running real good. Biting on this special rig." " No, we do not even have poles. We're headed to the Pacific." " Oh."

The day's temperature had reached 95 degrees, and it was dark by the time dinner could be prepared. Seeing a young man using a pay phone from the time we arrived to the time we went to bed, I joked that he was probably on the line with the young girl at Kettle Falls.

MONDAY, AUGUST 13TH, 2001

Debbie said that as she took her morning shower the soap and water ran off black, having to soap up twice to feel clean.

The day started having to fix the fuel line. While trying to change the in-line fuel line filter I put a twist in the metal line, which really ticked me off so I broke it off the rest of the way. A combination of tubing and rubber hose would fix it. Not finding the marine repair shop in Electric City with the directions given at the Motel office, I stopped at Braun's Automotive, found along the way, who said he would look at it.

Within ten minutes he investigated the problem. I offered my solution, and without comment he walked back across the street to the shop. A short period of time later, and not knowing if he was blowing me off, I walked into the shop and asked Paul, the owner, if he would be able to fix it. Paul turned around, holding the same type of hose and clamp assembly that I had been thinking would solve the problem, and said, "Is this what you want?"

I replied, "I am at the point of coming in the door, and you have me at the point of going out!" While paying the very reasonable charge, the owner of the car that I'd interrupted Paul from working on came in to find out when it would be done. Another tourist dropped by and said the petcock on her radiator was leaking and asked Paul if he might be able to look at it, being told to come back in the afternoon. I felt very fortunate at being helped so quickly, and a little bit guilty.

Paul gave us directions to the Elmer City Launch, which is about six miles downstream from Grand Coulee Dam on the right descending bank. We went on #155 through Elmer City, across the dam, up a hill, through a rock cut, and turned left towards a campground. By not taking the almost immediate right towards the campground, we missed the road that lead to the ramp and continued down the hill. Passing through an area marked 'Day Use Only,' I saw and went through an open gate on a gravel road that paralleled the major rock riprap'd river without finding a ramp. Retracing our route back to and through the open gate, we then saw an emblazed sign "Maintenance Trucks Only", contemplating our next move, a car with a young gal and four young kids pulled up next to us. She said, "I was driving the other way and saw you on the government road, so I turned around to see if you needed directions to the ramp. It's up by Spirit Campground," and she pointed back up the hill towards it. She reminded us of our neighborhood babysitter in Eagan, Jodi, who had taken care of Nate as an infant. Friendly, perky, she seemed way too young for so many kids; was she also doing day care?

Finally finding the ramp, all of us made the short run to the down side of Grand Coulee Dam, elevation being 1290'. During summer, a laser light show uses its massive facade as a projection screen. Grand Coulee Dam is the largest of all the dams on the Columbia, generating an enormous amount of power from its many turbines.

After dropping Debbie off at the ramp, Nate and I continued onto Rufus Woods Lake, the fifty-one mile pool formed by Chief Joseph Dam.

The next two paragraphs are from a US Corp of Engineer brochure, Chief Joseph Dam and Rufus Woods Lake.

> *The dam was named after a leader of a band of Nez Perce Indians. A man of peace, Chief Joseph was also a skilled military strategist and statesman. After a series of battles with the U.S. Army, following encroachment of Nez Perce lands by settlers, his band was overpowered in 1877 near Bear Paw, Montana. After several relocations, Chief Joseph spent his last years in exile on the Colville Indian Reservation, which borders the north shore of Rufus Woods Lake. He is buried on the reservation near there.*
>
> *Rufus Woods Lake was named in honor of the former publisher of the Wenatchee Daily World newspaper.*
>
> *Woods, a strong and vocal supporter of Columbia River development, used his editorial pages to argue for the construction of Grand Coulee Dam, Chief Joseph Dam and other projects in the Columbia River Basin.*

Debbie found the ramp on the left bank above Chief Joseph Dam, Elevation 956' Mile 545 above the mouth of Columbia, and went to the visitor center located inside the powerhouse. Not finding anyone staffing the visitor center, she picked up a brochure giving some details about Wells Dam, thirty-five miles downstream. We unloaded at a ramp on the left bank at the town of Bridgeport, just below Wells Dam. Since Wells Dam is only thirty miles from Chief Joseph, and not knowledgeable of any ramps in-between, a round trip with the three of us was the most logical and enjoyable thing to do. There were numerous shallow areas in the wide expanse of the reservoir. I tried to remember the downstream route so I could retrace it heading upstream since the channel wasn't marked.

From Bridgeport, we trailered to a ramp at Beebe Bridge Park, across the Columbia River from the town of Chelan. Nate and I had about eight miles of upstream travel to reach the downstream side of Wells Dam, and then a run of forty-two miles down river to Rocky Reach Dam, Elevation 707'. Debbie met us at Lincoln Rock State Park, where we camped for the night. When Debbie called her parents to touch base and let them know we were OK, Frank asked if we were getting enough sleep. Debbie's answer was that since it got dark at night, I did have to stop and rest.

TUESDAY, AUGUST 14TH, 2001

Seeing a Park Ranger on the way out of Lincoln Rock State Park, we asked about boat access points below Priest Rapids Dam since I had been unable to find information about that area. He said to look for motor homes parked next to the river above the Highway 240 Bridge as potential spots.

An older couple walking Great Danes stopped to talk with us upon seeing our Minnesota plates. They had lived twenty years in Rochester and still had family in the western part of Minnesota.

At 9:00, we launched the boat from the Rock Island Hydro Park, just below Rocky Reach Dam. Rock Island Dam is 31.6 miles downstream from Rocky Reach Dam. Because of the relatively short distance, we did the round robin up and back. With the river perfectly calm while passing underneath a railroad bridge during a train crossing, the upside down image of the bridge, train, nearby town and mountain all were reflected on the river surface. It was a fleeting moment not caught on camera but captured in memory.

As we got close to Rock Island Dam, Elevation 613', rock spires shot above and between the narrow span of the rivers banks. It was surrealistic, like navigating the moon's dry surface, except by boat! It took just over two hours to make the round trip. Depth typically ran about 140', with it going to 35' between spires.

We refueled The Boat and van en route to Crescent Bar Recreation Area, a la-di-dah ritzy golf resort area on a major sand bar with a boat ramp tucked behind the sweep of the river current. The boat launch had a 'daily parking fee' but since we were not parking, did not have to pay.

While launching the boat we noticed a big sign stating:

WARNING
You may encounter submerged hazards
Strong currents, Violent Winds, and waves
Floating debris, and fluctuating water levels

Nate and I headed upstream to the lower end of Rock Island Dam, and upon reaching, turned downstream towards Wanapum Dam, about thirty-five miles distant. Finding Debbie at a ramp close to Wanapum, we loaded The Boat not experiencing any particular problem that the sign at Crescent Bar Recreation Area had warned.

Earlier Debbie had found a nice ramp on the downstream side of Wanapum dam. In telling the desk attendant at a nearby museum that she was trying to find a boat ramp above the dam, was told to go back up the road to the first left. 'Had we arranged with the dam to be taken around since a truck with an empty trailer is available to do that?' Debbie also learned about a boat ramp located within the community of Desert Aire, a short distance upriver from Priest Rapids Dam.

Upon arriving at the ramp above Wanapum, she saw a white truck with an attached empty trailer marked - PUD (Public Utility District) For Official Use Only - parked there. During her brief wait, some teenagers came to the ramp to swim. One girl kept asking where the water had went, saying it was higher yesterday, much higher.

Wanapum Dam, named in honor of the Wanapum People from Priest Rapids, has a Z configuration with a length of 8,320 ft.

Trailering The Boat around Wanapum Dam to run the 18.7-mile distance to Priest Rapids Dam, we left with the understanding that we'd meet at a ramp I'd found marked on a map very close to the dam (not Desert Aire).

Not finding the ramp, Debbie drove to Priest Rapids Visitor Center where she talked to a man in a truck who said the only access close to the dam was at Desert Aire, a short distance upriver. Since I was expecting to meet her at the left bank next to Priest Rapids Dam, she looked for a way to get there. Following a gravel service road that led through desert like conditions of sand, sagebrush, and scrub trees, she found a place to park within sight of Priest Rapids Dam while still able to turn the van and trailer around. Upon seeing us arrive at the dam, she walked to the waters edge and shouted over the noise of an irrigation pump to meet her back up river at Desert Aire. There was a crude ramp there, but it appeared that it had been a long time since it had been used because there was a large mound of sand and gravel between it and the water. Only while returning to the van did Debbie see a sign warning it to be a rattlesnake area.

With us arriving first at Desert Aire, I asked a young Indian if this was Mountain Air? He replied, "No, Desert Aire". The heat and time spent on the water must be getting to me. There are actually two ramp areas there, one going directly into the reservoir, with the other one going to a lagoon, then the reservoir.

Eating lunch amongst the shade, we then headed to the downside of Priest Rapids Dam to find an access point with the goal being to make it to the Snake River confluence by nightfall.

Priest Rapids Dam, built by Grant County PUD, extends directly across the river at Priest Rapids with a length of 10,248 feet.

Grant County PUD pays for the operation of a major Chinook salmon fish hatchery next to Priest Rapids. The hatchery successfully raises and releases up to 10 million salmon each year.

We took the first unimproved road heading south below the dam, not much more than two tracks separated by desert scrub. It meandered its way to a river view, then turned southeast and paralleled the river. When the path came to a washed out gully with loose rocks and a deep drop, Debbie tried to persuade me to cross it and pick up the path on the opposite side. My thought was that even if a halfway decent ramp to unload The Boat even existed, low water level conditions and the lack of a controlled channel would make the use of the I/O iffy at best.

The next obstacle to open navigation was McNary Lock and Dam, over a hundred miles away. With McNary backing up a 62-mile pool when full, that left at least forty miles of unpredictable depth.

I made an executive decision to use the Zodiac for the seventy-three mile run from Priest Rapids to the where the Snake River joins the Columbia. This did not include the distance to power back up river to Priest Rapids Dam. I managed to turn the van and trailer around without crossing the washout.

The Zodiac was trip ready at the rivers edge in ½ hour. A new record considering that everything also needed transiting two hundred yards through rough rocky terrain in 105-degree temperature. Time was of the essence since it would take at least three hours of running at the top speed of 25 mph to reach the Snake.

In the short space of time between when Debbie carried three gas containers to the waters edge and when we pulled the inflated Zodiac to the river, it had come up six inches. The higher water level and fast river current caused the gas containers to start floating downstream, causing us to chase them down.

With an island separating us from the main flow of the river, Nate and I floated downstream in the shallow water to where it joined the main channel before being able to use the motor to head upstream.

Water was ripping through the narrow channel; Priest Rapids Dam must have just initiated a major release through its turbines.

One of the weirdest boats I'd ever seen was just leaving shore and heading into the swift current towards Priest Rapids Dam. It was similar to a small fiberglass bi-hull, but with out a deck. A child sat at opposite sides of the bow with two adults sitting on opposing sides in the stern with the motor in-between them. It was as if everyone had his or her own compartment to sit in. Upon experiencing the full strength of the current, they headed right back in.

We encountered two to three foot standing waves about a ½ mile below the dam.

It was 5:20 when we passed by Debbie, who had waited to make sure that no problems occurred going upstream. I had told her to expect to meet us at the Snake River Confluence at 8:20. The Boat would never have made it due to the many shallow areas along the way. While going around an island we saw two small deer with large antlers. The current was strong and tended to split its volume somewhat equally upon encountering an island.

I need to mention we were also boating through the Hanford Nuclear Government Site; with mostly mountainous terrain to the east and varying terrain to the west. This precluded us from making any stop whatsoever on most of the west bank and a good portion of the east bank.

It was 8:00 when we saw the bridges of the Tri-Cities (Pasco-Kennewick-Richland), with Nate thinking we'd made it. There was at least ten miles to go before reaching the Snake River confluence, with the Zodiac acting like Jell-O due to the temperature dropping 40 degrees since being inflated. Its rigidity had changed substantially. Not wanting to delay our arrival, we did not stop to add air to its three main chambers. The numerous brush fires occurring in central Washington obscured the setting Sun, causing darkness to settle in early.

About one mile from Sacajawea State Park on the east side of the Columbia, our planned meeting spot, we ran out of premixed gas. We needed to add a pint of oil to six gallons of gas. Nate poured a pint of two cycle outboard oil into a six-gallon tank, and started to fill it with gas from the Gas Pal while I switched fuel lines. Due to semi-darkness and the Zodiac bouncing in choppy river, the fuel spout came out of the tank after adding only two gallons, causing a small spillage. Cleaning the gas up the best we could, I figured two gallons would be more than enough to get us the rest of the way. I pulled on the rope starter and off we went. Ten feet! The motor did not want to start and stay running.

I told Nate to grab a paddle and work us closer to shore while I dinked with the motor. By the time he had the two-piece paddle assembled I figured out the problem. There was an excessive amount of oil in the gas mixture causing it to be to inflammable enough to power the motor. We added additional gas to the tank and shook to mix it. It took many pulls before it would start and stay running, with us off again.

About two minutes later we saw a waving flashlight on the left bank we were hugging. It was Debbie 'Shining us in!' She'd walked from the boat ramp to the swimming beach, unsure if the motor heard was ours.

After getting within hailing distance she said, "Go up the Snake". I said "OK" and started to take off. "Wait! The ramp is in a lagoon with a little opening just past all the trees and fishing piers."

We missed the lagoon entrance, only finding it upon turning back with Debbie once again signaling with the flashlight after running back to the ramp.

Between the time Debbie signaled us on the east bank of the Columbia and then on the north bank of the Snake, she encountered a park ranger who asked if it was her van at the ramp. Saying it was and that she had been waiting for us to arrive from Priest Rapids Dam, he said the park had closed a ½ hour ago. The ranger said to load as quickly as possible and honk as we went out so he could lock the gate.

It was 8:40 when we pulled into the cove, twenty minutes later than my prediction. It took longer than usual to deflate and load due to almost absolute darkness with the lights in the loading area of little help.

Debbie did her usual good job of navigating unfamiliar city streets. Having pushed hard all day to reach the Snake River confluence, I was wired. While Debbie drove she complained about my 'chattering.'

Following Columbia River's west bank and heading north we saw a sign with the word "camping" emblazed in the headlights with an arrow pointing left. The gates were open with the registration building having closed at 9:00. It now being 10:00, we pulled into unoccupied site #12. It took writing trip notes and reviewing maps of the Columbia River before I was able to relax enough to fall asleep.

WEDNESDAY, AUGUST 15TH, 2001

Having literally thrown everything in last night, some time had to be spent reorganizing. Partially due to the addition of the Snake Rivers flow, the rest of the 324-mile trip to the Pacific on the Columbia has a system of four lock and dams with a marked navigation channel that would enable us to use The Boat.

While preparing to launch at a ramp above the Columbia/Snake confluence I realized my prescription sunglasses were AWOL. I had kept them in a case until one of Debbie's lenses fell out and she started using them instead. Retracing our steps first back to a gas station, then the campground, Nate found them on the boat floor. They must have fallen out of my shirt pocket while checking the crankcase oil level. Get those glasses fixed so I can have my eyeglass case back!

Back to the ramp we went. We agreed to meet at either McNary Lock and Dam, 31.4 miles from the Snake, or John Day Lock and Dam 24.5 miles further. I wanted Debbie to take pictures of Nate and I locking through, and knowing that some locks have better visitor viewing facilities than others, it would be Debbie's call on which one worked out best.

It was interesting to travel the same section of river as last night, doing so in daylight and in the in relative comfort of The Boat. Shortly after the point where the Snake River joined, the river changed from choppy to rough so I slowed to twenty mph. The Columbia swept from Richland southeast towards Pasco, looped southwest almost 90-degrees, and then turned west.

Water became almost dead calm as the heading changed from SE to W/SW. A long distance separated the buoys that designate the navigation channel.

Outside of McNary Lock and Dam, I used VHF radio channel 14 to make contact. While I refer to the Seasprite as The Boat, my VHF license has the name River Runner. Using The Boat would sound confusing to a lock operator.

2001 COLUMBIA RIVER

"River Runner to McNary Lock." "McNary Lock, back." "River Runner would like to lock down." "Are you private or commercial?" "Private." "Our next scheduled lockage is at 2:30 PM.

It was now 12:30, so I idled towards a boat ramp on the right bank. With the depth gauge showing ten feet and the tachometer at 1000 RPM, I hit something hard enough to take a quarter-size chunk off one of the three blades. I do not understand how something could possibly have been so close to the surface. This was the second prop damaged this year already, with both done at about five mph. I had put over 10,000 miles on the original aluminum prop without major nicks.

While tied up at the boat ramp dock Nate said, "If Mom was here we could load up and go around". "Or if we had drugs for sale we could be commercial and be locked through immediately."

I started to walk up the hill to the lock to get a better idea of what was going on- When the camper van popped over the ridge! I said she looked, "Like the cavalry coming over the hill to the rescue". "You have saved me twice – "Shining me in last night" and showing up now so we can trailer around.

Debbie then told of a scare experienced while leaving a shopping center after buying ribbon to help slide her eyeglass lens back in place. Hearing an explosion, like a tire blowing, she stopped to check the van and trailer tires when she heard it again. It came from a bike shop.

Fortunately, for Nate and me, she decided to wait at McNary. From the fish-viewing platform, Debbie saw a barge lock down shortly before our arrival. Seeing us leave the lock approach without the lock chamber filling she thought, Uh Oh, the VHF radio isn't working, so off to the ramp she went.

Puzzled about McNary's lock schedule, I radioed from the boat ramp and asked; "Being from Minnesota and our first lockage attempt on the Columbia, why is there a lock schedule". The Lockmaster responded, "Because of water shortage we only do private boat lockages three times a day." I asked if he knew John Day's schedule, which he did not.

Thanking him, I said we would trailer around. We loaded The Boat and put in at a ramp about three miles downstream on the Oregon side. Using the River Cruising Atlas from Evergreen Pacific Publishing Ltd.

as a resource, a boat ramp 1/3 mile upstream from John Day on the Washington side after passing underneath railroad tracks would be our next meeting spot.

Nate and I cruised upstream to the downside of McNary, and upon reaching, turned downstream to cover the 24.5 miles to John Day. We had a pleasant run until the motor started crapping out again. Finding John Day Lock & Dam was easy, but trying to find a way underneath the railroad tracks was not. A closer inspection of what first appeared to be a small drain tube was actually 12-14 foot in diameter. We passed through it and followed a channel to a boat ramp where Debbie was waiting.

While loading, two construction workers living in a trailer next to the boat ramp working on a nearby road project talked with us. We headed west eight miles, crossing over the Columbia River on Highway Bridge 97 to Oregon, where we went back east six miles to a ramp on the downstream of John Day to the town of Rufus.

It was 5:30 when Nate and I were once again on the river and headed upstream to John Day. Our next meeting spot is to be at Horsethief Lake State Park on the Oregon side, twenty-two miles from John Day and 2 ½ miles above Dalles Lock & Dam.

Debbie saw us a couple times in the rough water caused by the almost constant high wind that flows through the Columbia Gorge on her way to Horsethief.

It was 6:50 when Debbie saw us passing by Cellio Park, with nine miles to go before reaching Dalles Lock and Dam. Not seeing us having major problems handling the rough water, she drove to Horsethief State Park to wait. It took rounding a minor bend for the full force of the wind to hit, with three waves going over the bow when the motor suddenly cut out, causing it to dip. It was slow progress fighting against the wind and waves, with the motor cutting out at critical times not helping.

Hiding out in the relative calm of a bend, I added gas and sprayed the carburetor with cleaner fluid hoping to alleviate the problem.

As we rounded an island around a turn in the river on the left bank, I saw a red navigation buoy to our right. Remembering the rule Red to the Right Returning **from** the sea, with us still going to the Pacific the marker should have been to our left. The depth gauge dropped to 3 1/2 foot while crossing. Nate's job was to watch the chart and channel buoys, while mine was to keep from sinking by taking waves over the open bow. Asking what the shallowest depth for the area on the chart was, his answer was three feet! Obviously we were not communicating very well. One big swell would have dropped us below that.

Shortly after getting back in the marked channel, we saw Debbie waving from a ramp on the right bank. Exchanging meaningless hand gestures, we continued onto Dalles Dam. While approaching the ramp at Horsethief Falls Sate Park, Debbie warned of its poor condition. I said that even if it was a mud ramp I would be happy to be off the river safely.

The Camp Host at Horsethief Falls Sate Park where we stayed the night said, "It's always windy in the Columbia Gorge. Maybe at night the wind might lie down, but usually not." He verified that the still hazy sky was due to wild fires. The trees at the campground looked permanently bent from the wind.

THURSDAY, AUGUST 16TH, 2001

With the wind still up, I spent the morning trouble shooting the motor. I changed the fuel and water separator filters, and cleaned the carburetor again. One of the spark plug wires did not seem to be seated on the distributor cap.

We left the park at 1:00 and headed for the Port of the Dalles ramp on the Oregon side to check water conditions. As we came down the steep hill on 197 and with the right turn signal on to pull into a Shell station, a car furiously honking its horn passed by. Checking the trailer lights, I found they were completely non-functional. No wonder I had been honked at. Suspecting a wiring failure, I decided to buy a circuit tester. The wind was howling even worse than at the campground with Debbie saying the wind was getting to her. Finding two contiguous parking spots right in front of a NAPA store in Dalles, Oregon, I spent $23 for a circuit tester. It showed the wiring was good up to the trailer. Pulling the bulbs out of the trailer, I found the dual filaments of each bulb burned out on both sides. One thing that helps keep unsealed bulbs from failing is to unplug the wiring harness before backing the trailer in. This keeps the bulbs from getting hot as the brake light goes on and off and failing upon hitting cold water. Don't forget to plug them back in after reloading. We hadn't checked to see if the lights were working after every launch, which is what should be done.

We launched The Boat at the Port of the Dalles, planning to run the two miles upriver to the downside of Dalles Lock & Dam, and then see what it took to fight our way into the wind and waves on the way back. Debbie would wait ten minutes after we went by heading downstream before leaving.

Traveling to the downside of Dalles against the rapids generated by its discharge was easier than heading downstream into the wind whipped waves.

A strange phenomenon occurs due to the strong wind that courses through the Gorge. The downstream current is picked up and blown back over itself, creating major waves.

Debbie watched as we went past, seeing us stop twice before disappearing around a bend heading west. Intending to wait until 4:20 before leaving, she tried to start the van at 4:18 in preparation. Nothing, not even a whir or click! Then seeing me walk up the ramp towards the van at 4:19, Debbie says it is now me coming to the rescue.

The westerly water fight had not gone well. With the open bow continuously dipping into oncoming waves, taking on water each time, the decision to return was easy. In defense, I'd discussed the need of a bow cover to shed water with Debbie nixing the idea thinking it was over kill.

Using the 12-volt Booster Pac to start the van, back to NAPA we went. This time the closest parking spot with a vehicle/trailer combo was several blocks away. With Nate and me alternately carrying the 'dead' battery to NAPA and testing at almost 100% charge, carried it back. With it again failing to turn over the starter, we carried it back, and bought a new one, which immediately started the van.

While at NAPA, I asked if the wind ever died down. The response being that today was 'normal' and gets worse. I changed the original plan and decided to go by road to Bonneville Lock and Dam and travel west to east. Why beat myself up when the wind and water can work for you? I had given up on using the locking facilities of the remaining three dams after bypassing the first. I would have felt guilty flushing water through the locking system during their drought period that would otherwise have run through hydroelectric generators. White caps and large rolling waves were evident as we traveled along I-84, which closely follows the Columbia River through the Gorge. Between Hood River and Meyer State Park the scenery changes. The Dalles hills are treeless, with sand and scrub brush, with the Hood River hills populated by thick pine trees growing amongst angular rocks. Port of Cascades Locks Marina, 4½ miles upstream from Bonneville, has a campground where we secured a spot looking directly over the river. There is an unused old lock there, a remnant of before the lock system was upgraded and consolidated.

FRIDAY, AUGUST 17TH, 2001

It was 7:20 as Nate and I headed downstream to Bonneville Dam, with Debbie waiting for us to pass upstream before leaving to meet us at Port of Dalles ramp. The wind was still up for the forty-five mile river run we'd have from Bonneville.

The waves got progressively larger and deeper the further east from Bonneville Dam we went. It is time to acknowledge that I am not a writer because if I were this portion of the trip would be a mini-novel in itself. We alternated sides of the river, always trying to stay in the lee of the wind and waves.

Gas was added twice, once shortly after starting. Since it seems the motor only cuts out when the fuel gets low, or after three hours of running, I tried to make sure the tank did not get low. The second time was as much to settle my nerves as to add gas. Finding a dock on the south side of river, we tied up to top off the tank. Trying to verify river progress by identifying our location, we walked up the hill to the restroom facilities. Taking advantage of them, we continued to walk up the drive to a latched chain link fence barring access from the other side. I lifted the latch, walked through, and saw the Do Not Enter sign that you would see upon approaching. There were additional postings that identified the area we'd docked at as a Native American only access.

Guesstimating an additional twelve miles to go once leaving the dock, we passed through an area very popular with wind surfers. In fact we literally passed through' *a bunch of wind surfers'*! This was the most harrowing segment of water I had ever traveled in The Boat; regardless of being a river, inland lake, or the Gulf. I did my best to avoid colliding with the wind surfers while climbing or descending ten-foot waves. It would have been an interesting legal case if I had injured one. My understanding of the rules regulating inland rivers with navigation channels is as follows; a recreational boat must yield the right of way to a sailing vessel, but a burdened vessel has the right of way. Is a sail boarder a sailing vessel? Was I a burdened vessel since I could not easily change course without taking on water? The best defense I would have had is that is that there was no way to make a radical change of course quick enough without sinking myself. The best analogy I can compare it to is; picture yourself on a summer's night braving your way to the grill from the shelter of the house and encountering a swarm of mosquitoes. Do you try to avoid each one or maintain the shortest route to the grill? There was one near encounter with a sailboarder, who managed to steer to our stern while shouting something unintelligible on the way by.

Sometimes we caught up to waves and sometimes they caught up to us. In cresting the larger waves, we actually **SURFED** down their slope. The open bow would plow into the tail of the wave ahead of us. My attempt to describe how close we came to stuffing the bow, filling the boat with water, defies my use of the English Language. I thought about putting the boat in reverse, to keep from submarining ourselves, but didn't. I was already putting it in neutral to keep from accelerating down the wave crest. Many times the entire bow was only two inches above the wave we were plowing into. Looking back at the high following sea, going into reverse would have submerged us just as surely.

My greeting to Debbie at the Port of Dalles ramp was one of the biggest understatements I have ever made, "That Sucker was Rough!" Followed by, "You could not pay me to do that again! That's because the boat would have sunk and have to be pulled up off the bottom!" Just for the record, no water came aboard. I'd done a good job of piloting.

Trying to hide my doubts about making it to Port of Dalles ramp without sinking, I asked Nate his thoughts. His reply, "We've been through worse".

We decided to travel to the mouth of the Columbia by road, accomplishing two things; One, to scout out accesses along the way, Two, enable Nate and me to run the ever-widening Columbia west to east; using the prevailing wind flow to our advantage.

Stopping at Chinook Public Ramp five miles from the Pacific on the Washington side, we talked to two men who had just come in from fishing with their twenty-two foot cuddy cabin because of rough water. They advised us to stay away from the Washington side as the navigation channel closes down heading east. They said there were two tide cycles per day; with a seven-foot variance between high and low. Tomorrow's 7:00 AM low tide would leave the channel just out from the ramp only one and a half foot deep. They told two stories; one of a forty-five foot boat overturned by waves after grounding on a sand bar, and another about a father and son who lost an engine and drifted onto a shallow bar in heavy waves and jumping out just before it sank.

Having been 'On the Edge' earlier, I was apprehensive about completing the trip to the Pacific. I pulled out the chart and analyzed it in detail. We should have stayed on the Oregon side where the 'maintained' channel of the Columbia runs fairly close to shore. It was time to find a camping spot, so we drove to Fort Canby State Park, Washington. Finding they were full, we turned back looking to find the first campground with an opening. Every campground along the way was wall to wall with RV's. Not seeing a FULL sign at a an RV camp in Ilwaco, the first town west of Fort Canby, Debbie got in a line ten deep to register. The lady asked, "Dry Camping?" It turns out 'dry camping' means you stay overnight in their large parking lot, the only facility being an over worked toilet shared with the other 100 vehicles.

OK, OK, I exaggerate; there were separate Men/Women toilets and at $10.98 cheap enough.

Two reasons why the campgrounds were full; it was the weekend, and 'The Salmon' were running.

SATURDAY, AUGUST 18TH, 2001

Doing the tourist thing, we returned to Fort Canby and hiked up to the lighthouse that overlooks Cape Disappointment. Debbie asked, while videotaping the expanse of water off to the west, "Is there an island out there?" Using binoculars, what first appeared to be an island was actually a large concentration of fishing boats. While returning on the hiking trail, we talked with a couple who had also had trouble finding a place to camp. "They tried to give us a spot without a fire pit. Hello! Who would want to go camping without a fire?"

Crossing over the wide expanse of the Columbia on the 101-bridge we found a ramp at Hammond, Oregon about eight miles from Mile Zero, the 'official' ending of the Columbia. Lots, & lots, & lots, of empty boat trailer/tow vehicles filled the lot. Fortunately, it was 'late' in the day for an angler so there was not a line at the ramp to unload.

As the three of us made the run to Mile Zero, we fought wakes of the mostly larger boats that had 'FISH' on their mind! The only rule that seemed to apply was 'FISH.' I am going to where the fish are so get out of my way, my big wake is your problem!

It would have been nice to clear the fishing boat flotilla and hit open water, but that would have required fighting through the dragnet of crisscrossing fishing lines and risk their entanglement in the prop. We had crossed over 'The Bar,' the point at which you can look to 180 degrees to the right and left and not see land.

While dropping Debbie back at the ramp, we agreed to meet next at Port of Kalama Marina, Mile 75 on the Columbia. The motor started cutting out again, this is getting old! Our arrival to the marina coincided with that of Debbie. With Nate videotaping an odd-looking ocean-going vessel while passing in front of the breakwater, Debbie thought we hadn't seen the marina.

We ate lunch and discussed where to meet next after refueling. I wanted to stop at Jantzen Beach for the night, thirty miles distant. Debbie thought it was too close to the Portland, Oregon metro area to find camping so we settled on Chinook Landing, forty-five miles away. At 5:30, we arrived at Chinook with the motor cutting in and out.

Seeing a sign on I-84 indicating camping facilities, we exited and followed another sign for a specific campground up a 10% grade for a mile and a half only to find it FULL. I decided to go back to Cascade Lock where we stayed two nights ago, arriving in time to get the last 'official' spot. Later arrivals set up camp in an open area. The 'Class of 81' was having a reunion at the picnic shelter.

SUNDAY, AUGUST 19TH, 2001

It was 9:00 as Nate and I headed west after launching from just below Bonneville Dam, using the North Bonneville ramp. The final twenty-five miles of the Columbia started out choppy, then calming with the motor problem getting worse. Our arrival to Chinook Landing marked another major milestone towards accomplishing my goal. The boat was on the trailer and everything organized for the trip to Bozeman, Montana by 11:40 AM.

Kevin, now a third year Montana State mechanical engineering student, was using the Aeorstar and snowmobile trailer to haul what he needed from Lakeville to equip his off campus apartment. He was a groomsman in a wedding that was to take place today and had called Debbie's parents when leaving Minnesota last Wednesday. They'd not received the promised call saying he'd arrived safely. Kevin is normally very responsible, so naturally we were worried. With the predetermined plan to pick up the Aeorstar and snowmobile trailer on our way back to Lakeville and with Debbie's parents not receiving the confirmation call that he had arrived safely, we were understandably in a hurry to make sure he was OK.

I suppose you wonder why we don't use cell phones. There is not a simple answer. First, there is the expense, considering it would take two for us to communicate. Then considering the areas traveled, reliability is an issue due to mountainous terrain and sometime remote areas. The real answer quite simply is that neither Debbie nor I like them. We'd been able to find each other so far and enjoyed our quiet time away from the wired and wireless world. Having emergency contact numbers, an AT & T calling card, and touching base with parents or neighbors on a regular basis had thus far worked.

As we traveled I-84 east, the areas of the Columbia River that had been so rough had hardly a white cap. I guess the wind and waves do go down if you wait long enough. Originally planning to boat the Snake River to its upper limit of navigation, we did not do it due to our concern for Kevin and the fact that I finally had had enough of boating for the summer.

It would have required going through four locks and dams and travelling 147 miles from its confluence with the Columbia.

Traveling most of the night, at 11:00 AM we arrived to the address of the apartment complex in Bozeman that Kevin had given us. Seeing the Aerostar and snowmobile trailer parked there provided some relief. No one answered the door to the ground level apartment. Peeking in, I saw beer cans and bottles all over the place. Seeing the back door patio glass sliding glass door open, with the screen door shut, I walked around and into the apartment. Still no Kevin, and with an ample supply of beer spread between two refrigerators, I helped myself while we awaited his return. About three hours later Pixie heard Kevin inserting his key and started barking. He had been horseback riding with two friends and had no idea anybody was in the apartment. One of his friends said, "You should have seen the look on his face when he heard the dog barking!" I had purposely hid the camper van and boat to surprise him.

As to why so many beer cans, full and empty, were in our 20-year-old son's apartment; the bachelor and after wedding party were held there. The many adults present at both had done the buying. Kevin, having left Debbie's parents telephone number in Lakeville, used the Internet to look it up. He'd called several times with no answer. The Internet number was wrong.

After returning home with the two vehicles, both pulling trailers, I took The Boat out for a spin on our lake. The cutting out problem was now solid so I took it to a husband/wife repair shop in Rosemount. He repaired boats and she did upholstery. I checked back the following week and found out they had gone on vacation. A caretaker was answering the phone and watching over the place. With The Boat backed up to a service door, not the spot left at, I assumed it was fixed. Wanting to winterize it before I left for the Southwest on a non-boating vacation, decided to pull it home. The caretaker could not find a bill so I said have it mailed upon the owners return. I took the boat out for a test run and it ran perfectly.

Not having received the bill during my three-week vacation, I drove there and asked what I owed. Remembering working on the boat, but not what needed fixing, he said it was probably just the choke sticking. What do I owe you" "No charge". He had worked on it before and we had gotten to be friends.

23

2002 CLARK FORK, PEND OREILLE, FLATHEAD, & YELLOWSTONE RIVERS

My goal of going East to West by water has become an obsession rather than a passion. I planned to start this year's trip from where I had dumped the kayak on the Big Hole and take it to the Jefferson. Then go over the Continental Divide, pick up the Clark Fork, to the Pond Oreille, and stop at Albeni Falls Dam, last years starting point. I explored buying a raft to run rougher sections and decided not to since I no longer had the grip to handle paddles in white water conditions. Before attempting a start with the canoe, we'd explore down river conditions. Behind the camper van, we'd be towing the snowmobile trailer with the inflated Zodiac and the canoe on an overhead rack.

SUNDAY, JUNE 23RD, 2002

Debbie, Nate, and I stayed overnight at the now familiar Bozeman Montana Interstate I-90 rest stop.

MONDAY, JUNE 24TH, 2002

We continued west on I-90 to I-15 South, taking the sixth exit and followed the frontage road to Glen Bridge as a starting point to check out access areas and river conditions. For the record, the entire length of the Big Hole is non-motorized.

Using a hydrographic chart from 'The Big Hole River' map of Montana Afloat as a reference, I knew peak river flow is typically in May. Colder weather had slowed the above average snowfall mountain melt this year.

Glenn access is 22.4 miles above the Jefferson, with the town of Glenn at an altitude of 4980.' We talked with anglers preparing their inflatable while watching the high fast river flowing by.

Heading northwest, we checked out Browns Bridge and Salmon Fly access points. It was not encouraging to see water running fast and high past both.

While following a dirt/gravel road some distance trying to find Maiden Rock access, we met a truck with Colorado plates whose driver said the road led to a mountain lake. I retraced our route and took a left turn at the only other major fork. We stayed on it until reaching an overhead ranch sign spanning the road width. It may have been the correct road, but I did not feel right driving through. Retracing our route again, we saw a rancher herding cattle across the road using an ATV and a dog. Not the way you'd typically picture an Out West Cowboy.

We found the next Maiden Rock access. There are two; the first heading upstream provided by the Department of Fish and Wildlife, the second maintained by the Bureau of Land Management. This is a beautiful area, isolated, with sparsely covered scrub brush bluffs ascending from both sides of the river.

Next to the road leading to the river, I saw a temporary sign warning that the next bridge had a clearance of less than three feet! That made my decision to stay off the Big Hole easy. Already having doubts about Nate's and my ability to handle the canoe in high fast water, we didn't need the added danger of low clearance bridges. What else would we unexpectedly encounter? Log jambs? Dangerously low overhanging trees?

Another thing weighing on my mind was the long-range plan to pick up the Clark Fork River on the other side of the Continental Divide after finishing the Big Hole-Jefferson connection. There is a nineteen-mile white water section of it called Alberton Gorge with Class IV (very difficult) rapids. I already knew we would not attempt to boat it; and instead take a professionally guided raft.

I wanted to go East to West as much as possible without the on-water assistance of guides or watercraft that weren't ours. So I rationalized not finishing the Big Hole and decided to find the first logical place where motor use is allowed heading west.

The only reason for picking the Big Hole, Jefferson, to the Missouri route was to have the least land distance between rivers heading east and west as is possible, regardless of the number of water miles it would take to do so. Having stated that as my original goal, it would have been stupid to attempt it knowing I might drown and possibly take Nate with me in the process.

The Continental Divide is a defining point for which way rivers flow. As the crow flies, less than thirty miles separates the Big Hole, flowing mostly southeast, from the Clark Fork. The Clark Fork flows northwest about two-hundred miles before joining the Pend O' Reille, which flows to the Columbia and then to the Pacific.

The new goal became to find the shortest distance between the Missouri rivers water flowing east and the Clark Forks heading west **and** do so safely without the assistance of a for hire raft or fishing guide. Looking at the Montana highway map, I found it to be about 132 miles between Holter Dam on the Missouri and the town of Paradise where the Clark Fork snakes east then turns northwest.

Decision made! Paradise here we come.

Viewed looking west, I-90 closely follows the Clark Fork for about 165 miles, then at the St. Regis exit the river takes a sharp turn back east. Twenty-four highway miles later is the town of Paradise, elevation 2489'.

The town of Paradise has an interesting story behind its name. Supposedly there was a saloon there called Pair O' Dice, and upon the Milwaukee Railroad establishing a division point nearby changed the spelling for moral reasons, without actually changing pronunciation.

Rather than start immediately from Paradise, I wanted to get a feel for river conditions. While driving alongside the Clark Fork on Hwy

200 for thirty-three miles, we saw it running fast with white water several places.

Figuring the water below Thompson Falls Dam at the Idaho/Washington border would be somewhat regulated, I decided to start there the following day and do the upriver stretch after it calmed a bit.

While staying at Riverfront RV Park, with the river not actually visible from our campsite just below the dam, I got fired up reviewing maps. The approximately two-hundred-fifty mile portion of water initially intended to travel and now skipped would have required paddling, and going through many dangerous sections. After barely making it out when I'd put a snowmobile through the ice in January 1989, almost drowning in the sea kayak, and losing fingers in the lawn mower accident, more caution needed to be exercised if I wanted to see any of my unborn grandchildren.

TUESDAY, JUNE 25TH, 2002

It took a fair amount of time to prep for the day. Nate pumped the Zodiac up to the proper pressure, I loaded gear, and Debbie made a good breakfast.

With a full load of fuel, we headed in search of the closest ramp to Thompson Falls Dam. Thompson Falls State Park, about four miles downstream from the dam, had a nice ramp. While unloading, George, representing American Water Survey, asked questions for a study. He actually answered more questions than he asked. The only resource I'd came up with for the area was a pamphlet produced by Washington Water Power. It only generically showed access points between Thompson Falls, Noxon Rapids, and Cabinet Gorge Dams. George told Debbie of a place called Monroe Flats, not identified on the pamphlet. She would take the road leading to Noxon Dam viewpoint, cross RR tracks, take two lefts, and follow a rough road to the river's edge. Locals with four-wheel drives used it as an access. We'd probably have to move some logs to load up.

Nate and I took off upriver, quickly encountering fast water. We wound our way through major rock formations, running rapids while doing so. Stopping just short of actually seeing Thompson Falls Dam, we videotaped the water boiling around the bend below it.

Turning downstream for the approximate twenty-five mile run to Noxon Rapids Dam and running with the rapids was more to my liking. While enjoying the run to Thompson Falls Dam, it hadn't allowed any time to get acclimated to fast water again. While going with the flow you have the option of using minimum throttle to direct the boat through rapids. Going upstream, faster is better unless you hit rocks taking out the prop. Ideally I should be using a jet drive lower unit, which takes about 35% more horsepower to get the same speed, resulting in being less fuel efficient.

The ever-varying view was always dramatic, with the snow-capped mountains visible beyond the tree and rock studded banks evoking a childhood memory of a backlit lamp that was next to my bed when I was sick for a year. The lamp had a panoramic shot of exactly the same type of scenery I was now seeing. While seemingly in the wilderness, signs of civilization were evident from the collection of plastic bottles and cans picked up along the way. Having reached Noxon Rapids Dam, it took Nate's Santa Claus Christmas present of two-way radios to find Debbie. It took moving four or five large semi-floating logs to reach shore where we then wheeled the Zodiac to the point where Debbie had parked the van. I picked up a strangely shaped piece of driftwood as a souvenir.

Finding George taking his survey at the overview on the downstream side of Noxon, we thanked him for the good directions given. The volume of water pouring out of the dam was amazing! You had to practically yell to hear each other above the roar.

Arriving at Pilgrim Creek Recreational Facility, the first access below Noxon Dam east of the town of Noxon, we found it gated shut. A sign indicated the closure was temporary due to the spraying of a lawn chemical. Even with the best of plans, things happen that you can not foresee. We found a workable access one-half mile downstream.

While running the three miles back up stream against the heavy discharge of the dam we saw several Bald Eagles. They were swooping down attempting to nab fish from the turbulent water; one came within ten feet of us. We did not see a successful catch.

The fast water encountered heading upstream only continued two miles downstream past our launch point. The rest of the eighteen-mile distance between Noxon and Cabinet Gorge Dam required avoiding the heavy wood drift that seemed to raft together. About five miles from Cabinet Gorge Dam, and now in Idaho, we passed under a one-lane bridge where Debbie was standing. Conversing over the radios we found she'd been unsuccessful in trying to find the unmarked route to the Heron County Boat Launch described in the Washington Water Power pamphlet. After making several false attempts and inquiring locally without success she'd parked at the end of the bridge and waited for us. I said we'd continue to the dam and upon returning let her know of any access point along the way.

Cabinet Gorge Dam is tall at 208 feet while only 600 foot long.

Coming back upriver, we stopped about one-half mile short of the bridge at a gravel ramp. Not knowing if it was public or private, Nate and I knocked at a travel trailer parked there to inquire. Not getting an answer, we went to the house next door. I pushed a button inside the garage thinking it was a doorbell, only to have it start closing the garage door. As it started to rattle shut, I pushed it again to reverse direction. When no one came to investigate why the garage door had operated, I found and rang the real doorbell. A woman talking on a cell phone answered the door. I explained the situation, and she graciously gave permission to use the ramp. After Nate relayed her directions to Debbie over the walkie-talkie about how to get from the bridge to their place, he then went to the end of the long gravel driveway so she would not miss it.

In the fifteen minutes it took Debbie to arrive, we became friends. Her last name was Fitche, and her husband, Paul, was a semi-truck driver. They owned some surrounding land on which they'd raised cattle for a number of years. Calvin, her son, gave us directions to a downstream access point called Johnson's Creek. Just after we'd loaded the Zodiac, a semi pulled in. It was Paul, who had 'Rat Pack' painted on the cab.

Calvin's directions put us on a scenic twisty local road. While stopped at a junction and unsure of which direction to go, a passing driver asked if we were OK. Saying we were looking for a boat ramp, he gave directions to a private ramp owned by a group that you were supposed to be a member of in order to use. Not a member himself, he said if anybody hassled us to tell them Jerry White said it was OK. We checked it out but due to being late in the day and wanting to find a closer access to the dam, decided to continue driving. We crossed over the Clark Fork River into the town of Clark Fork, Elevation 2100', and headed back southeast on Hwy 200. Finding River Delta Resort, they gave us a riverfront RV site right on the river with the view of the high country beyond it spectacular.

WEDNESDAY, JUNE 26TH, 2002

The day did not start out well. After hand wheeling the loaded Zodiac to their ramp, I started the motor. The tell tale stream of water indicating the water pump is working was not coming out. We pulled the Zodiac back to the campsite and switched motors. While putting the four-horse on, I wished we'd brought the fifteen-horse Honda normally carried on the back of the I/O. After pulling the Zodiac back to ramp we were off for real.

Sort of! In trying to proceed upstream for the one and a half mile trip to Cabinet Gorge Dam, we could not. Instead of seeing shoreline whiz by, we were stationary. With the motor wide open, we just held our own against the fast current, as if anchored. Oh well, we'd head downstream instead.

The Clark Fork enters Lake Pend Oreille about twenty miles below Cabinet Gorge Dam. From there we'd have about seventy-miles to go before arriving at Albeni Falls Dam, the point from where we'd started last year.

How to gain access to the lake was confusing with many wooden barriers blocking entry. Other than controlling floating debris from entering the lake or a remnant of the logging era, I do not know their purpose. Locating a gap, we sneaked through and entered the huge lake.

Fortunately it was dead calm since about thirty-five miles of open water was between us and to where it narrows back to a river.

Nate's walkie-talkies paid off again as we contacted Debbie waiting at a ramp near the town of Hope. With it being out of the way to stop and everything going well, we agreed to meet at Sandpoint, an easily identifiable location since this is the only place a bridge crosses the lake. While slowly motoring across the dead still lake we passed a sailboat under motor power.

Teenagers making the scene dominated the crowded public beach where Debbie waited in the nice day. The layover was more like a pit stop because I was concerned about darkness setting in before arriving at Albeni Falls Dam.

It took every turn of the prop to make the ramp at Albeni Falls Recreation Area to keep from being swept towards Albeni Falls Dam in the fast current at 6:40.

Having been to the downside of Albeni Falls Dam last year, I had made another river connection!

For some reason the camping facilities at the recreation area were closed so we stayed at Priest River Campground.

THURSDAY, JUNE 27TH, 2002

It being Nate's 16th birthday, we asked how he'd like to celebrate it. He wanted to go to a place with a pool so we headed back east on rural roads to Missoula, Montana, the closest place we knew of having one.

Large towns have so many chain outfits such as Burger King, Pizza Hut, McDonalds, Midas, etc; they all seem the same, offering little in the way of local character. While passing through small towns in Idaho, we got a kick out of the names of some local businesses; Squeaky's Welding, Melody Muffler, The Outlaw Bar with 'A friendly' placed above the word outlaw, and Dad's Auto Wrecking. About two miles east of the town of Hope was a campground called Beyond Hope, and in Clark Fork was The Squeeze On Inn housed in a small narrow building.

The previously skipped section of the Clark Fork between Thomson Falls and Paradise did not seem to be carrying as much water as on

Monday. While following Hwy 200 East past the point where the Flathead River joins the Clark Fork I had an inspiration. Why not travel the Flathead from the town of Dixon, the point at which its direction sharply changes from due south to almost straight west, to its junction with the Clark Fork thirty miles later?

Hwy 200 closely follows the Flathead through a valley for about twenty-five road miles enabling me to view most of its westerly route. While running fast, I did not see any rapids. Due to a broad flood plain, it looked relatively easy to stay away from areas where the river flowed through tree and brush areas.

We found out we were on the Flathead Indian Reservation while checking out the access point at Dixon. A sign there stated permits are required to gain water access, with no motor use being allowed from March 15th to June 30th to protect nesting waterfowl. Paddling the canoe did not seem dangerous, let's do it!

I stopped at the small Post Office in Dixon, one of just a few buildings comprising the town, and asked about purchasing a permit. The sole female employee, new to the area, did not know where they were sold. She suggested we go north towards the main reservation. Since I'd promised Nate a campground with a pool, we continued on to a KOA in Missoula.

While Nate and I were in the pool, Debbie went shopping for his birthday dinner. Debbie had told Nate she was going to make his cake in the microwave and he believed her even after seeing the store bought cake.

FRIDAY, JUNE 28TH, 2002

Just as were ready to leave the campground, a 60'ish woman asked help to reposition her motorcycle in the enclosed trailer she was towing. In helping Naomi, I learned she'd started riding after retiring from teaching English and was delivering her accumulation of teaching materials to a niece who had just started teaching.

Heading back north to buy a permit, we saw a sporting goods store in Ronan with a display sign in the window 'permits here.' As he filled out the $8.00 permit, I asked about river conditions from Dixon to the

Clark Fork. The going was easy except for the three-mile portage at Perma Bridge. What? He was pulling my leg, but it never hurts to ask local conditions from someone in the know.

Debbie fixed our previously skipped breakfast while Nate and I prepared to launch the canoe from Haskins Landing in Dixon. I was almost baptized again while slipping and falling *into* the canoe while pushing into the swift current.

Nate and I paddled nonstop for four hours, averaging six mph. Even with the swift current, there was a forty-five minute stretch towards the end where we fought a headwind and would not have made progress without digging in and paddling hard. Debbie took pictures and radioed from various points to make sure things were going OK.

At some point she drove ahead to find a good meeting spot, which we had not looked for while passing through twice before. The last two miles of the Flathead had some exciting spots requiring maneuvering to avoid dangerous rocks. The permit seller only half kidded about portaging, lower water levels could make this a hazardous area.

Debbie waited by the Hwy 135 Bridge, just above where the Flathead joins the Clark Fork close to the town of Paradise. Due to swift current, I pulled in some distance upstream of the bridge to check out places to swap the canoe for the Zodiac and four- horse. I walked through head high weeds and brush to where Debbie stood on the other side of a barbed wire fence. She thought it best I continue onto the bridge and exchange there, with her having parked about 1/8 of a mile away. Without going into ad nausea of detail, it was the portage from hell! The exchange required going over barbed wire, through poison ivy, and up and down steep boulder banks in hot humid weather.

It is a thirty-five mile straight-line distance between the Highway 135 Bridge and Thompson Falls Dam. Right after passing under the bridge, I saw a very nice level access point on the opposite bank. Debbie decided to play her 'Bad Decision Card,' a family vernacular term generically equivalent to a 'Get Out Of Jail Free Card' in Monopoly.

We ran through more rapids than initially envisioned. While a white water rafter would have considered them a mere nuisance to setting up for more serious ones yet to come, I was apprehensive. The river looped more than I initially thought, with each bend potentially presenting an obstacle or situation I may not be able to handle. Professional river guides, whether white water or fishing orientated, know what is around each bend and can position the watercraft with seemingly little effort or forethought.

I usually stayed to the outside of a bend, except for a couple places where the water was especially turbulent. On those, I would hug just to the inside staying right next to the curl of the white water. The water that did splash over the front was at an enjoyable level.

It was 7:30, and an anticlimactic event, upon our arrival to Thompson Falls Ramp, completing my version of traveling East to West by water. More people than you might imagine have traveled the Mississippi from Lake Itasca to New Orleans, stopping short of entering the Gulf, with a few traveling the entire distance. Very few people have completed an East West route. I have not heard of anyone who has done the Lake Itasca to the Gulf, Lake Winnipeg to the Mississippi, and an East West route.

I am not trying to detract from the individuals who have spent so much time and energy paddling canoes and kayaks down the Mississippi and Missouri. It took me fourteen years, four vehicles, five watercraft, four outboard motors, several false starts, and a lot of help and understanding from the family over the years to accomplish my 99% plus motorized water trips. A dream, unless pursued, will always be a dream.

The owner of River Front RV Park came out to greet us, recognizing the van from our stay four days ago. He was amazed at where we had been, as he did not know of anyone else even having been on the still flood stage Clark Fork River.

While talking about the day's trip, Nate said he had felt jinxed. Asked why, he jokingly replied, "Mom kept saying, I'll see you in Paradise."

By not finishing The Big Hole and skipping over a major portion of the Clark Fork, we were way ahead of our planned return. I decided to check out the Yellowstone from the point at which Debbie and I had taken out from on the guided raft trip two years ago.

SATURDAY, JUNE 29TH, 2002

Having Kevin's new fall address in Bozeman, we drove by to check it out. Two of his roommates were just moving into the nice three-story townhouse with a two-car garage. It's not the type of place that normally comes to mind when thinking of off-site college housing.

While travelling Hwy 89 towards Yellowstone National Park we checked out various accesses points along the way. Camp spots tend to fill quickly next to the park so we felt fortunate to secure a spot without hookups at Rocky Mountain Campground in Gardiner. Just as we returned from a long walk, a Greyhound bus type camper arrived at the office. I commented that they would surely have a reservation. But, No. They ended up right next us in the overflow area. In the process of pulling in, they hit a staked concrete marker doing major cosmic damage. In my opinion, it was the driver's fault. Every time the woman directing him said to stop, he'd continue another three feet.

Then 'the wife' got in trouble. Kevin was working a night job stocking major grocery stores with soft drink products and we wanted to check in with him. Debbie waited until 11:00 MST, 12:00 CST, to call since he did not get up until then. While walking to the pay phone, Debbie, the perennial teacher, pointed out different star constellations to Nate and was quietly telling him which ones they were. As they neared the public phone one of the owners reprimanded them for being too loud, 'Quiet Time' had started at 10:30 and he was getting complaints. I got a kick out of her being 'talked to' since she is one of those persons who always plays by the rules.

SUNDAY, JUNE 30TH, 2002

While unloading at Carbella access, 17 ½ miles out of Gardiner, a gentleman came over and told me that motors are not allowed. I said, according to the Montana Boating Laws booklet, the only restriction on the Yellowstone is a ten horsepower limit in certain counties. As we talked, I told of various trips. His reply was the now umpteenth 'you should write a book.'

Our starting elevation was around 5000' with Gardiner being at 6160.' If looks could kill, Nate and I would have been dead many times over while covering the first fifty miles. We passed many anglers; some in waders, some on the bank, and some in the occasional raft. Several of them pulled out cell phones, and I assume called someone to report what they perceived is a violation upon seeing us using the four-horse on the Zodiac. When passing the anglers, I always went as far to the opposite bank as possible I was using minimum throttle, just enough to maintain steering. Seeing a group of four fly fishermen, three of them had one on the line at the same time.

Nate and I met Debbie about forty miles below Carbella at Carter Bridge for lunch. The river had dropped about 400 foot in elevation, doing so on a relatively consistent basis. Besides the beautiful backdrop of the mountains; Eagles floated overhead, occasional deer were next to the waters edge, and a flock of lamas grazed. Yes, lamas. Just being on the river is enough to evoke feelings as to the 'why?' of our existence.

While Nate and I enjoyed being on the cool flowing water, Debbie was suffering in the hot muggy day on shore. Expecting to find Debbie right after passing through Livingston and while going under what I later assume to be one of the two Interstate 90 bridges in especially fast flowing water we came in 'Hot,' slamming into shore. Nate quickly jumped out with a rope so I would not be swept past, completely surprising a male who was sleeping with several empty beer cans lying next to him. Saying that we were looking for the Hwy 89 Bridge, I asked if this was it. He said yes, but since Debbie wasn't around, I showed him our river and highway maps to help verify our location. Then with him changing his mind by saying it was further on, we hopped back in and were gone. I've often wondered since if he went back to sleep, and upon waking, thought our quick fleeting encounter had been a dream. Coming in 'Hot' is a term that might only make sense to me. It means trying to come to a stop at a certain point with a second attempt not being possible, similar to the principle of a Space Shuttle landing where a second approach is not an option.

Finding Debbie at the next bridge, I asked her to check out a place called Grey Bear to stay for the night.

Our starting elevation was around 5000' with Gardiner being at 6160.' If looks could kill, Nate and I would have been dead many times over while covering the first fifty miles. We passed many anglers; some in waders, some on the bank, and some in the occasional raft. Several of them pulled out cell phones, and I assume called someone to report what they perceived is a violation upon seeing us using the four-horse on the Zodiac. When passing the anglers, I always went as far to the opposite bank as possible I was using minimum throttle, just enough to maintain steering. Seeing a group of four fly fishermen, three of them had one on the line at the same time.

Nate and I met Debbie about forty miles below Carbella at Carter Bridge for lunch. The river had dropped about 400 foot in elevation, doing so on a relatively consistent basis. Besides the beautiful backdrop of the mountains; Eagles floated overhead, occasional deer were next to the waters edge, and a flock of lamas grazed. Yes, lamas. Just being on the river is enough to evoke feelings as to the 'why?' of our existence.

While Nate and I enjoyed being on the cool flowing water, Debbie was suffering in the hot muggy day on shore. Expecting to find Debbie right after passing through Livingston and while going under what I later assume to be one of the two Interstate 90 bridges in especially fast flowing water we came in 'Hot,' slamming into shore. Nate quickly jumped out with a rope so I would not be swept past, completely surprising a male who was sleeping with several empty beer cans lying next to him. Saying that we were looking for the Hwy 89 Bridge, I asked if this was it. He said yes, but since Debbie wasn't around, I showed him our river and highway maps to help verify our location. Then with him changing his mind by saying it was further on, we hopped back in and were gone. I've often wondered since if he went back to sleep, and upon waking, thought our quick fleeting encounter had been a dream. Coming in 'Hot' is a term that might only make sense to me. It means trying to come to a stop at a certain point with a second attempt not being possible, similar to the principle of a Space Shuttle landing where a second approach is not an option.

Finding Debbie at the next bridge, I asked her to check out a place called Grey Bear to stay for the night.

SATURDAY, JUNE 29TH, 2002

Having Kevin's new fall address in Bozeman, we drove by to check it out. Two of his roommates were just moving into the nice three-story townhouse with a two-car garage. It's not the type of place that normally comes to mind when thinking of off-site college housing.

While travelling Hwy 89 towards Yellowstone National Park we checked out various accesses points along the way. Camp spots tend to fill quickly next to the park so we felt fortunate to secure a spot without hookups at Rocky Mountain Campground in Gardiner. Just as we returned from a long walk, a Greyhound bus type camper arrived at the office. I commented that they would surely have a reservation. But, No. They ended up right next us in the overflow area. In the process of pulling in, they hit a staked concrete marker doing major cosmic damage. In my opinion, it was the driver's fault. Every time the woman directing him said to stop, he'd continue another three feet.

Then 'the wife' got in trouble. Kevin was working a night job stocking major grocery stores with soft drink products and we wanted to check in with him. Debbie waited until 11:00 MST, 12:00 CST, to call since he did not get up until then. While walking to the pay phone, Debbie, the perennial teacher, pointed out different star constellations to Nate and was quietly telling him which ones they were. As they neared the public phone one of the owners reprimanded them for being too loud, 'Quiet Time' had started at 10:30 and he was getting complaints. I got a kick out of her being 'talked to' since she is one of those persons who always plays by the rules.

SUNDAY, JUNE 30TH, 2002

While unloading at Carbella access, 17 ½ miles out of Gardiner, a gentleman came over and told me that motors are not allowed. I said, according to the Montana Boating Laws booklet, the only restriction on the Yellowstone is a ten horsepower limit in certain counties. As we talked, I told of various trips. His reply was the now umpteenth 'you should write a book.'

Twenty plus river miles and two bridges later we arrived at Grey Bear. Debbie found the main road blocked by a downed tree and had used a poor secondary road to arrive there. With the area inundated by mosquitoes, we mutually agreed to meet at Otter Creek, ten more river miles.

With Otter Creek access not allowing camping, we loaded up and found a campsite at Spring Creek Campground.

Having gone eighty-five river miles and dropping about 1000 feet of elevation, I considered it a good day.

Spring Creek Campground had an unusual attraction; Reggie, a fourteen-year old black bear. He'd been born in the wild, one of three cubs. According to the information posted on his large enclosure, a mother will only take care of two. The owners adopted and hand raised him. When little, he used to ride around the large campground on a trailer. As he'd gotten bigger, was confined to a large pen adapted to seasonal needs.

A young girl named Madison, after one of the Three Forks that comprise the Missouri, was celebrating her birthday after having seen her namesake for the first time.

While looking over river maps in preparation for tomorrows run, I did some serious soul searching and concluded that I was not really looking forward to it with any real enthusiasm, and was in fact somewhat dreading it.

The maps showed that the next one-hundred-eight miles included three sets of rapids and five diversion dams with another 1000-foot drop of elevation. Theoretically four of the diversion dams are avoidable if you pick the correct route through the maze of islands, with the fifth being a mandatory portage. The days had gotten increasingly hotter, with decreasingly less shade available. I knew the scenery would stay much the same due to having paralleled the Yellowstone's route on Interstate 90 & 94 many times. Another thing that bothered me was the now lack of horsepower in case I had to power back upstream due to picking a blocked channel.

Loving July 4th celebrations, and having been invited to a birthday party July 3rd on the Mississippi River, greatly influenced my decision to stop after a short run tomorrow.

Having attained my goal to put as much water under me East/West without professional assistance as much as possible, traveling the Yellowstone was 'extra credit' on the way home. When I told Debbie and Nate of my decision, they were happy. We'd all had enough.

The Yellowstone is considered the longest free-flowing river in the lower 48 states of the U.S. at 678 miles. The first hundred miles lies within Yellowstone National Park and is not open to floaters. I had the Montana Afloat maps covering the next 211 miles, which showed the three rapids and five diversion dams mentioned above. Finally, I'd been able to get a no longer printed copy of 'Treasure Of Gold', which covers the rest of the Yellowstone's distance to where it joins the Missouri at the Montana/North Dakota border. It showed five more diversion dams and one set of rapids. I would disagree with the term free flowing considering there are ten diversion dams, six of them spanning the entire width of the river. I don't know the height of the highest diversion dam that spans the entire width of the Yellowstone, but I suspect less than ten feet depending upon the seasonal flow.

MONDAY, JULY 1ST, 2002

We put back in at Otter Creek, intending to stop twenty miles later at Bratten. The Yellowstone was running very fast and at full bank.

Debbie exited I-90 at Greycliff and used a frontage road to reach an access about eight miles short of Bratten, intending to take our picture while passing. I surprised her by finishing our trip there instead of continuing onto Bratten.

I will borrow from part of Debbie's father, Frank May, retirement speech to describe how I felt when I stopped river traveling because it fits so well.

> *While on a backcountry gravel road a travelling salesman hit and killed a cat darting out of the ditch. Wanting to do the right thing he drove up the lane of the closest farmhouse and in telling he'd hit a cat, asked if they had one. Saying they had more than one, asked what it looked like. The*

salesman then cocked his neck and went limp with his tongue hanging out of the side of his mouth. No, No, what did it look like before you hit it? He then pulled his arms up close to his face, emulating a cat showing complete fright.

Frank then equated the story with his teaching career. Initially frightened and naïve, the years wore on, taking their toll to the point where he felt like the limp cat.

I'd started out naïve and ambitious, with each trip taking its toll. I was now the limp cat!

EPILOGUE

Looking back I need to thank all of the people who helped me along the way. First and foremost is Debbie. She not only accompanied me in the canoe, Zodiac, and The Boat, she was also chief cook, radio man, and chase vehicle. Then there are the two sons, Kevin and Nate, who, while not really given a choice, were mostly helpful and agreeable. We did a strange combination of combining family vacations and boating adventures. And finally I have to thank all of the named and unnamed, mentioned and unmentioned people met along the way, who truly made this experience worth happening.

Looking forward, and still liking adventure. Cousin Dick(1989) and I took five self guided fishing trips to northern Saskatchewan over the next five years. Using our inflatable's we had varied trips ranging from being dropped off and picked up at the same location by a float plane, to travelling a 'winter' road 120 miles, taking 12 hours to do so before the start of fishing, to being dropped off by a float plane, camping on an island, and having to be trucked out on a very rutted road after being stranded due to rough water for the float plane to land on.

Since the trip in 2002, Debbie and I have traveled extensively in our RV, including a seven week trip to Alaska.

Kevin is now a Lieutenant Colonel in the Air Force, and Nate is a Major in the Air Force.

www.ingramcontent.com/pod-product-compliance
Lightning Source LLC
Chambersburg PA
CBHW021438070526
44577CB00002B/211